Judaism Transcends Catastrophe
God, Torah, and Israel Beyond the Holocaust

Volume III

The Torah Teaches

Jacob Neusner
Editor

Mercer University Press
Macon, Georgia

ISBN 0-86554-492-1

The Torah Teaches

Edited by
Jacob Neusner

Libray of Congress Cataloging-in-Publication Data

Judaism transcends catastrophe: God, Torah, and Israel beyond the Holocaust/
    Jacob Neusner, editor.
    x + 210 pp.   6" x 9" (15 x 23 cm.)
    Includes bibliographical references.
    Contents:
    v. 1. Faith renewed: the Judaic affirmation beyond the Holocaust
    v. 2. God commands.
    v. 3. The torah teaches
    1. Holocaust (Jewish theology). 2. Holocaust, Jewish (1939–1945) — Influence.
    BM645.H6J83   1994   296.3'11   94-38718
    ISBN 0-86554-460-3 (v. 1)
    ISBN 0-86554-461-1 (v. 2)
    ISBN 0-86554-492-1 (v. 3)

Contents

The Received Faith: The Torah in the Dual Torah
Jacob Neusner

Part One—Revelation

Revelation
Shalom Rosenberg

Understanding Revelation
Abraham J. Heschel

Part Two—Torah

Celebrating the Revelation at Sinai
Eugene B. Borowitz

Not by Bread Alone
Jakob J. Petuchowski

Part Three—Commandments

Commandments
Yeshayahu Leibowitz

Torah and Law
Emanuel Rackman

Part Four—Particular Commandments of the Torah: The Sabbath and Prayer

Preface

The polemic of this anthology, which is meant to be a highly crafted statement and not merely a collection of this and that, a political portrait of ephemerally important folk, is simply stated: "God after Auschwitz" endures as of old, and that is the God of Sinai, known to us through the Torah. Eternal Israel after Auschwitz has not only survived but remained faithful to its election, loyal to its covenant, and true to its vocation of exploring what it means to form a kingdom of priests and a holy people. To be born that eternal Israel, or to find a place in that Israel, for those who are there, abides God's ultimate act of grace: so eternal Israel has always affirmed, and so, whether in or after Auschwitz, eternal Israel today confesses. That confession and affirmation adumbrate not intellectual problems but spiritual mysteries; it is how life is defined and lived for me, and for all of us who embody in our time and place the remnant of that eternal Israel.

In this anthology, I mean to offer the reader the occasion to take up enduring issues of theology as Judaic theologians in our own day have framed those issues. For Christianity, as much as Judaism, formulates its religious experience in the theological categories represented here: (I) the encounter with God in history; (II) finding God in the world, or how we meet God in the here and now (here: God); (III) responding to revelation, or God's self-manifestation (here: Torah); (IV) forming the community of the faithful, in Christian language, the body of Christ (here: eternal Israel), as well as (V) theological thinking about theology. So far as the two religious traditions, Christianity and Judaism, are conceived within a single, shared structure, what Judaic thinkers define as their discipline and task bears relevance to Christian thinking about the same category, and the contrary also is the case. These are the issues of the five volumes:

(1) for the Holocaust in particular, how a religious reading of the massacre of millions of Jewish children, women and men has defined the issues of the last half of the twentieth century, the bases for the affirmation of God beyond the Holocaust (thus: "Judaism transcends catastrophe");

(2) for God, how we know God, where we meet God, the meaning of prayer, other forms of religious encounter and experience;

(3) for the Torah, the definition of the Torah as God's self-manifestation; the issues of how we mediate between the form of that manifestation, which is to say, writing of a particular age, and eternal truths that are made manifest;

(4) for Israel, we want to know how people have thought about the vocation and election of Israel, not only in the aftermath of the Holocaust and the foundation of the state of Israel, but in more enduring categories as well; and how these categories that endure—this is the way of life that God has given us for our service to God, this is the life of faith that we lead in the Torah—have formed a system for the interpretation of what happens in the here and now.

(5) for theology, the account of how theologians have defined their work, the program they have defined for their heirs, the philosophically-minded religious intellectuals of the coming century.

My purpose is to afford access for faithful Christian and Judaic readers to a kind of religious thinking and writing, profoundly Judaic in character, that is possessed of acute relevance but at the same time subjected to wasteful neglect. As I explain in the Introduction, people suppose that "after Auschwitz theology," or "post-Holocaust theology," must deal with only one question, which is, the problem of evil. But that supposition is only partly right, therefore entirely wrong. In fact, Judaic theology from 1945, all of its in one way or another a response to the catastrophe of the German murder of millions of Jews by reason of nothing they ever did but only what they were, which is, born of one Jewish grandparent.

No thinker whom we read in these pages wrote a single line in the oblivion of forgetting or ignoring the revelation of absolute evil that has taken place in our time. But the important thinkers, those whose writing will instruct the coming century, brought to the Holocaust the issues of transcendence, the classical categories and enduring doctrines of the Torah the world calls "Judaism." That is why I think it important to afford access here to moments of theological reflection that form in a variety of idioms and voices a single cogent work sustained, rigorous thought. In post-Holocaust writings I aim to show coherence, cogency, consistency; proportion and balance; authority and commanding mastery; in all, the classical tradition of Judaic theology as it has come to expression in diverse, authentic formulations in our time. I do so in the conviction that first-rate minds provide the rest of us with a model and a standard for our own religious thought, and much first-rate work is encompassed in these pages.

I address Christian as well as Judaic readers because the issues of Christian theology, framed in their own idiom to be sure, run along the same lines as those facing eternal Israel. We want to know what the world can reveal about God, so do they. We explore the responsibilities of the covenant with God that defines our being, so do they. We want to understand what it means to be "Israel," meaning, the people of God assembled before Sinai and children of Abraham, Isaac, and Jacob, and so, by their own word, do they. The dilemmas of faith and temptations of unbelief—how can an all-powerful God have made the world to be what it now is, for instance— confront us both. Judaism and Christianity share a common heritage of revelation, Judaism's written Torah (a term explained in the Introduction), and Christianity's Old Testament. Whatever one of us learns about God in the here and now and in revelation is going to lay claim upon the attention of the other, since by our own word both of us maintain that each party worships and loves the same, one and unique God (along with Islam).

That explains why I choose as my publisher a press conducted by academic colleagues who without apology stand for a clear and explicit religious position, and my publisher has chosen my work because of its comparable recognition that I here make an uncompromisingly religious statement. I take pride in presenting this anthology through the medium of this Southern Baptist university press; valuing the written Torah ("the Old Testament") as the word of God, just as eternal Israel does, that university and its press form an appropriate medium for an account of how God speaks in our place and time. And through theologians' intellect, as much as through saints' deeds and prayers, in responding, we answer the call that comes first and provokes response. Our response may not be the one God wants, but it is an authentic response to a call that, in the end, we maintain, comes to us from God.

Religious faith begins with God, not with us, for the world does not witness to God, but, more often than not, against Him. For me it follows that revelation, in the Scripture we share, the Torah/Bible, forms the beginning of our diverse religious thought. Theology for each of us follows rules of disciplined and rigorous reflection that God in the Torah/Bible has exemplified and that the words of God in the Torah/Bible embody. It is not for us to know why God has made the world the way it is, or to understand the reason why ancient Israel endures through the three great faiths that identify with it, rather than only through us, Israel after the flesh and (we think) the spirit too. But that is how it is, and how it has been for long enough, now, as to defy easy explanation. None of us conceives that theological negotiation is possible; each party believes its torah is the Torah, and that is how God has made us. That Baptists can find in an anthology of Judaic theology a work worthy of their publication forms a tribute to both the Baptists and the intellectual achievement of the theology of Judaism portrayed here. I do not know why God chooses to be heard in one way by Baptists in the Bible, in another way by Holy Israel in the Torah, but I do know that the faith of the Baptists and the steadfastness of holy Israel attest to the glory of one and the same God, and I honor their service as they mine.

This is no history of Judaism either, nor do I promise a thumb-nail account of how nearly two thousand years of thought took place prior to the last half of this century. Right at the outset, I lay out the issues of the Holocaust and then turn to the classical categories. But in each volume, I mean to offer perspective on the issues at hand. That is why I begin with a brief account of how, in the formative age of Judaism and its canon, catastrophe has elicited rational reflection, and, for volumes two through four, how the categories find definition: God, Torah, and Israel in the definitive documents of Judaism. In volume five, the counterpart is my own position on the next task in the theology of Judaism. In these opening statements I offer perspective on what is to follow.

Then I turn to the repertoire of writings on these same topics in our own time, not a survey of popular opinion, which is irrelevant to theology, but a re-presentation of informed thought, which embodies the theological voice. Each speaker is given a brief introduction, in which I explain what I find important in what is to be said.

Readers here take up not individual thinkers' whole systems, but specimens of thought of a number of thinkers on classical problems.

Since I have placed this anthology into the categorical context of Christian theology, I call attention to four other books co-authored by Bruce D. Chilton and myself, on the problem of comparative theology, the first three on the comparison of theological structures, the fourth on the comparison of theological systems, of Judaism and Christianity. These are as follows:

Christianity and Judaism: The Formative Categories. I. Revelation. The Torah and the Bible. Philadelphia: Trinity Press International, 1995.
Christianity and Judaism: The Formative Categories. II. The Body of Faith: Israel and Church. Philadelphia: Trinity Press International, 1996.
Christianity and Judaism: The Formative Categories. III. God in the World. Philadelphia: Trinity Press International, 1997.
Judaeo-Christian Debates. Communion with God, the Kingdom of God, the Mystery of the Messiah. Minneapolis: Fortress Press, 1997.

These works are free-standing but may prove of interest to Judaic and Christian readers interested in the comparison and contrast of the two great traditions of Scripture.

No work of mine can omit reference to the exceptionally favorable circumstances in which I conduct my research. I edited these three volumes as part of my labor of research scholarship, expressed through both publication and teaching at the University of South Florida, which has afforded me an ideal situation in which to conduct a scholarly life. I express my thanks for not only the advantage of a Distinguished Research Professorship, which must be the best job in the world for a scholar, but also of a substantial research expense fund, ample research time, and some stimulating and cordial colleagues. In the prior chapters of my career, I never knew a university that prized professors' scholarship and publication and treated with respect those professors who actively and methodically pursue research.

The University of South Florida, and all ten universities that comprise the Florida State University System as a whole, exemplify the high standards of professionalism that prevail in publicly-sponsored higher education in the U.S.A. and provide the model that privately-sponsored universities would do well to emulate. Here there are rules, achievement counts, and presidents, provosts, and deans honor and respect the University's principal mission: scholarship, scholarship alone—both in the class room and in publication. Here at last I find integrity, governing in the lives of people true to their vocation and their mission.

Jacob Neusner
Distinguished Research Professor of Religious Studies
University of South Florida, Tampa

Introduction

This five-volume anthology systematically presents how the enduring issues of the Judaic faith have transcended catastrophe and shaped the mind of the age beyond. The occasion—a half-century after the liberation of the remnant of suffering Israel, God's holy people, from the German death factories—invites the question, how has the faith, Judaism, recovered its voice? Or has that faith fallen silent, unable to speak beyond the abyss? We know the answer and here celebrate the fact of the renewal of holy Israel, God's people, in the faith of the Torah. That is what this set of theological anthologies proposes to spell out.

Now, had Israel then cast off its covenant with God and thrown its lot in with Satan, the rest of humanity would have deplored but understood its tragic end. But that is not what has happened. With the turning of the century and the daily passing of the generation that accomplished the physical feat of surviving, the time has come to take note of what has taken place among us all. An entire people, overcoming despair and renewing hope, embodied the faith of Job: even though He has slain so great a part of us, yet shall we all trust in Him. It is on that foundation, and only on that foundation, that holy Israel has surpassed death and tasted resurrection. And every faithful Jew who practices Judaism takes part in that resurrection—beyond the shadow of the valley of death, where, in ways we cannot understand, God was with us.

The Torah—the faith's own name for itself—governs holy Israel in God's compelling voice. Nothing has changed. The commanding voice of Sinai has overwhelmed the cacophany of death. For it is now clear that from 1945 to today we have witnessed one of the remarkable moments in the history of theology in the West, Judaic and Christian alike: the power of rigorous thought to think about events that in advance none could even have imagined. The theological minds of eternal Israel in our own day have met a challenge of which few in prior generations can have taken the measure. The Torah (or "Judaism") has triumphed, transcending radical evil, in classical terms, meeting Satan and through holy Israel affirming the living God made manifest in the Torah.

That is not to be taken for granted. Surveying the ruins of the ancient civilization of European Judaism, few imagined that the faith would renew itself, large parts of the Jewish people reaffirming despite and against it all that God rules, God loves. The past half-century has witnessed the unfolding of one of the great religious dramas of all time: how people survived evil beyond imagining and affirmed their heritage of faith. When Israel, the Jewish people, looked outward, around and backward, from 1945, so far as the eye could say lay ruins: villages and towns where the Torah had been proclaimed for a thousand years, now bereft of the presence of holy Israel; great cities, once vital with the vivid affairs of eternal Israel, now in ruins. With everything that flourished in 1939, homes, families, entire societies, now a mass of ashes and an empire of death, who can then have predicted what in fact took place? For it was not the mass-apostacy that the failure of faith would have provoked, but the determination, among religious Jews (Judaists) and secular ones alike, to reaffirm, renew, rebuild. What happened then was not to have been predicted at all: the rebirth of eternal Israel, the reaffirmation of its loyalty to God's word in the Torah, the renewal of faith in the one and only God of all ages. For not only did the remnants of the people, Israel, emerge from death factories where Satan ruled, they renewed their lives by forming a new political entity, the State of Israel, and by rebuilding throughout the world beyond the religious community of Israel that embodies Judaism, that is, the Torah, in the here and now.

Many find in the creation of the State of Israel the response of the people, Israel, to the Holocaust. And they surely find good reason for their view. But the challenge of the Holocaust to faith vastly outweighed the political crisis in which the Jewish people in Europe found itself. And it is here, in particular, that the remarkable renaissance of love for God and obedience to the Torah (variously construed to be sure) formed a response equal in power, but greater in weight and meaning, even to the political one involved in state-building. Israel, the holy people, did more than found the State of Israel. It also found its way to Sinai, once more taking up in these times, in this place, the yoke of the Kingdom of Heaven. Having emerged from the kingdom of Hell, this entire religious community now bears witness to the presence of the living God.

They affirmed the enduring covenant with God. They resumed the holy life of the faith. By word and deed they proclaimed the hope for the salvation of Israel and humanity through the Messiah. So the people Scripture sets forth as God's first love renewed its sustained, and sustaining, life of loving loyalty and obedience to God's Torah. Satan was vanquished by Israel's faith beyond the Holocaust. So, a calamity in many ways unique in history survived, Israel's remarkable rebirth marked the transcendence of catastrophe such as the world has seen only seldom. Why turn to theology to call attention to the renewal of religion? It is because in the profound reflections of the intellectuals of this religion the order, rationality, and coherence of events and faith emerge. Here we find not a narrow theodicy—beyond dogged faith, what theodicy is necessary, and facing the Holcaust, what theodicy is possible?—but a broad and nourishing theology of renewal.

To that religious experience of affirmation and rebirth, theology devotes its best intellectual energies in the pages of these five volumes. Here we see how the first-rate thinkers of the people, Israel, addressed the crisis of the day, on the one side, but also took up the disciplines and tasks of the classical theological heritage of the Torah, on the other. If no generation in the history of Judaism has confronted so critical a catastrophe, none was better served by its thinkers. Even our sages of blessed memory, who carried the Torah beyond the ruins of the Temple and reconstructed the kingdom of priests and the holy people through the Mishnah and the Talmud, accomplished no more towering achievement, nor did they face more intidimating obstacles to faith, than have the theologians of our own half-century.

The anthology shows the ways in which the important Judaic theologians writing in English have thought about the five issues that could not be avoided and had to be met head on: the defining hour of the Holocaust, then the three principal categories of the theological structure of Judaism: God, Torah, and Israel, meaning the eternal people to whom God spoke at Sinai, and then the challenge of the coming century. We here encounter not descriptions of opinion or historical accounts of what various people have thought about the Holcaust, God, Torah, and eternal Israel, and the tasks of theology for generations to come. Rather we read in their own words the theologians' propositions, arguments, passionate advocacy of particular positions. This is theology not recorded but lived in vivid intellects, how thoughtful, rigorous, demanding and restless minds have taken up the critical, anguished issues of a living faith at its time of crisis. The writers assembled here show diverse capacities of learning, acumen, perspicacity, and wit; some write one way, some another. But all of them do precisely what theologians in the traditions of Islam, Christianity, and Judaism are expected to achieve. That is the formulation in well-crafted prose of faith seeking understanding through processes of rationality; sustained and vigorous argument concerning the solution of conceptual problems of a religious character. More than mere philosophers of religion speaking about matters in general, mediating commanding revelation (for Judaism: the Torah) and rigorous, worldly reason, these writers reshape conviction and conscience into intellectually compelling statements of an entirely rational order.

A generation of theologians of Judaism, the one from World War II to the end of the Cold War, which faced the enormous intellectual challenges of the Holocaust, the founding of the State of Israel, now completes its work. The earlier figures, represented by the names of Berkowitz, Herberg and Heschel, have gone to their rest, and the later ones, represented by Borowitz, Fackenheim, and Vogel, now bring their thought to fruition and wisely undertake their valedictory statements. The next generation has yet to coalesce; we simply cannot at this time predict the shape and structure of thought; Judaic theology out of the most recent generation proves still ephemeral and has yet to find either its voice or its agenda. But in the moment of ebb tide, as the waters eddy and seek their new force, a backward perspective illuminates; we can at least take the measure of the high tide that has flowed out. So it is time to inquire into how rigorous religious intellectuals asked themselves the urgent questions precipitated by the greatest catastrophe Israel, the eternal people, has ever faced.

This anthology of five volumes about theological thinking about the Holocaust, God, Torah, and eternal Israel and Judaic theology of the second half of the twentieth century and beyond allows us to take stock of what has happened in the Judaic intellect. The anthology demonstrates that the classic and enduring—chronic in a healthy sense—issues of religious truth, not solely the critical and painful—acute—issue of evil and theodicy, elicited intelligent and profound thought over the past half-century. Not only so, but much that has been written endures as a legacy and a heritage for the thoughtful among the faithful in the century that is now dawning. It is meant to showcase important discussions on the principal categories of the theology of Judaism in the period from World War II to the end of the Cold War.

What makes such an anthology urgent is not only the passing of a generation. It is also that, in general, Jews present themselves as a wholly secular social entity, and the media of religious expression common among their Christian neighbors do not define how Jews make their religious statement. It is the simple fact that while the Jews are a social entity of a single religion, Judaism, or no religion at all (acceptance of any religion other than Judaism marks a person, in functional terms, as no longer part of the Jewish people), the proportion of Jews who also are Judaists, that is, practitioners of Judaism, varies but hardly encompasses the entire community. Not only so, but even among Judaists, serious encounter with the intellectual heritage of Israel takes place only in modest proportion. Faith without learning (an oxymoron in Judaic piety) is very common; faith surpassing understanding, which two generations from 1945 to the present in fact embodied, is not fully grasped.

God

It follows that, because of the prevailing secularity of the Jews' public discourse (and not merely its mediocrity), the modest place accorded to Judaists in the scheme of the Jews' ethnic existence, and the uncomprehending disdain for the reality of God's presence in and through eternal Israel, many, Jewish and gentile, have missed the astonishing intellectual events of our time. If attentive to the better publicized theological discourse, the more discerning will have judged the theological response to the Holocaust shallow and predictable. If God is all-powerful, then what does the Holocaust tell us about God? And if God is not all-powerful, then the Holocaust "proves" there is no God. So the issue of theodicy has exacted, and not only from theologians by any means, many sleepless nights. Many people now suppose that the only theological issue important in Judaism is theodicy, which is to say, theologies that focus upon "God after Auschwitz."

All Judaic theology from 1945 and onward, I think, for centuries to come, will have to qualify as "after-Auschwitz"-theology, not only for chronological reasons, but for substantive ones. We have learned facts about this world that, before the rule of Satan, we could never have conceived. A central religious task of rigorous thinking will always require confrontation with these facts, as much as, for the prophets, the demise of Northern Israel and the destruction of Jerusalem in 586 precipitated deep thought on how God acts in history. But what the catastrophe teaches, how eternal Israel has responded, the commanding voice of Sinai, the renewed encounter with the living God in prayer and acts of service—these all together form that theology in the shadow of the Holocaust. The reason is that, beyond the shadows, there has been much illumination: eternal Israel, responding to the living God, renewed its covenant in the Torah. That is the story of the rebirth of Judaism throughout the world, on the one side, and the message, too, of the theologians whom we meet in these five books. In an exact sense, for all who mourn for Israel's millions, murdered by the Germans from 1933 through 1945, every breath is an act of affirmation: we, Israel, choose to live, despite it all, because of the call of the One to whom we respond.

That is why all Judaic theology is a "Holocaust-theology." But few presently understand that every piece of religious expression, encompassing the entirety of Judaic theological writing, forms a response to the issue of the Holocaust; there is no other fact of transcendent religious character that compares in our time, or, many would maintain, in all time. Here I show a different picture. It encompasses not only the re-affirmation of God beyond the gates of Hell. It extends also to how thinkers have worked on a wide front, all of them under the shadow of the catastrophe of the Holocaust, but all of them engaged by classic issues and the revealed Torah. True, that statement contradicts how people presently assess the condition of eternal Israel and of Judaism. Any observer, following public life, would have supposed there has been paralysis in the encounter with the classic challenges to systematic thought.

I here make manifest that that is not the case. I show how thought has taken place in the main lines of theology of Judaism not despite the Holocaust nor solely in response to the Holocaust but in the renewal of the religious life of reflection in the aftermath of the Holocaust: how people mediated between new experience and received truth. The enduring categories of thought —God, Torah, Israel—continue to form the definitive outline of truth. For that forms the challenge to thought, which is to say, the religious mind transcends events and transforms them into enduring truth, making occasion into eternity. For the secular Jews, these questions come to formulation in secular speech: fiction, poetry, film, music; and they are given a secular articulation in politics and social thought. For the religious Jews there is yet another response. It takes two forms, the inchoate, profound expression of live as it is lived under the covenant with the Almighty: the life of faith and trust, hope, patience, and service, which the Torah teaches. And, it takes the second form of reflection on the meaning and truth of that life, reflection in the form of not only prayer or poetry or artful gesture, but sustained and rigorous thought, lucidly set forth in crafted prose. Secular Jews dominate the public square. But religious ones— Judaists, not only Jews—have also found voices, and in this anthology, these voices gain their hearing.

Israel

In this same context—the distinction between the secular and the religious in the life of the Jews—a further complication must be introduced. When in the theology of Judaism we speak of "Israel," we do not mean the State of Israel in particular but the eternal, holy people. That people, of whom Scripture speaks, to whom God gives the Torah, of course encompasses the Jewish part of the population of the State of Israel, but it is not limited to that one sector of the Jewish people, not at all. In fact, the name, "Israel," bears a variety of meanings. In the Torah, "Israel" always speaks not of a place nor yet of a state but only, invariably, of the people Israel, the extended family of Abraham and Sarah, Isaac and Rebecca, Jacob and Leah and Rachel; the kingdom of priests and the holy people. In all Judaic theology, and in all Jewish ethnic writing, before 1948, when people spoke of "Israel" they meant the Jewish people. All other usages in which "Israel" appeared referred to the same sense, e.g., in Hebrew, "land of Israel," did not mean, "the land, Israel," but "the Land that belongs in particular to Israel, the people." In the liturgy of Judaic prayer, "Israel" refers to the elect people of Israel, to whom God gave the Torah, wherever they live; it does not refer to a particular place or to a particular group of Jews as distinct from all others.

The confusion between the received, theological meaning carried by the word "Israel" began in 1948, when the Jewish State, founded by the Zionist movement, to which, as a matter of fact, most of the Jews in the world and in the Land of Israel subscribed, called itself "the State of Israel." Now that formulation, "the State of Israel" by contrast quite properly speaks of the Jewish state, located in the Land of Israel (as the Jewish people have always known that place). When the Psalmist speaks of "The guardian of Israel does not slumber nor sleep," he means, of course, "the guardian of the holy people," and not "the guardian of the Land of Israel," or obviously of "the political entity, the State of Israel." "Israel" as the holy people to whom God revealed the Torah, identified in the here and now as Israel the Jewish people, obviously should not to be confused with the contemporary State of Israel, a this-worldly fact, to be sure bearing profound religious meaning to Judaism. Since people refer to the State of Israel simply as "Israel," I distinguish the State of Israel from the holy people of Israel of whom the Torah speaks by referring to the latter as "eternal Israel." That will sidestep the difficulties in sense and meaning brought about by calling a secular state by a name that bears its own, distinct theological referent.[1]

So it is time to distinguish the ethnic from the religious, the secular from the theological, out of the voices of a half-century of pained and anguished reflection upon, not merely response to, the catastrophe of the ages that took place between 1933 and 1945. For those who see Israel not as an ethnic group alone but as God's people, those who interpret the world not in its own terms alone, but as testimony to the Almighty, those who distinguish this world's facts from eternal truths, those who view humanity "in our image, after our likeness," the issues surpass ethnic testimony about sound social policy or political action. Judaists, without apology, without shame, see the world under the aspect of God's rule, find in the Torah surpassing truth, appreciate the Israel of this world in its transcendent setting.

Torah

The profoundly secular character of the Jews' public life and therefore shared discourse in the USA and Europe obscures the equally deep, rooted religious faith of Judaists' inner life. This book and its companions give testimony to the living faith, Judaism—which calls itself "the Torah," which sees itself as the "Israel" of which the Torah speaks and which identifies itself as the statement of the eternal God, creator of heaven and earth, ruler of all worlds, and ultimate redeemer of humanity. Specifically, they show how Judaic thinkers, rooted in the absolute and unshakeable givenness of God's presence in history and rule over Israel, responded in rigorous, rational, theological ways to the defining moments of our day.

Theology in this context refers to systematic and rigorous reflection on religious questions; faith seeking understanding through processes of rationality; sustained and vigorous argument concerning the solution of conceptual problems of a religious character. In Judaism, theology has taken a variety of forms, important ideas expressing themselves through patterns of behavior as much as through propositions of belief. But in times past, and in our own day, rigorous and systematic religious thought has yielded a harvest of sustained, proportioned, coherent theological writing. This anthology means to portray how Judaic theology in the past half-century has conducted its work of making sense of the world measured by the dimensions of

(1) the Holocaust events themselves
(2) the revealed Torah
(3) the one, unique, and only God who is made manifest in the Torah at Sinai
(4) the eternal, holy nation, Israel, God's first love
(5) the presence, in eternal Israel, of rigorous, philosophically-insistent intellects and their theological program for time to come.

Knowing what we have learned in this awful century, how do we read the Torah, think about the power and mercy of God, make sense of the mystery of Israel? And what tasks face us in the coming generation?

The Holocaust: What makes the theological adventure of Judaic religious thought compelling and of broad interest to a wide audience of religious faithful, Christian and Judaic alike, over the past fifty years? The gates of the death factories, built by the Germans in World War II, closed finally in 1945. No event in the history of humanity bears more profound implications for our understanding of Torah, Israel, and God, not the fall of Man and Woman, not the Golden Calf, not the exile of the lost tribes, not the destruction of the Temple in 586 B.C.E., nor again in 70, not the massacre of Rhineland Jewries in the First Crusade, nor the expulsion of the Jews from Spain, nor the advent of Communism, nor the empowerment of Fascism and Nazism. Seen by themselves or all together, these turnings in time made sense on the received cartography of the known ways, God's and humanity's. But the received solutions to the problem of evil—Job's or Jeremiah's for instance—for many proved insufficient, incommensurate to what now has happened. Consequently, Judaic thinkers writing in the American language faced a challenge of reflection, critical thought, and sustained, rigorous intellection. Some directed their attention to the problem of evil and the issue of theodicy.

God, Torah, Israel

But others took up the ancient discipline of rationality in quest of religious truth and broadened the discussion. The Holocaust for them presented the occasion, even the provocation. But it did not define the issues. These, for eternal Israel, had been determined at Sinai, when, God having made the world and brought Israel into being and assembled the holy people before the mountain, completed the trilogy by giving the Torah. Creation, revelation, redemption defining the workings of the unfolding system that Sinai set forth, God, Torah, and Israel constituted the structure by which all reality, here and above, natural and supernatural, would be ordered. So for those who surpassed the occasion, the Holocaust stood for a new beginning in the unending encounter, in intellect, with the living God of Sinai's Torah.

Now, a half-century later, it is time to take stock of the work of a generation that has run its course. Clearly, two distinct kinds of theology require attention, "Holocaust-theology," and "theology that takes account of the Holocaust." The former, as is clear, rightly insist that all thought within the Torah find its defining program in the catastrophe of 1933–1945 (whether or not completed by the miracle of 1948 to the present day represented by the creation of the State of Israel, the Jewish state, in the Land of Israel). The latter carry forward the classical program of Judaic theological thought—how to live the holy life that God has commanded to covenanted Israel, how to reflect intelligently on the defining categories of that sanctified community's existence, God, Torah, Israel. Among these latter thinkers, the Holocaust found full recognition; but those events were not permitted to silence thought or impose upon the full and transcendent program of intellectual reflection constraints of what are, ultimately, an adventitious character. For they did not permit episodes to define eternal issues, but only to contribute new facts to the contemplation of those issues. So far as the Holocaust contained defining moments on the character of humanity and the holiness of Israel, it was to make, and it did make, its full, ample, and necessary contribution. But the Holocaust for this second set of writers, the more classical ones in education and sensibility, was to be faced within the received and eternal framework of the Torah.

The Theological Adventure in Contemporary Judaism

Ample evidence, part of which is laid out in these five anthologies, demonstrates that, transcending catastrophe, great intellects of Judaism accomplished two remarkable tasks of an intellectual character, and they did so forthrightly and courageously.

First, they faced head-on what came to be called "the Holocaust." A formidable corpus of writing by systematic thinkers of Judaism took up the problems of religious belief presented by the events of 1933–1945, when millions of Jews, men and women and upwards of a million children, were murdered by reason of not their faith but the mere fate of having been born into a Jewish family. In fiction, poetry, film, music, as well as in the media of sustained and rigorous thought in the form of ideas carefully crafted and persuasively set forth, the issue of the catastrophe was framed. Certainly, no generation has ever confronted a more insistent or formidable challenge than finding ways to think theologically about the unthinkable.

The faithful of Christianity and Judaism alike have found in the results not only important religious ideas, commensurate to the enormous dimensions of the challenge, but also the occasion for the renewal of faith. That is why the religious response to the Holocaust has rightly won for itself so rich a response of public appreciation. These anthologies do not have to provide a reprise of that protracted chapter in post-Holocaust theology of Judaism. But within the demanding discipline of reasoned thought about religious questions that theology comprises, a specific, theological formulation of matters was set forth. And that has to be appreciated to make sense of everything else. The achievement of the theologians—as distinct from philosophers, poets, film makers, composers, novelists, moralists, and publicists—was to insist that the Holocaust ask not a thin question of theodicy, but a thick question of encounter: God was there, the Torah was there, with eternal Israel in Auschwitz.

Second, some of these same thinkers and others as well in the same period, under the shadow of the same tremendous events, furthermore took up the received agenda of Judaic theology, that is, the program of mediating between revelation, the Torah, and the present hour that defines the work of theology in that religious tradition. From the formation of the classical and authoritative writings of Judaism, called all together "the Torah," to our own day, each generation has taken up the labor of making its own what the ages had handed on, the fundament of faith for which the Torah stands. The past half-century has witnessed a remarkable display of how enduring and historically-rooted intellectual traditions have taken over and made their own the newest of humanity's, and eternal Israel's, discoveries. When thinking about God, Torah, and Israel, the three generative categories of thought, the Judaic theologians took up an age-old discipline of continuous reflection, always aware of the catastrophe in Europe, but never struck dumb by it. This corpus of religious thinking of a rigorous character in Judaism shows us how Judaism not only faced the Holocaust but also, through appeal to enduring theological disciplines, transcended it as well. And it is to that labor of intellectual transcendence that these three anthologies are devoted.

What justifies the work in the proportions that characterize these anthologies—the Holocaust forming only part of the portrayal of the encounter with God in our time —is simple. While ready access to the first of the two massive enterprises of Judaic theology, both in its conventional form and in the unconventional formulations of the second half of the twentieth century, is easily gained in numerous and widely-appreciated works, to the second labor, the more classical, few have afforded an opening. That is to say, we may readily find anthologies of Judaic theological and Jewish ethnic responses to the Holocaust, and many of these have rightly enjoyed a massive hearing. But the paramount status rightly accorded to the theological challenge of the Holocaust has tended to obscure this other kind of theology that the generation beyond the Holocaust has formulated.

That is the theology that has continued the ages-old discussion of the enduring issues of Judaic faith to which the greater part of these volumes is devoted. Theologians of mighty power met the challenge, only to find their work neglected in favor of other kinds of expression, because of the paramount secularity characteristic of the Jewish world. For the secular taste, the Holocaust validated atheism; God could not stop those events, so is not God; or God could stop them but did not do so, so is evil. For the religious perception, God is always, everywhere, eternally God, without qualification, condition, or apology. In the context of the iron, incorruptible faith of eternal Israel from its origins to today, silence before the unknowable hardly defined a task beyond accomplishment. So the secular reading of the Holocaust prevailed in public life.

But of course for those of us who find our being in God's Israel and the purpose of our being in God's Torah, the Holocaust is reduced in its dimensions when treated as an event only in this world's terms. So reading the Holocaust in the narrowly political, secular, and ethnic reading of the catastrophe—or in terms essentially secular people assume pertain to theology impoverishes. More happened at Auschwitz and the other capitals of evil embodied than this world contains. And we have known the reality of pure evil from of old; for our paradigm, if there is no ultimate evil, there also is no meaning to the ultimate redemption. And God is diminished. But in the structure of a this-worldly reading of existence that predominates in Israel, the Jewish people, as distinct from eternal Israel in the here and now, how the received, enduring dimensions of the Torah are to be measured has scarcely attracted attention.

Theodicy

The issues of religious encounter with the living God that religious Jews— practitioners of Judaism, called Judaists—find urgent but secular, ethnic Jews scarcely acknowledge are not addressed in theodicy alone, or in declarations that there was a God but he died in Auschwitz and similar formulations. Consequently, when people take up the examination of the theology of Judaism in the generation now completing its work, they take for granted one issue defines discourse. That issue is the one of theodicy, framed as "God after Auschwitz." People have taken for granted that, when we turn to theology, all we shall discuss is what we can know about God in light of the revelations of systematic murder of the people, Israel, in Europe. That is a legitimate issue; it is not the only one.

It is a broadly held impression that, in the aftermath of the murder of nearly six million Jews in Europe in world war II and also the creation of the State of Israel, the theology of Judaism has given itself over to the enormous problem of theodicy presented by the former, and the political concerns defined in response to the creation and maintenance of the latter. So God is no longer God in creation, revelation, and redemption, as Judaism has always encountered God. God is now subject to human judgment, requiring explanation and defense. But we in holy and eternal Israel have known more about God than the works of this day's history. We have defined our existence in more dimensions than the political and the empowered. Not only so, but theologians, who undertake in each generation to mediate the Torah to the acutely-present moment, have set forth rigorously argued systems, or components of systems, that provide rational and philosophically-defensible re-presentations of the received and revealed Torah of Sinai.

It is time to right the balance. That is not by an opposite and equal distortion, namely, re-presenting the theology of Judaism in the last half-century under the aspect of Sinai but not of Auschwitz. No theologian of Judaism has imagined such a vision; it were folly. All theologians of Judaism from 1945 onward have written in full consciousness of the events of 1933 to 1945, and every one of them in every line acknowledged those events. No religious thinking in Judaism has aimed at obscuring or diminishing the dreadful power of the ultimate revelation of evil—the counterpart and opposite of Sinai. But all of those represented in these pages have conducted the theology of Judaism in a different way.

The Holocaust-theologians start where they finish: at Auschwitz, The theologians who transcend catastrophe and move, as time moves, beyond the Holocaust, conduct their thought in a different realm. They surpass calamity and transcend the Holocaust by continuing the ancient and lasting conversation with the Torah, speaking of this morning's headlines in the language of eternity. Specifically, theologians who carry on beyond the Holocaust do so by placing that theology of Judaism in its own, enduring context, under the aspect of Sinai that of course illuminates all life, all time, all being, even unto death. What some have called "the commanding voice of Auschwitz" then is taken in to the commanding voice of Sinai. In this setting, one immense event casts its shadow over all that has come before and over all that will follow; but it is not the whole of time, nor does it set forth the entirety of truth.

Theology

I have throughout used a term not defined at all, "theology." An entire volume in this anthology, the final one, is devoted to the Judaic definition of theology. But to begin with, we turn to the definition of the particular kind of thinking that is represented in these anthologies: theological thinking, not philosophy, not "Jewish thought" (which rarely is defined but generally means, Jews thinking about Jewish things), and not history, literature, or anything else but itself.

To state matters simply: theology philosophically sets forth religion. That statement paraphrases the definition of Ingolf U. Dalferth,

> Theology is not philosophy, and philosophy is not a substitute for religious convictions. But whereas religion can exist without philosophy, and philosophy without religion, theology cannot exist without recourse to each of the other two. It rationally reflects on questions arising in pre-theological religious experience and the discourse of faith; and it is the rationality of its reflective labor in the process of faith seeking understanding which inseparably links it with philosophy. For philosophy is essentially concerned with argument and the attempt to solve conceptual problems, and conceptual problems face theology in all areas of its reflective labors.[2]

Accordingly, by the definition of theology that is before us, what we here examine is contemporary Judaic theologians' systematic and rigorous reflection on religious questions; faith seeking understanding through processes of rationality; sustained and vigorous argument concerning the solution of conceptual problems of a religious character.

To understand the claim of this anthology, a clear definition of theology is required at the very outset. For that purpose I reverse the elements of the definition provided by Dalferth. The predicate becomes the subject in this way:

> (1) *where* we have rational reflection on questions arising in religious experience and the discourse of faith,
> (2) *there* we have theology.

When we find reflective labor on the rationality—the cogency, harmony, proposition, coherence, balance, order, and proper composition—of statements of religious truth, e.g., truth revealed by God, then we have identified a theological writing. In these pages I present numerous, sustained examples of reflective labor on the rationality of statements of religious truth and consequence:

> God commands.
> The Torah teaches.
> Eternal Israel endures.

Those three theologoumena encompass the entire theology that Judaism has maintained and today sustains as God's truth. They form Judaism in its theological manifestation.

Concern with argument, the attempt to solve conceptual problems—these characterize that writing. By themselves, of course, they do not mark a writing as theological. Argument concerning conceptual problems yields theology when the argument deals with religion, the conceptual problems derive from revelation. Only the source of the givens of the writing—revelation, not merely reasoned analysis of this world's givens—distinguishes theology from philosophy, including, as a matter of fact, philosophy of religion. But that suffices.

To make this point clear, let me refer to the canonical documents and how they make their points. Take for example that splendid formulation of religion as philosophy, the Mishnah. The Mishnah states its principles through method of natural history, sifting the traits of this-worldly things, demonstrating philosophical truth—the unity of one and unique God at the apex of the natural world—by showing on the basis of the evidence of this world, universally accessible, the hierarchical classification of being. That is a philosophical demonstration of religious truth. The Talmud of Babylonia states its principles through right reasoning about revealed truth, the Torah. The Torah (written, or oral) properly read teaches the theological truth that God is one, at the apex of the hierarchy of all being. That is a theological re-presentation of (the same) religious truth. But that re-presentation in the two Talmuds (and in the Midrash-compilations, not treated here) also exhibits the traits of philosophical thinking: rigor, concern for harmonies, unities, consistencies, points of cogency, sustained argument and counter-argument, appeal to persuasion through reason, not coercion through revelation. In our time, as through the past centuries, in Judaism, the methods of philosophy applied to the data of religious belief and behavior produced theology. The method of philosophy shapes the message of religion into a re-statement characterized by rationality and entire integrity.

Since I have made reference to the received and classical documents of Judaism, a very brief account of the sources out of which all authentic Judaism thought proceeds is here required. That is important for the understanding of the opening chapter of each of these volumes, which provides the starting point of all Judaic theological thought, which is, the canonical definition of the several categories that form Judaism. A brief account of that authoritative canon must start with the end-product, which is, the Torah as defined at the end of the formation of Judaism.[3] For many people, both Christian and Jewish, take for granted that "Judaism" is pretty much the same thing as "the Old Testament," and if they know the word "Torah" at all, they mean by it "the Pentateuch," the Five Books of Moses, Genesis, Exodus, Leviticus, Numbers, and Deuteronomy.

But Judaism is no more the religion of the Old Testament alone than Christianity is the religion of the New Testament alone. "Torah" for Judaism is the counterpart to "Bible" for Christianity. Just as Christianity reads the Old Testament in the light of the New, so Judaism reads what it knows as "the written Torah" in the complementary and fulfilling setting of "the oral Torah." So to understand the enduring conversations about religious truth that theologian of Judaism conducts, we have to acquire a very exact knowledge of the sources of religious truth that the Torah comprises. What then is this "Torah" that forms "the Bible" for Judaism?

It is the Torah in two media, written and oral. That Torah, called in due course "the one whole Torah of Moses, our rabbi," was formulated and transmitted by God to Moses in two media, each defining one of the components, written and oral. The written is Scripture as we know it, encompassing the Pentateuch, Prophets, and Writings. The oral part of the Torah came to be written down in a variety of works, beginning with the Mishnah, ca. 200 C.E. The canon of the Judaism the theology of which is described here is made up of extensions and amplifications of these two parts of the Torah. The written part is carried forward through collections of readings of verses of Scripture called Midrash-compilations. The oral part is extended through two sustained, selective commentaries and expansions, called talmuds, the Talmud of the Land of Israel, a.k.a. the Yerushalmi (ca. 400 C.E.), and the Talmud of Babylonia, a.k.a., the Bavli (ca. 600 C.E.).

In literary terms, then, the formation of Judaism reached its fruition in extensions of the oral Torah and the written Torah. For the oral Torah, the formative age came to its conclusion when the Talmud of Babylonia set forth the theological statement of Judaism by expressing the religious convictions of the Talmud of the Land of Israel in accord with a profound reconsideration of the philosophical norms of the Mishnah, ca. 200. C.E. Joining the method of the Mishnah to the messages of the prior Talmud, the framers of the second Talmud thereby defined the theological, including the legal, norms of Judaism. For the written Torah, the Midrash-compilations of the successive ages, corresponding to the two Talmuds and associated with them, carry forward the same modes of discourse and express in their ways the same hermeneutics.

The Talmuds' distinctive hermeneutics, which contains within itself the theology of the Judaism of the dual Torah, is exposed not in so many words but in page-by-page repetition; it is not articulated but constantly (even tediously) instantiated; we are then supposed to draw our own conclusions. The unique voice of the second of the two Talmuds, the Talmud of Babylonia, which bears that hermeneutic, speaks with full confidence of being heard and understood; and that voice is right; we never can miss the point. For the hermeneutic itself—insistence on the presence of philosophy behind jurisprudence, law behind laws, total harmony among premises of discrete and diverse cases pointing to the unique and harmonious character of all existence, social and natural—properly understood, bears the theological message: the unity of intellect, the integrity of truth.

As the Mishnah had demonstrated the hierarchical classification of all natural being, pointing at the apex to the One above, so the second Talmud demonstrated the unity of the principles of being set forth in the Torah. The upshot is that Judaism would set forth the religion that defined how humanity was formed "in our image, after our likeness," not to begin with but day by day: in the rules of intellect, the character of mind. We can be like God because we can think the way God thinks, and the natural powers of reason carry us upward to the supernatural origin of the integrity of truth—that sentence sums up what I conceive to be the theological consequence of the Talmud's hermeneutics.

The Talmud of Babylonia therefore forms the pinnacle and the summa—what we mean when we speak of "Judaism"—because from the time of its closure to the present day it defined not only Judaic dogma and its theological formulation but also Judaic discourse that carried that dogma through to formulation in compelling form. Not only so, but the entire documentary heritage of the first six centuries of the Common Era was recast in that Talmud. And that body of writing was itself a recapitulation of important elements of the Hebrew Scriptures and in its basic views indistinguishable in theological and legal character from elements of the Pentateuch's and Prophets' convictions and requirements. Scripture itself ("the written Torah") would reach coming generations not only as read in the synagogue on the Sabbath and festivals, but also, and especially, as recast and expounded in the Talmud in the school houses and courts of the community of Judaism.

Other received documents that had reached closure during that long period of time—the Mishnah, the Tosefta, the Talmud of the Land of Israel itself, the score of Midrash-compilations—furthermore flowed into the Talmud of Babylonia. So each prior writing found its proper position, in due proportion, within the composite of the Bavli. And the Bavli made of the entire heritage of the revealed Torah, oral and written, not a composite but a composition, whole, proportioned, coherent. That is what I mean by, "the Talmudic re-presentation," that is, the second Talmud's re-presentation of the Torah given by God to our rabbi, Moses, at Mount Sinai.

That re-presentation was accomplished through one medium: a governing, definitive hermeneutics, the result of applied logic and practical reason when framed in terms of the rules of reading a received and holy book. I need not hide my conviction that the persuasive power of the Talmud's hermeneutics explains the Talmud's success in taking the primary position in the canon of Judaism. That conviction admittedly is subjective, resting as it does on the unprovable premise that ideas and attitudes account of conduct and social policy. But it is the indubitable fact that the second Talmud effected the re-presentation of all that had gone before. Given the Talmud's priority of place among all Judaic writings, before and since for all time, I set forth an objective fact when I maintain that the Talmud also stated in its distinctive way, through its particular hermeneutics, the authoritative theology of the Judaism for which it formed the summa. Religious belief and right behavior to express that belief —both would find definition in its pages, exposition and exegesis in accord with its modes of analytical thought. With the Bavli, the theological text had been inscribed; all the rest was commentary.[4] The commentary would flourish from then to now; the exegesis of that exegesis would define the future history of Judaism.

For the later history of Judaism, from late antiquity to the present day, theology would take a distinctive, and I think, unique form. It provoked rigorous argument, rather than merely laying out well-defined propositions. In this way it guided the conduct of theological thought, rather than merely defining its propositions and syllogistic goals. When the sages of Judaism chose to make their statements of norms, they began in the Talmud, worked within its categories, framed their ideas in accord with its intellectual discipline, and spoke in its language about its problems. They did so in the (descriptively-valid) conviction that the Talmud had made the full and authoritative statement of the Torah of Sinai, oral, covering the Mishnah and Midrash-compilations, and written, covering Scripture, as well. That is why everything to come would validate itself as a commentary to the text set forth by the Talmud out of all the prior texts that all together comprised the Torah.

It remains to explain that a well-known Judaism is not treated here. Specifically, In this setting, I do not address "the Judaism of Holocaust and Redemption," which from 1967 to the very recent past enjoyed enormous power in the life of American Jews. It was the Judaic religious system formed around the events of the Holocaust in Europe and the creation of the State of Israel, and held that the principal task of the Jews (not "eternal Israel") is to remain Jewish (without a supernatural definition of what that meant, that is, without a Judaism) and to support through political and philanthropic activity the State of Israel. It was enormously influential among American Jews, accounting to them why they should remain different from gentiles, but defining the difference in this-worldly terms, with no bearing on the conduct of everyday life and affairs. Profoundly secular in every way, that Judaism elicited the kind of devotion that, under other circumstances, religions ordinarily do.

But as a matter of fact, by any definition of religion and theology, that Judaism was no religion and had no theology. It was, and in its surviving pockets still is a chapter of the politics and sociology of Jewish Americans, itself an element in the politics and sociology of Americans in general. "Holocaust and Redemption" writing has no place in the theology of Judaism, except as rigorous theologians have transformed the issues, as they have, into the occasion for profound theological reflection. "The Judaism of Holocaust and Redemption" formed a Judaic system—an account of the way of life, world view, and definition of the social entity of a particular version of "Israel," but even though powerful in Reform and Conservative Judaisms, it was not a Judaic religious system, lacking as it did a serious confrontation with God and with issues of transcendence and holiness.[5]

Clearly, my focus is on issues of faith seeking understanding, the rational, philosophical construction of religious belief. It is not on the facts of who said what; I do not describe what pretty much everybody has thought, and I entirely ignore the institutional embodiments of the faith in the partisan seminaries and organizations of synagogues, e.g., Reconstructionist, Orthodox, Reform, Conservative, humanistic, and the like. In these pages the sects of contemporary Judaism play no role at all, because the issues that divide them are trivial and personal. Not only so, but locally-important theologians are not surveyed, since the criteria of selection emphasize the excellence of thought, not the ephemeral influence of the thinker. None of the worldly facts of episodic popularity bears theological consequence; all form mere accidents of local politics and sociology.

Episodically-famous personalities, joined to such institutions and occasions of ritual celebration by them, mean nothing. Mediocrity lays no claim upon the future. We are not here to celebrate platitudes and banalities. Conventional thinking fails the challenges of classical faith, and routine and full minds do not require a hearing that is not compelled by politics. Writers in the English language, and those whose works translated into English, that are not treated here are not neglected; they are rejected. Nor do I choose to pay attention to what by the standards of the Torah are simply heresies, on the one side, or rationalizations for apostasy, on the other. That is why I ignore some local icons, whose writing I find merely homiletical, on the one side, and theologians whose theology consists of the announcement that there is no God, on the other. For different reasons, neither class of theologians of Judaism deserves a hearing when the faithful come together rigorously to analyze the faith.

At stake here are issues alone. And I should maintain the catholic character of the writing, coming as it does from theologians identified with Orthodox, Reform, Conservative, and other Judaisms, resident in the English-speaking world or overseas, justifies that decision. Here are no party platforms nor partisan voices, celebrated here but unknown there, but rather, sober efforts at purveying truth—God's truth, so far as, in this world, we gain access to it. That is why this anthology presents not a historical-biographical repertoire covering everybody who was around at that time, but a sampler of vivid thinking and provocative, engaged writing. I bear sole responsibility for the judgments represented by inclusion and exclusion; nothing is tacit.

I have chosen writing that means to persuade, not merely inform; writing from heart to heart; writing that sets forth in the medium of words a deeply-felt religious sentiment, attitude, emotion, or conviction. In these pages readers meet embodiments of faith, hope, love for God, in the words of exemplary figures. That is why readers may expect to be not merely informed as to information but invited to participate in the thought and argument of interesting minds on important questions. When people go to a museum formed as a storehouse, they acquire information; they are left inert and unchanged. But when they go to a museum designed to teach, instruct, and engage, they enter into the experience of what is placed on display. They are affected and changed. Here they describe in vigorous advocacy of propositions, fully analyzed, amply documented, the encounter with God that has brought regeneration and renewal after the unparalleled catstrophe of our century.

Endnotes

[1] I have spelled out the many meanings imputed to "Israel" in various Judaic religious systems in my *Judaism and its Social Metaphors. Israel in the History of Jewish Thought* (New York: Cambridge University Press, 1988).

[2] Ingolf U. Dalferth, *Theology and Philosophy* (Oxford: Basil Blackwell Ltd., 1988) vii.

[3] By "Judaism" throughout these pages I mean one Judaic system in particular, the Judaism of the dual Torah, oral and written. The canon of that Judaism in particular is what is described in this and following paragraphs. Other Judaic systems have flourished and do today. Here the focus is upon the system that predominated and now continues, in a variety of modulations, to define Judaism for most practitioners of (a) Judaism, and to provide a principal source for all the others. That operative definition is descriptive, of course. All of the Judaic theologians represented in this anthology appeal to that one canonical literature and acknowledge its authority and authenticity as represented of God's revelation to eternal Israel.

[4] We of course should not ignore the fact that the labor of extension, amplification, application, and commentary in the richest sense went forward, and now goes forward, in a variety of directions. But no contemporary Judaic system begins elsewhere than in the Talmud and the oral part of the Torah represented by it. In the seminaries of all Judaic systems, and in the synagogues of all contemporary Judaisms, the Torah is presented in both the written and the oral components, though, I hasten to add, different Judaisms take up, each its own position on what fits into that entire Torah and how the Torah ia to be received and re-presented.

[5] Reading that Judaism in its correct, secular framework, I have dealt with that matter at some length in *Stranger at Home. Zionism, "The Holocaust," and American Judaism* (Chicago: University of Chicago Press, 1980).

Chapter 1

The Received Faith:
"The Torah" in the Dual Torah

Jacob Neusner

Through the Torah that God is made manifest. The religion, Judaism, finds its origin in God's revelation of the Torah to Moses at Mount Sinai and takes as its purpose living in accord with the covenant that God made with holy Israel, the people, through the Torah at Sinai. It follows that the purpose of Judaism is to live in accord with what we know God has commanded us as an act of love and grace: to know God through the Torah.

We have used two kinds of words in that statement, descriptive and native, "Judaism" and "the Torah." They refer to the same thing; "the Torah" and "Judaism," coincide, the former word speaking within the faith, the latter about it. Both words refer to that way to God and the love and service of God that has been taken by "Israel," the word in quotation marks referring not to the contemporary state of Israel or indeed to any political or ethnic entity at all, but to that holy people—the kingdom of priests and the holy nation—to which the Hebrew Scriptures refer. Israel is that social entity to which God gave the Torah, and gives the Torah through all ages when that same holy, eternal Israel assembles in synagogues to hear the written Torah proclaimed, and in study halls to hear the oral Torah studied.

Two sentences that say the same thing show what is at stake in the distinction between the neutral and the native:

> [1] In the secular, descriptive terms, rigorous, "sustained reflection upon revelation forms the theology of Judaism."
>
> [2] "Study of the Torah as the Talmud presents the Torah teaches us the will of God." In the native language of Judaism, we say the same thing in words that speak of knowing God through the Torah.

The two words, "Judaism" and "Torah," then correlate, though each imposes its own logic and discipline. When, in ordinary speech in the West, we want to speak of the religion set forth by the Torah, we call it "Judaism." That is, the whole, complete, authoritative, fully-composed religion, with its system comprising a way of life, world view, and theory of the social entity, Israel, is Judaism (for the secular language of the West) or is what the Torah presents (for the theological language of the faith).

"The Torah" being the native category, understanding "the theology of Judaism" as that theology came to full and systematic expression in its authoritative document requires an inquiry into the nature and structure of the Torah. The inquiry into nature and structure encompasses the media designated with the status of Torah, the persons, books, gestures, hierarchical authority in the social order, modes of thought and expression, that fall into the category, Torah, and require orderly systematization as a single, coherent statement. Indeed, that statement—the theology of Judaism comes to realization in the Torah—self-evidently forms a redundancy, since "theology of Judaism" in one language of thought is the same as "the Torah" in the other. And both "theology of Judaism" and "the Torah" cover the same ground in a deeper sense, since each promises the same thing as the other: knowledge of God and God's will for humanity, so, to repeat: *through the Torah that God is made manifest.*

But what is it about God that is made manifest in the Torah? The answer is, specifically, it is through the intellection—the modes of thought, the attitudes, the ways of reasoned communication—exemplified in the Torah that we know the mind of God. That means, what defines humanity and what defines God, in rationality, is the same thing: we are consubstantial in mind. It follows that, first, the category, "Torah," defines the theology of Judaism, and, second, knowledge of the Torah tells us how God thinks. We shall now see that these allegations are natural—fully native—to the documents of Judaism.

Then the entire theology of Judaism may be expressed in the language of the Torah in a formulation that accommodates both Western, academic language and the forms of speech of the Torah: it is through the Torah—God's own manifestation to Moses and holy Israel, and God's self-manifestation—that faithful Israel knows God. Now let me state the theology of Judaism in the language of the Torah, once more joining the two categories, native and secular: the Torah is the sole medium of God's revelation; it bears the unique message of God; and the Torah also conveys the correct method for the inquiry into the medium in quest of the truthful message: all three. Through learning in the Torah we know God.

We may then identify the theology of this Judaism—that is to say, the truth of the Torah—with the following formulation: "all our knowledge of divine truth . . . depends on God's prior self-manifestation; there is no knowledge of God unless he reveals and we reason."[1] That formulation of contemporary philosophical theology in correct, academic language accurately and completely describes the entire program of the theology of Judaism. It is hardly necessary once more to translate into the language of Judaism, but an appropriate counterpart language for the same position may be identified in the liturgical setting when the Torah is proclaimed to faithful Israel at worship: "Blessed are you, Lord, our God, who has chosen us from among all nations by giving us the Torah. Blessed are you, who gives the Torah," and, at the end, "Blessed are you, Lord, our God, who has given us the true Torah and so planted within us life eternal. Blessed are you, who gives the Torah." When we know how through the Torah Israel knows God, we know the theology of Judaism. And then, about God there is nothing more to be known.

Now this brings us to the second point, namely, how the Torah reveals God's intellect and ours as well. What, exactly, is to be known about God in the theology of Judaism, or, phrasing the question in the native category: "what does the Torah say about the Holy One, blessed be he?" Obviously its messages are many, from an account of attributes ("the Lord, the Lord is merciful and long-suffering"), to the story of immediate encounter ("you shall not see my face. . . ." ". . . the thin voice of silence"), and, above all, to the detailed and insistent account of what God commands Israel and covenants himself to do in regard to Israel. That, after all, is the principal message of the Torah par excellence, which is the Pentateuch. But the Torah not only sets forth propositions—things God is, has done, or wants of us. "Our sages of blessed memory" notice that the Torah also lays out sentences God has said. Since through language we reveal not only what is on and in our minds, but also the very working of our minds, through the language of the Torah we gain access to God's mind. Humanity is like God specifically in intellect: God and the human being are joined in a common rationality.

God is bound by the same rules of logical analysis and sound discourse that govern sages. In the following story we find an explicit affirmation of the priority of reasoned argument over all other forms of discovery of truth:

II.1A.   *There we have learned:* **If one cut [a clay oven] into parts and put sand between the parts,**

B.   **R. Eliezer declares the oven broken-down and therefore insusceptible to uncleanness.**

C.   **And sages declare it susceptible.**

D.   **And this is what is meant by the oven of Akhnai [*m. Kelim* 5:10].**

E.   *Why* [is it called] the oven of Akhnai?

F.   Said R. Judah said Samuel, "It is because they surrounded it with argument as with a snake and proved it was insusceptible to uncleanness."

2.   A.   *It has been taught on Tannaite authority:*

B.   On that day R. Eliezer produced all of the arguments in the world, but they did not accept them from him. So he said to them, "If the law accords with my position, this carob tree will prove it."

C.   The carob was uprooted from its place by a hundred cubits—and some say, four hundred cubits.

D.   They said to him, "There is no proof from a carob tree."

E.   So he went and said to them, "If the law accords with my position, let the stream of water prove it."

F.   The stream of water reversed flow.

G.   They said to him, "There is no proof from a stream of water."

H.   So he went and said to them, "If the law accords with my position, let the walls of the school house prove it."

I.   The walls of the school house tilted toward falling.

J. R. Joshua rebuked them, saying to them, "If disciples of sages are contending with one another in matters of law, what business do you have?"

K. They did not fall on account of the honor owing to R. Joshua, but they also did not straighten up on account of the honor owing to R. Eliezer, and to this day they are still tilted.

J. So he went and said to them, "If the law accords with my position, let the Heaven prove it!"

K. An echo came forth, saying, "What business have you with R. Eliezer, for the law accords with his position under all circumstances!"

L. R. Joshua stood up on his feet and said, "'It is not in heaven' (Deut 30:12)."

3. A. *What is the sense of,* "'It is not in heaven' (Deut 30:12)"?

B. Said R. Jeremiah, "[The sense of Joshua's statement is this:] For the Torah has already been given from Mount Sinai, so we do not pay attention to echoes, since you have already written in the Torah at Mount Sinai, 'After the majority you are to incline' (Ex. 23:2)."

4. A. *R. Nathan came upon Elijah and said to him, "What did the Holy One, blessed be he, do at that moment?"*

B. He said to him, "He laughed and said, 'My children have overcome me, my children have overcome me!' "

b. Baba Mesia 59A-B

The testimony of nature is null. The (mere) declaration of matters by Heaven is dismissed. The Torah now forms the possession of sages, and sages master the Torah through logical argument, right reasoning, the give and take of proposition and refutation, argument and counter-argument, evidence arrayed in accord with the rules of proper analysis. Then the majority will be persuaded, one way or another, entirely by sound argument: and the majority prevails on that account.

If God rejoices at the victory, in the give and take of argument, of the sages, it is because God is subject to the same rules of argument and evidence and analysis. Then if we want to know God, we shall find God in the Torah: not in what the Torah says alone, but in how the Torah reaches conclusions, meaning, not the process of argument, but the principles of thought. God has revealed these in the Torah, and in them we encounter God's own intellect. That is why it is the fact that the theology of Judaism sets forth knowledge of God as God is made known through God's self-revelation in the Torah.

It follows that the Torah reveals not only what God wants of humanity through Israel, but what (humanity can know of what) God is. The being of God that is revealed in the Torah—by the nature of that medium of revelation, the Torah itself, made up of words we know and sentences we can understand and forming connections we can follow and replicate—is God's will and intellect. Within the religion of the Torah called Judaism, therefore, there is ample occasion to take up the labor of learning not only what, but how God thinks. What is at stake in that lesson is how we too should conduct intellection. And the upshot will be, if we think the way we should, we may enter deep into the processes of the Torah and so reach propositions in the way in which God has thought things through too. The theology of Judaism provides an account of what it means to know God through the Torah, a sentence that is made up of two equivalent and redundant clauses: [1] theology of Judaism proves . . . and [2] know God through the Torah. What makes that theology interesting is its special sense of what knowing God through the Torah involves, requires, and affords: knowing what it means rightly to know. Three steps lead to that simple conclusion.

First, knowing God and striving to be holy like God—"Let us make Man in our image . . . after our likeness," "You shall be holy, for I the Lord your God am holy,"—define the lessons of the Torah or "Judaism."

Second, that knowledge is both unique and also sufficient: it is only through the Torah that knowledge of God comes to humanity. The Torah comes to Israel in particular because of God's decision and choice: God gave the Torah, or, in the language of liturgy, ". . . who gives the Torah."

Third, knowledge of God depends not only on God's self-revelation through the Torah. It requires also humanity's—therefore, uniquely, Israel's—proper grasp of the Torah. And that requires active engagement: sagacity, wit, erudition and intelligence. Gifts of intellect form instruments of grace: elements of God's self-revelation. The reason is that by thinking about thought as much as thinking thoughts, we ask the deeper question about what we can know about God, which is, God's thoughts in God's words, which, rightly grasped, expose God's thoughts.

Proper inquiry after God in the Torah therefore requires sound method: right questions, proper modes of analysis, reliable use of probative evidence, compelling reasoning. These are media of revelation accessible to humanity, to which through the Torah (in its oral as much as in its written components) and its everywhere-unitary rules of reasoning we gain access. For the Torah comes to Israel in the medium of language—some of it written down right away, at Sinai, some of it orally formulated and transmitted and only later on written down—and Israel knows God. Knowledge of God comes through not the silence of wordless sentiment nor inchoate encounter in unarticulated experience, nor through the thin voice of silence alone, a silence without words. Knowledge of God reaches us solely through the reflection afterward on what has been felt or thought or said by the voice of silence.

Now modes of bringing upward into the form of language knowledge of God begin with the writing down of the Torah itself, which, for Israel, records not only God's will but the actual words God used in stating that will to Moses, our rabbi. Therefore knowledge of the grammar and syntax of God's thought, learned through mastery of how to read the words themselves, which words pertain here, which there, and what conclusions to draw about God, on the one side, and what humanity embodied in Israel, on the other—that knowledge begins in the right reading of the

Torah. The authentic theologians of Judaism then are our sages of blessed memory, who know how, and, also, the reason why behind the how.

The religious system reaches its statement, in the case of this Judaism, in documents, even though, as we have already seen in the story about right conduct with women and right word choices, other media besides closed writings serve the same purpose. Still, the principal statement is made by a single, formidable, sustained writing, which—now speaking in description and fact,—from the time of its closure to our own day made, now makes, the summary-statement of Judaism, and, in centers where people study the Torah, defines the curriculum. That sustained, systematic exposition, through one instance after another, of the right reading of the Torah in both its media comes to Israel now as in the past in a single document, the Talmud of Babylonia.

That statement of fact describes the centrality of the Talmud in the future curriculum of the Judaic intellect, the priority of the Talmud from the time of its closure in ca. 600 C.E. to the present time. For "Judaism" is Judaism, and the Talmud of Babylonia is the authoritative statement of the Torah that that Judaism embodies. The Talmud is the prism, receiving, refracting all light. To state the proposition in academic language: into that writing all prior canonical (that is, authoritative) documents flowed; from it, all later canonical writings emerged; to it all appeal is directed; upon it, all conclusions ultimately rest. Now in the language of the Torah itself: study of the Torah begins, as a matter of simple, ubiquitous fact, in the Talmud.

Proof of these simple propositions on the Talmudic re-presentation of the Torah, which is to say, Judaism's statement of its theology, its norms of action and reflection and of the authority that sustains them and signifies right from wrong, derives from the character of Judaic discourse. In all times, places, and writings, other than those rejected as heretical, from then to now, the Talmud formed the starting point and the ending point, the alpha and omega of truth; justify by appeal to the Talmud, rightly read, persuasively interpreted, and you make your point; disprove a proposition by reference to a statement of the Talmud, and you demolish a counterpoint. In reading the written Torah itself, the Talmud's exegesis enjoy priority of place. Scripture rightly read reaches Israel in the Talmud (and Midrash) or can be shown, at least, not out of line with them. Even greater consequence attaches to action. In all decisions of law that express theology in everyday action, the Talmud forms the final statement of the Torah, mediating Scripture's rules.

Innovation of every kind, whether in the character of the spiritual life or in the practice of the faith in accord with its norms, must find justification in the Talmud, however diverse the means by which validation is accomplished. The schools and courts of the holy community of Israel studied the Torah in the Talmud and applied its laws. The faithful emulated masters of the Torah in the Talmud and accepted their instruction. Even in modern times, when, rejecting the self-segregation of "the people that dwells apart," Judaic systems took shape intending to integrate holy Israel into the common life of the nations where Jews lived, those systems acknowledged the authority of the Talmud, whether by proposing to validate a profound change in the social policy of holy Israel by appeal to its norms or by attempting to invalidate the entire received theory of Israel's society by discrediting the Torah in some detail or in its entirely. The authority of the document found its most profound recognition in the centrality accorded to it even by those who undertook to overturn that authority.

The premise is then shown to generate yet another principle, reaching upward, at a different terrain altogether, into other cases. Do the cases presuppose contrary principles? Do the principles express conflicting premises? Then the disharmony demands detailed attention, a work of harmonization not of detail nor yet of principle but of the most abstract formulations of premise. Right reasoning and its rules hold the whole together.

To what end? Clearly, knowing how to decipher the signals of dialogue allows us not only to come to conclusions but, more to the point, even to recreate an argument, one that would lead from out here, in the real world of cases and examples, inward, into the profound reaches of the Torah, where at the deepest structure we grasp what we can of God's will and intellect. The Talmud makes it possible to replicate the modes of thought that yielded principles and rules. The Torah then forms the data out of which, in our joining of the issue, we may find at the layers of abstraction and generalization the rules of reasoned reality: the world attests to the intent and mind of its Maker. The integrity of truth, its unity and coherence—these traits of intellect attest to God's mind, from which all things come, to which all things refer. The rules of life therefore came to this worldly expression within, and to those with wit and patience, would be fully exposed in all their unity and integrity, by, the Torah.

So the stakes of the second Talmud prove formidable indeed. That is why the theology of Judaism (in academic language) forms a statement of what it means to know God; and that theology defines what it means to know God in terms both particular but wholly accessible to the mind of all creation endowed with sensibility. God is wholly other, but God has given the Torah, so revealing to holy Israel both the terms of endearment—what God wants of Israel—and also the terminology thereof: the how and the why behind the what.

The Torah defines above all relationships, how God loves humanity, how humanity is to respond in deed and deliberation. Then the Torah comes to Israel in an encounter ("dialogue"), first between Moses and God, then between the disciple and the master, replicating the relationship between Moses and God. It follows that the critical moment comes at the encounter of master and disciple, where here and now, both enter into the situation of God and Moses.

That conception of relationship reaches definition in three ways, concrete, abstract, and mythic, in the following, first the concrete rule:

I.   A.   [If he has to choose between seeking] what he has lost and what his father has lost,
      B.   his own takes precedence.
      II.C. . . . what he has lost and what his master has lost,
      D.   his own takes precedence.
II.   E.   . . . what his father has lost and what his master has lost, that of his master takes precedence.
      G.   For his father brought him into this world.
      H.   But his master, who taught him wisdom, will bring him into the life of the world to come.
      I.   But if his father is a sage, that of his father takes precedence.

Mishnah Baba Mesia 2:11

Now the abstract statement of the theological fact:

A.   Moses received the Torah at Sinai and handed it on to Joshua, Joshua to elders, and elders to prophets. And prophets handed it on to the men of the great assembly. They said three things: Be prudent in judgment. Raise up many disciples. Make a fence for the Torah.

Abot 1:1

Third, the explicit mythic formulation of how the relationship of master to disciple replicates the relationship between God and Moses:

A.   *Our rabbis have taught on Tannaite authority:*
B.   What is the order of Mishnah-teaching? Moses learned it from the mouth of the All-powerful. Aaron came in, and Moses repeated his chapter to him and Aaron went forth and sat at the left hand of Moses. His sons came in and Moses repeated their chapter to them, and his sons went forth. Eleazar sat at the right of Moses, and Itamar at the left of Aaron.
C.   R. Judah says, "At all times Aaron was at the right hand of Moses."
D.   Then the elders entered, and Moses repeated for them their Mishnah-chapter. The elders went out. Then the whole people came in, and Moses repeated for them their Mishnah-chapter. So it came about that Aaron repeated the lesson four times, his sons three times, the elders two times, and all the people once.
E.   Then Moses went out, and Aaron repeated his chapter for them. Aaron went out. His sons repeated their chapter. His sons went out. The elders repeated their chapter. So it turned out that everybody repeated the same chapter four times.

We conclude with yet another concrete formulation of the theology in terms of everyday rules of conduct:

F.   On this basis said R. Eliezer, "A person is liable to repeat the lesson for his disciple four times. And it is an argument a fortiori: if Aaron, who studied from Moses himself, and Moses from the Almighty—so in the case of a common person who is studying with a common person, all the more so!"

G. R. Aqiba says, "How on the basis of Scripture do we know that a person is obligated to repeat a lesson for his disciple until he learns it [however many times that takes]? As it is said, 'And you teach it to the children of Israel' (Deut 31:19). And how do we know that that is until it will be well ordered in their mouth? 'Put it in their mouths' (Deut 31:19). And how on the basis of Scripture do we know that he is liable to explain the various aspects of the matter? 'Now these are the ordinances which you shall put before them' (Exod 31:1)."　　　　　　　　　　　　**Bavli Erubin 54B**

We see, therefore, what is at stake in the Talmud, its study in the right way, its transmission in the proper manner: knowledge of God, such as God makes manifest through the Torah. And that is the only knowledge of God that (this) Judaism maintains we have.

Accessible only in the living encounter, at the Torah, of the master and the disciple, the Talmud set forth the Torah as Israel received—and now receives—it night and morning through all time. What that abstract statement means in concrete terms then is simple. In reconstructing its arguments, analyzing its initiatives of proposition and objection, argument and counter-argument, thrust and parry, movement of thought and momentum of mind, the Talmud's disciples formed their minds, framed their modes of thought, in the encounter with the Torah. And, in making up their own statements, the best of them could therefore claim (though none of them ever did) to think the way God thought about the things about which God thinks: the rules of life as set forth in the Torah.

For the framers of the Bavli, what it means to be "in our image, after our likeness," is not only to act like God ("You shall be holy as I the Lord your God am holy: just as I am merciful and long-suffering, so must you be merciful and long-suffering," "You shall be holy, for I the Lord your God am holy:" That is to say, "if you sanctify yourselves, I shall credit it to you as though you had sanctified me, and if you do not sanctify yourselves, I shall hold that it is as if you have not sanctified me" [*Sifra* 195:1.3A–B]). To be "in our image" is also to think in full consciousness, in accord with articulated rules of rationality, like God. The Torah teaches how God speaks, therefore how God thinks—but it is only in the Talmud that we find a sustained and articulated effort to show in detail the meaning of that how.

From the time of its closure to the present, this Talmud has served as the summa of Judaism. The Judaic systems that succeeded from then to now have referred back to the Bavli as authoritative; formulated their statements in relationship to the Bavli, often in the guise of commentaries or secondary expositions of statements made in it; taken over the Bavli as the backbone for the law and culture that these continuator- and successor-systems proposed to set forth. To establish a truth, appeal to the highest court formed by those who have mastered the Bavli, its commentaries, codes, and accompanying response, alone would serve. Not only so, but until the twentieth century, all Judaisms classified as heretical formed their heresies in response to the Bavli's norms. So far as by "classic," we mean, authoritative, enduring, and defining, the Bavli is Judaism's classic. Now, since the Bavli is only one among the score or more large and important documents of classics of the formative age, we have to ask ourselves, why among all the documents of Judaism did the Bavli gain priority, indeed utter hegemony?

What characterizes the Bavli and not any prior document seen whole is the sustained and relentless search for the unitary foundations of the diverse laws, through an inquiry into the premises of discrete rules, the comparison and contrast of those premises, the statement of the emergent principles, and the comparison and contrast of those principles with the ones that derive from other cases and their premises—a process, an inquiry, without end into the law behind the laws. What the Bavli wants, beyond its presentation of the positions at hand, is to draw attention to the premises of those positions, the reasoning behind them, the evidence that supports them, the argument that transforms evidence into demonstration, and even the authority, among those who settle questions by expressing opinions, who can hold the combination of principles or premises that underpin a given position.

The real difference between the Bavli and all prior documents of the oral Torah, including the earlier Talmud emerges from one trait: the Bavli's completely different theory of what it wishes to investigate. And that difference derives why the framers of the Bavli's compositions and composites did the work to begin with. The outlines of the intellectual character of the work flow from the purpose of the project, not the reverse; and thence, the modes of thought, the specifics of analytical initiative—all these are secondary to intellectual morphology. So first comes the motivation for thought, then the morphology of thought, then the media of thought, in that order.

The difference between prior writings of the Oral Torah and the Bavli is the difference between fact and truth, detail and principle, jurisprudence and philosophy; the one kind of writing is a work of exegesis in search of system, the other, of analysis in quest of philosophical truth. The Yerushalmi, the first commentary to the Mishnah, for instance, presents the laws, the rule for this, the rule for that—pure and simple; "law" bears is conventional meaning of jurisprudence. The Bavli presents the law, now in the philosophical sense of, the abstract issues of theory, the principles at play far beneath the surface of detailed discussion, the law behind the laws. And that, we see, is not really "law," in any ordinary sense of jurisprudence; it is law in a deeply philosophical sense: the rules that govern the way things are, that define what is proportionate and orderly and properly composed.

The Bavli's framers are interested in conclusions and outcome; but for them the deep structure of reason is the goal, and the only way to penetrate into how things are at their foundations is to investigate how conflicting positions rest on principles to be exposed and juxtaposed, balanced, and, if possible, negotiated, if necessary, left in the balance. The Bavli's author manages to lay matters out in a very distinctive way. And that way yields as a sustained, somewhat intricate argument (requiring us to keep in the balance both names and positions of authorities and also the objective issues and facts) what the Yerushalmi's method of representation gives us as a rather simple sequence of arguments. If we say that the Bavli is "dialectical," presenting a moving argument, from point to point, and the Yerushalmi is static, through such a reductive understatement we should vastly misrepresent the difference. The Bavli's presentation is one of thrust and parry, challenge and response, assertion and counter-assertion; theoretical possibility and its exposure to practical facts ("if I had to rely . . . I might have supposed. . . ."); and, of course, the authorities of the Bavli are even prepared to rewrite the received Tannaite formulation. That initiative can come only from someone totally in command of the abstractions and able to say, the details have to be this way; so the rule of mind requires; and so it shall be.

The Bavli attained intellectual hegemony over the mind of Israel, the holy people, because its framers so set forth their medium that the implicit message gained immediacy in the heat of argument—so that, as a matter of fact, argument about the law served as a mode of serving God through study of the Torah. But its true power derived from the message: that the truth, like God, is one—and the unity makes all the difference. In the Bavli, the written Torah, with its proclamation of the unity and integrity of the one true God, reached its climax in the demonstration of the unity and integrity of truth: God's mind and humanity's mind are one, which is how humanity can, to begin with, know God at all. Now we want to know precisely what it means in Judaism to meet God in the Torah, which is to say, to know God the way Judaism maintains we do.

What happens to us—Israel—in Torah-study that does not happen to us in any other activity is one important thing: by Torah-study we are changed in our very being, not alone as to knowledge or even as to virtue and taxic status, but as to what we are. Knowledge does not only inform, it transforms. Through learning in the Torah we become something different from, better and more holy than, what we were. Through that learning we meet God, God's mind and our mind coming together in shared rationality. How do we know that we have been changed by Torah-study? The marks of the transformation emerge in the supernatural power that we have by reason of our (new) knowledge, learning in the Torah. When (mere) knowledge so transforms the knower that he or she is deemed transformed into something utterly different from the condition that had earlier prevailed, when one was marked by ignorance.

Torah-study produces knowledge that is transitive and transformative, joining the two quite distinct categories: intellect and personal salvation or regeneration. That jarring juxtaposition, identifying ignorance (not knowing a given fact) with the personal condition of unregeneracy, relates what need not, and commonly is not, correlated: the moral or existential condition of the person and the level of intellectual enlightenment of that same person. Knowledge of the Torah, as portrayed in the

Talmud and related writings quite specifically, changed a person and made him (never her—until the twentieth century!) simply different from what he had been before or without that same knowledge: physically weaker, but also strengthened by power that some might call magical, but that they called supernatural.

Before proceeding, let me give a good example of what I mean by knowledge of Torah represented as transformative and salvific. I can point to a story that explicitly states the proposition that the obeying the Torah, with obedience founded on one's own knowledge thereof, constitutes a source of salvation. In this story we shall see that because people observed the rules of the Torah, they expected to be saved. And if they did not observe, they accepted their punishment. So the Torah now stands for something more than revelation and life of study, and (it goes without saying) the sage now appears as a holy, not merely a learned, man. This is because his knowledge of the Torah has transformed him. Accordingly, we deal with a category of stories and sayings about the Torah entirely different from what has gone before. We find at Y. Taanit 3:8 one among numerous examples in which the symbol of the Torah and knowledge of the Torah bear salvific consequence, a claim never set forth in behalf of knowledge, let along knowledge of the Torah, in the Mishnah:

> [IIA] As to Levi ben Sisi: troops came to his town. He took a scroll of the Torah and went up to the roof and said, "Lord of the ages! If a single word of this scroll of the Torah has been nullified [in our town], let them come up against us, and if not, let them go their way."
>
> [B] Forthwith people went looking for the troops but did not find them [because they had gone their way].
>
> [C] A disciple of his did the same thing, and his hand withered, but the troops whet their way.
>
> [D] A disciple of his disciple did the same thing. His hand did not wither, but they also did not go their way.
>
> [E] This illustrates the following apophthegm: You can't insult an idiot, and dead skin does not feel the scalpel. **y. Ta'anit 3:8**

What is interesting here is how taxa into which the word Torah previously fell have been absorbed and superseded in a new taxon. The Torah is an object: "He took a scroll. . . ." It also constitutes God's revelation to Israel: "If a single word. . . ." The outcome of the revelation is to form an ongoing way of life, embodied in the sage himself: "A disciple of his did the same thing. . . ." The sage plays an intimate part in the supernatural event: "His hand withered. . . ." Here the Torah is a source of salvation. How so? The Torah stands for, or constitutes, the way in which the people Israel saves itself from marauders. This straightforward sense of salvation will not have surprised the author of Deuteronomy. But in our documents, there is more to the relationship of the Torah to salvation than mere obedience to its rules.

For now we discern an approach to the mere learning of the Torah—as distinct from obedience to its rules—that promises not merely intellectual enlightenment but personal renewal or transfiguration or some other far-reaching change. Now we confront a Torah, knowledge of which not merely informs or presents right rules of conduct, but which transforms, regenerates, saves. In that context and by these definitions, the theory of the Torah and of Torah-study promises a fully-realized transformation to those who study and therefore know the Torah. They gained not merely intellectual enlightenment but supernatural power and standing. In this context, that encompassed such salvation as would take place prior to the end of time. The new learning defined as the consequence of Torah-study changes not merely the mind but the moral and salvific condition of the one who engages in that learning transformation.

At issue is not mere learning, therefore, and at stake is not only knowledge. We deal with a religious statement, which tells us how to know and love God. And at the center of that statement is this simple conviction: when I study the Torah, I encounter God.

C.   R. Hananiah b. Teradion says, "[If] two sit together and between them do not pass teachings of Torah, lo, this is a seat of the scornful. . . .

E.   "Two who are sitting, and words of Torah do pass between them—the Presence is with them, as it is said, 'Then they that feared the Lord spoke with one another, and the Lord hearkened and heard, and a book of remembrance was written before him, for them that feared the Lord and gave thought to His name' (Mal 3:16)."

G.   I know that this applies to two.

H.   How do I know that even if a single person sits and works on Torah, the Holy One, blessed be he, sets aside a reward for him? As it is said, 'Let him sit along and keep silent, because he has laid it upon him' (Lam 3:28)."   **Avot 3:2**

A.   R. Halafta of Kefar Hananiah says, "Among ten who sit and work hard on Torah the Presence comes to rest,

B.   "as it is said, 'God stands in the congregation of God' (Ps 82:1).

C.   "And how do we know that this is so even of three? Since it is said, 'And he judges among the judges' (Ps 82:1).

E.   "And how do we know that this is so even of two? Because it is said, Then they that feared the Lord spoke with one another, and the Lord hearkened and heard (Mal 3:16).

F.   "And how do we know that this is so even of one? 'Since it is said, In every place where I record my name I will come to you and I will bless you' (Exod 20:24)."   **Avot 3:6**

"Knowing God" or bringing God into one's study circle certainly represent desirable goals of illumination. But these do not encompass the transformative experience promised the one who knows in the Talmud later on. Why not? Because even though God has joined my study-circle and brought the divine presence to rest among the disciples, we still do not then claim supernatural powers as the consequence.

That conclusion is drawn in the two Talmuds and related Midrash-compilations, where a quite different theory of Torah-learning predominates. It is the simple fact that knowledge of the Torah changes the one who knows. He becomes physically weaker, but gains, in compensation, supernatural powers. The legitimating power of the Torah and study thereof imputed in the pages of the Talmud of the Land of Israel is explicit: knowledge of the Torah changes a man into a sage and also saves Israel. The Torah then involves not mere knowledge, e.g., correct information, valid generalization, but saving knowledge.

One important qualification is required. Knowledge is not the only medium of salvation. Salvation, as before, derives from keeping the law of the Torah. Keeping the law in the right way is the way to bring the Messiah, the son of David. This is stated by Levi, as follows. "If Israel would keep a single Sabbath in the proper way, forthwith the son of David would come" (*y. Ta'anit* 1:1.IX). But the issue of not doing but (mere) knowing, of salvation through study of the Torah, is distinct.

To the rabbis the principal salvific deed was to "study Torah," by which they meant memorizing Torah sayings by constant repetition, and, as the Talmud itself amply testifies, (for some sages) profound analytic inquiry into the meaning of those sayings. This act of "study of Torah" imparted supernatural power. For example, by repeating words of Torah, the sage could ward off the angel of death and accomplish other kinds of miracles as well. So Torah formulas served as incantations. Mastery of Torah transformed the man who engaged in Torah learning into a supernatural figure, able to do things ordinary folk could not do. In the nature of things, the category of "Torah" was vastly expanded so that the symbol of Torah, a Torah scroll, could be compared to a man of Torah, namely, a rabbi. Since what made a man into a sage or a disciple of a sage or a rabbi was studying the Torah through discipleship, what is at stake in the symbolic transfer is quite obvious.

The Torah is then identified with and personified by the sage; so he is changed because of what he knows. That is a material and palpable claim, not a mere mode of ascription of great sanctity, lacking any concrete consequence, the vastly expanded definition of the symbol of "Torah." The claim that a sage (or, disciple of a sage) himself was equivalent to a scroll of the Torah forms a material, legal comparison, not merely a symbolic metaphor.

A.   He who sees a disciple of a sage who has died is as if he sees a scroll of the Torah that has been burned.   **y. Mo'ed Qatan 3:7.X**

I.   R. Jacob bar Abayye in the name of R. Aha: "An elder who forgot his learning because of some accident which happened to him—they treat him with the sanctity owed to an ark [of the Torah]."   **y. Mo'ed Qatan 3:1.XI**

In both instances actual behavior was affected. That view is expressed in stories indicating the belief that while a sage is repeating Torah sayings, the angel of death cannot approach him.

F.   [Proving that while one is studying Torah, the angel of death cannot touch a person, the following is told:] A disciple of R. Hisda fell sick. He sent two disciples to him, so that they would repeat Mishnah-traditions with him [The angel of death] turned himself before them into the figure of a snake, and they stopped repeating traditions, and [the sick man] died.

G.   A disciple of Bar Pedaiah fell ill. He sent to him two disciples to repeat Mishnah-traditions with him. [The angel of death] turned himself before them into a kind of star, and they stopped repeating Mishnah-traditions, and he died.

y. Mo'ed Qatan 3:5.XXI

Repeating Mishnah traditions thus warded off death. It is hardly surprising that stories were told about wonders associated with the deaths of various rabbis. These validated the claim of supernatural power imputed to the rabbis. A repertoire of such stories includes two sorts.

First, there is a list of supernatural occurrences accompanying sages' deaths, and, second, we have a claim of specific miracles that were done by Heaven when a great sage died. The former are as in the following

A.   When R. Aha died, a star appeared at noon.

B.   When R. Hanah died, the statues bowed down.

C.   When R. Yohanan died, the icons bowed down.

D.   They said that [this was to indicate] there were no icons like him [so beautiful as Yohanan himself].

E.   When R. Hanina of Bet Hauran died, the Sea of Tiberias split open.

F.   They said that [this was to commemorate the miracle that took place] when he went up to intercalate the year, and the sea split open before him.

G.   When R. Hoshaiah died, the palm of Tiberias fell down.

H.   When R. Isaac b. Elisheb died, seventy [infirm] thresholds of houses in Galilee were shaken down.

I.   They said that [this was to commemorate the fact that] they [were shaky and] had depended on his merit [for the miracle that permitted them to continue to stand].

J.   When R. Samuel bar R. Isaac died, cedars of the land of Israel were uprooted.

K. They said that [this was to take note of the fact that] he would take branch [of a cedar] and [dance, so] praising a bride [at her wedding, and thereby giving her happiness].

L. The rabbis would ridicule them [for lowering himself by doing so]. Said to them R. Zeira, "Leave him be. Does the old man not know what he is doing?"

M. When he died, a flame came forth from heaven and intervened between his bier and the congregation. For three hours there were voices and thunderings in the world: "Come and see what a sprig of cedar has done for this old man!"

N. [Further] an echo came forth and said, "Woe that Samuel b. R.R. Isaac has died, the doer of merciful deeds."

O. When R. Yosé bar Halputa died, the gutters ran with blood in Laodicea.

P. They said [that the reason was] that he had given his life for the rite of circumcision.

Q. When R. Abbahu died, the pillars of Caesarea wept.

R. The [gentiles] said [that the reason was] that [the pillars] were celebrating. The Israelites said to them, "And do those who are distant [such as yourselves] know why those who are near [we ourselves] are raising a cry?"

y. 'Abodah Zarah 3:1.II

BB. One of the members of the patriarchate died, and the [burial] cave folded over [and received the bier], so endangering the lives [of those who had come to bury him]. R. Yosé went up and took leave [of the deceased], saying, "Happy is a man who has left this world in peace."

CC. When R. Yosé died, the castle of Tiberias collapsed, and members of the patriarchate were rejoicing. R. Zeira said to them, "There is no similarity [between this case and the miracle described at BB]. The peoples' lives were endangered, here no one's life was endangered. In that case, no pagan worship was removed, while here, an idol was uprooted [so, consequently, the event described in BB was not a miracle, while the event described here was a miracle and a sign of divine favor]."

y. 'Abodah Zarah 3:1.II

What is important in the foregoing anthology is the linkage between the holy deeds of the sage and the miracles done at their demise. The sages' merit, attained through study of Torah or through acts of saintliness and humility was demonstrated for all to see. So the sage was not merely a master of Torah. But his mastery of Torah laid the foundations for all the other things he was: he was changed into something other than what he had been before he studied the Torah, and all else follows.

Thus far what I have shown is only that sages studied the Torah and also that sages through study of the Torah gained supernatural standing (e.g., when they were buried) and power, which they imputed to their knowledge of the Torah. What I have yet to demonstrate is that knowledge of the Torah itself changed the sage in such a way that he not only could manipulate the supernatural power inhering in the Torah but also could himself join in the processes of forming the Torah. For I have alleged that the man himself was transformed through Torah-study. And what I have already offered in evidence demands an explanation of how that transformation took place. For the allegation that knowledge in particular changes the person can itself refer to a merely instrumental power: if I know thus and so, I can do such and such. At stake in the Yerushalmi's theory of the Torah was much, much more.

Specifically, if I know the Torah, I can join in the making of the Torah, and that claim in my behalf as a sage forms solid evidence of the allegation that studying the Torah not only endows one with power but actually changes the man from what he had been into something else. He had been ordinary, now he is not merely powerful but holy. And his holiness is shown by the fact that, just as we study the Torah in its written and oral forms, so we may study the Torah in its quotidian form: the sage himself, his gestures, his actions then forming precedents valid within the practice of the Torah itself. And when I allege that because we have studied the Torah, we are changed so that I can now join in the process of revealing the Torah, studying the Torah provides an experience of transformation, regeneration, and salvation. Accordingly, I have now to demonstrate that the supernatural status accorded to the person of the sage endowed his deeds with normative, therefore revelatory power.

What the sage did had the status of law; the sage was the model of the law, thus having been changed, transformed, regenerated, saved, turned by studying the Torah into the human embodiment of the Torah. That view of Torah-study as transformative and salvific—now without explicit appeal to deeds in conformity to the law, though surely that is taken for granted—accounts for the position that the sage was a holy man. For what made the sage distinctive was his combination of this-worldly authority and power and otherworldly influence. The clerk in the court and the holy man on the rooftop praying for rain or calling Heaven to defend the city against marauders, in the Yerushalmi's view were one and the same. The tight union between salvation and law, the magical power of the sage and his lawgiving authority, was effected through the integrative act of studying the Torah. And that power of integration accounts for the successor-system's insistence that if the sage exercised supernatural power as a kind of living Torah, his very deeds served to reveal law, as much as his word expressed revelation.

The capacity of the sage himself to participate in the process of revelation is illustrated in two types of materials. First of all, tales told about rabbi's behavior on specific occasions immediately are translated into rules for the entire community to keep. Accordingly, he was a source not merely of good example but of prescriptive law. Here is a humble and mundane case of how that view came to expression.

> X.　R. Aha went to Emmaus, and he ate dumpling [prepared by Samaritans].
> Y.　R. Jeremiah ate leavened bread prepared by them.

Z.   R. Hezekiah ate their locusts prepared by them.

AA.   R. Abbahu prohibited Israelite use of wine prepared by them.

y. 'Abodah Zarah 5:4:III

These reports of what rabbis had done enjoyed the same authority, as statements of the law on eating what Samaritans cooked, as did citations of traditions in the names of the great authorities of old or of the day. What someone did served as a norm, if the person was a sage of sufficient standing.

Far more common in the Talmud are instances in which the deed of a rabbi is adduced as an authoritative precedent for the law under discussion. It was everywhere taken for granted that what a rabbi did, he did because of his mastery of the law. Even though a formulation of the law was not in hand, a tale about what a rabbi actually did constituted adequate evidence on how to formulate the law itself. So from the practice of an authority, a law might be framed quite independent of the person of the sage. The sage then functioned as a lawgiver, like Moses. Among a great many instances of that mode of generating law are the following.

A.   Gamaliel Zuga was walking along, leaning on the shoulder of R. Simeon b. Laqish. They came across an image.

B.   He said to him, "What is the law as to passing before it?"

C.   He said to him, "Pass before it, but close [your] eyes."

D.   R. Isaac was walking along, leaning on the shoulder of R. Yohanan. They came across an idol before the council building.

E.   He said to him, "What is the law as to passing before it?"

F.   He said to him, "Pass before it, but close [your] eyes."

G.   R. Jacob bar Idi was walking along, leaning upon R. Joshua b. Levi. They came across a procession in which an idol was carried. He said to him, "Nahum, the most holy man, passed before this idol, and will you not pass by it? Pass before it but close your eyes."

y. 'Abodah Zarah 3:11.II

The example of a rabbi served to teach how one should live a truly holy life. The requirements went far beyond the measure of the law, extending to refraining from deeds of a most commonplace sort. The example of rabbinical virtue, moreover, was adduced explicitly to account for the supernatural or magical power of a rabbi. There was no doubt, in people's imagination, therefore, that the reason rabbis could do the amazing things people said they did was that they embodied the law and exercised its supernatural or magical power. The correlation between learning and teaching, on the one side, and supernatural power or recognition, on the other, is explicit in the following.

A.　R. Yosé fasted eighty fasts in order to see R. Hiyya the Elder [in a dream]. He finally saw him, and his hands trembled and his eyes grew dim.

B.　Now if you say that R. Yosé was an unimportant man, [and so was unworthy of such a vision, that is not the case]. For a weaver came before R. Yohanan. He said to him, "I saw in my dream that the heaven fell, and one of your disciples was holding it up."

C.　He said to him, "Will you know him [when you see him]?"

D.　He said to him, "When I see him, I shall know him." Then all of his disciples passed before him, and he recognized R. Yosé.

E.　R. Simeon b. Laqish fasted three hundred fasts in order to have a vision of R. Hiyya the Elder, but he did not see him.

F.　Finally he began to be distressed about the matter. He said, "Did he labor in learning of Torah more than I?"

G.　They said to him, "He brought Torah to the people of Israel to a greater extent than you have, and not only so, but he even went into exile [to teach on a wider front]."

H.　He said to them, "And did I not go into exile too?"

I.　They said to him, "You went into exile only to learn, but he went into exile to teach others."　　　　　　　　　　　　　　　　**y. 'Ketubot 12:3.VII**

This story shows that the storyteller regarded as a fact of life the correlation between mastery of Torah sayings and supernatural power—visions of the deceased, in this case. That is why Simeon b. Laqish complained, EF-, that he had learned as much Torah as the other, and so had every right to be able to conjure the dead. The greater supernatural power of the other then was explained in terms of the latter's superior service to "Torah." The upshot is that the sage was changed by Torah learning and could save Israel through Torah.

Precisely how did sages explain the transformation effected by study of the Torah? It was by appeal to the character of the saints of Scripture. Seeing Scripture in their own model, they took the position that the Torah of old, its supernatural power and salvific promise, in their own day continued to endure among themselves. By studying the Torah, they turned themselves into the model of those sages whose holy deeds the Torah recorded: Moses, David and Isaiah being called rabbis, for instance. In consequence, the promise of salvation contained in every line of Scripture was to be kept in every deed of learning and obedience to the law effected under their auspices. Learning in the Torah was salvific because it turned ordinary men into saints in the model of the saints of the Torah.

That fact helps us to understand the constant citation of Scripture in the context of sages' rulings and doings. It was not to establish authority alone. Rather, it was to identify what was happening just then with what had happened long ago. The purpose was not merely to demonstrate and authenticate the *bona fide* character of a new figure of salvation, but to show the continuity of the salvific process, a process then that relied for its persistence upon learning in particular. The act of study of the

Torah, in the system before us, had to be endowed with supernatural status, supernatural power to save, because the act of learning formed the medium for the transmission of not merely the lessons, but the supernatural power, of old. The Torah presented not merely rules but examples of holiness, and salvation lay in sanctification: "Today, if you repent," that is, conform now, as not before: accept transformation, regeneration, salvation.

It followed that the pattern and promise of salvation contained therein lay within their way of life: studying the Torah in discipleship. That is the meaning of the explicit reading of the present into the past—the implicit arrogation of the hope of the past to the salvific heroes of the present: themselves. To state matters simply, if David, King of Israel, was like a rabbi today, then a rabbi today would be the figure of the son of David who was to come as King of Israel. It is not surprising, therefore, that among the many biblical heroes whom the Talmudic rabbis treated as sages, principal and foremost was David himself, now made into a messianic rabbi or a rabbinical Messiah. He was the sage of the Torah, the avatar and model for the sages of their own time. That view was made explicit, both specifically and in general terms. If a rabbi was jealous to have his traditions cited in his own name, it was because that was David's explicit view as well.

In more general terms, both David and Moses are represented as students of Torah, just like the disciples and sages of the current time. David is represented as a devoted student of the Torah. Here is one re-presentation of a biblical story in the mode of an academic tale:

> A.   It is written, "And David said longingly, 'O that someone would give me water to drink from the well of Bethlehem [which is by the gate]'" (1 Chron 11:17).
>
> B.   R. Hiyya bar Ba said, "He required a teaching of law."
>
> C.   "Then the three mighty men broke through [the camp of the Philistines]" (1 Chron 11:18).
>
> D.   Why three? Because the law is not decisively laid down by fewer than three.
>
> E.   "But David would not drink of it; [he poured it out to the Lord, and said, 'Far be it from me before my God that I should do this. Shall I drink the lifeblood of these men? For at the risk of their lives they brought it']" (1 Chron 11:18, 19).
>
> F.   David did not want the law to be laid down in his own name.
>
> G.   "He poured it out to the Lord"—establishing [the decision] as [an unattributed] teaching for the generations, [so that the law should be authoritative and so be cited anonymously]. (*y. Sheqalim* 2:4.V.)
>
> O.   David himself prayed for mercy for himself, as it is said, "Let me dwell in thy tent for ever! Oh to be sage under the shelter of thy wings, selah" (Ps 61:4).
>
> P.   And did it enter David's mind that he would live for ever?
>
> Q.   But this is what David said before the Holy One, blessed be he, "Lord of the world may I have the merit that my words will be stated in synagogues and schoolhouses."

> R.   Simeon b. Nazira in the name of R. Isaac said, "Every disciple in whose name people cite a teaching of law in this world—his lips murmur with him in the grave, as it is said, 'Your kisses are like the best wine that goes down smoothly, gliding over lips of those that sleep" (Song 7:9).
>
> S.   "Just as in the case of a mass of grapes, once a person puts his finger in it, forthwith even his lips begin to smack, so the lips of the righteous, when someone cites a teaching of law in their names—their lips murmur with them in the grave."

y. Sanhedrin 2:6.IV

David as a model of the disciple of the sage is represented in the following for the virtue of conscious and zealous Torah-study.

> O.   "I will awake the dawn" (Ps 5:7, 8)—I will awaken the dawn; the dawn will not awaken me.
>
> P.   David's [evil] impulse tried to seduce him [to sin]. And it would say to him, "David. It is the custom of kings that awakens themm. And you say, I will awake the dawn. It is the custom of kings that they sleep until the third hour [of the day]. And you say, At midnight I rise." And [David] used to say [in reply], "[I rise early] because of thy righteous ordinances (Ps 119:62)."
>
> Q.   And what would David do? R. Phineas in the name of R. Eleazer b. R. Menahem [said], "[He used to take a harp and lyre and set them at his bedside. And he would rise at midnight and play them so that the associates of Torah should hear. And what would the associates of Torah say? 'If David involves himself with Torah, how much more so should we.' We find that all of Israel was involved in Torah [study] on account of David."

y. Berakhot 1:1.XII. (trans. by Tzvee Zahavy)

This extract has shown us how the Talmud's authorities readily saw their concerns in biblical statements attributed to David. "Water" meant "a teaching of Torah." "Three mighty men" were of course judges. At issue was whether or not the decision was to be stated in David's own name—and so removed from the authoritative consensus of sages. David exhibits precisely those concerns for the preservation of his views in his name that, in earlier sections, we saw attributed to rabbis. All of this, as we have noted, fully reveals the rabbis' deeper convictions when we remember that David, the rabbi, also was in everyone's mind David, the Messiah. Enough has been set forth to suggest that I mean to represent the supernatural theory of the transformation effected by the study of the Torah as the centerpiece of the Yerushalmi and related Midrash-compilations.

But our evidence suggests precisely the opposite, for, as a matter of fact, even the stories contained in the Talmud of the Land of Israel in which the priority and sanctity of the sage's knowledge of the Torah form the focus of discourse prevent me from doing so. Time and again, knowledge of the Torah forms a way-station on a path to a more distant, more central goal: attaining *zekhut*, the heritage of virtue and its consequent entitlements. Torah-study is one means of attaining access to that heritage, of gaining *zekhut*. There are other equally suitable means, and, not only so, but the merit gained by Torah-study is no different from the merit gained by acts of supererogatory grace. Since, in the Yerushalmi and related Midrash-compilations, it is points of integration, not of differentiation, that guide us to the systemic problematic, we must take seriously the contingent status, the standing of a dependent variable, accorded to Torah-study in such stories as the following:

C.   There was a house that was about to collapse over there [in Babylonia], and Rab set one of his disciples in the house, until they had cleared out everything from the house. When the disciple left the house, the house collapsed.

D.   And there are those who say that it was R. Adda bar Ahwah.

E.   Sages sent and said to him, "What sort of good deeds are to your credit [that you have that much merit]?"

F.   He said to them, "In my whole life no man ever got to the synagogue in the morning before I did. I never left anybody there when I went out. I never walked four cubits without speaking words of Torah. Nor did I ever mention teachings of Torah in an inappropriate setting. I never laid out a bed and slept for a regular period of time. I never took great strides among the associates. I never called my fellow by a nickname. I never rejoiced in the embarrassment of my fellow. I never cursed my fellow when I was lying by myself in bed. I never walked over in the marketplace to someone who owed me money.

G.   "In my entire life I never lost my temper in my household."

H.   This was meant to carry out that which is stated as follows: "I will give heed to the way that is blameless. Oh when wilt thou come to me? I will walk with integrity of heart within my house" (Ps 101:2).   **y. Ta'anit 3:11.IV**

What I find striking in this story is that mastery of the Torah is only one means of attaining the *zekhut* that had enabled the sage to keep the house from collapsing. And Torah-study is not the primary means of attaining *zekhut*. The question at E provides the key, together with its answer at F. For what the sage did to gain such remarkable *zekhut* is not to master such-and-so many tractates of the Mishnah. It was rather acts of courtesy, consideration, gentility, restraint.

These produced *zekhut*, all of them acts of self-abnegation or the avoidance of power over others and the submission to the will and the requirement of self-esteem of others. Torah-study is simply an item on a list of actions or attitudes that generate *zekhut*. Here, in a moral setting, we find the politics replicated: the form of power that the system promises derives from the rejection of power that the world recognizes—legitimate violence replaced by legitimation of the absence of the power to commit violence or of the failure to commit violence. And, when we ask, whence that sort of power? the answer lies in the gaining of *zekhut* in a variety of ways, not in the acquisition of *zekhut* through the study of the Torah solely or even primarily. But, we note, the story at hand speaks of a sage in particular. He has gained *zekhut* by not acting the way sages are commonly assumed to behave but in a humble way.

In context of this story, *zekhut* then may prove a virtue dependent upon the situation of the Torah and its study, in consequence of which we should have to impute to the supernatural theory of the value of study of the Torah systemic priority, indeed centrality, finding in the new learning the key to the Yerushalmi and related Midrash-compilations as a whole. But that is, in fact, not so. At hand is not a religious system in which the transformation of the individual through salvific knowledge provides the compelling answer to the question of personal salvation. A different question stands at center-stage, and a different answer altogether defines the dramatic tension of the theatrical globe. At stake, as we shall now see, is a public and a national question, one concerning Israel's history and destiny, to which the individual and his salvation, while important, are distinctly subordinated. Not Torah-study, which may generate *zekhut*, but *zekhut* itself defines what is at issue, the generative problematic of the system, and only when we grasp the answer provided by *zekhut* shall we reach a definition of the question that precipitated the systemic construction and the formation of its categories, principal and contingent alike.

The importance of the transformative theory of the study of the Torah in no way diminishes when we recognize the subordinate position of the Torah in the Yerushalmi and related Midrash-compilations. In unifying the distinct categories of learning and not deeds or virtue but one's personal condition in the supernatural world, the recasting of the category of the world-view from an intellectual and even a moral to a salvific and a supernatural indicator, encompassing data not formerly noted or even assembled at all, shows the successor-system's novel power of integration. If Torah-study changes us not only in my knowledge or even virtue but my relationship to Heaven, endowing us with the supernatural power, then the system as a whole signals a union of Heaven and earth that was formerly unimagined. What we know concerns not only earth but Heaven, the power that knowledge brings governs in both realms.

Study of the Torah changed the one who studied because through it he entered into the mind of God, learning how God's mind worked when God formed the Torah, written and oral alike and (in the explicit view of *Genesis Rabbah* 1:1) consulted the Torah in creating the world. And there, in the intellect of God, in their judgment humanity gained access to the only means of uniting intellect with existential condition as to salvation. The Mishnah had set forth the rules that governed the natural world in relationship to Heaven. But knowledge of the Torah now joined the one world, known through nature, with the other world, the world of supernature, when, in the end, intellect merely served in the quest for salvation. Through Torah-study sages claimed for themselves a place in that very process of thought that had given birth to nature; but it was a supernatural process, and knowledge of that process on its own terms would transform and, in the nature of things, save. But, in the end, Torah proves contingent and instrumental. Knowing God involves something other than mere mastery of learning and tradition. As we have already noted, there is something more important than Torah-study. Let us now turn to *zekhut*, a quite different way of knowing God. We know God not only through the Torah, but through acts of supererogatory, self-effacing mercy: service to others that no one can demand or command, but that God respects and values, and to which God, uncoerced, can respond. These are the acts that yield *zekhut*, which, as we have seen, transcends even a life of Torah-learning.

While people suppose that the Torah forms the symbolic center of Judaism, and study of the Torah the critical action, so that women, excluded from academies, find no place in Judaism at all, in fact when we reach the systemic center, we find that "the study of Torah" does not outweigh all else, not at all. Even the stories contained in the Talmud of the Land of Israel in which the priority and sanctity of the sage's knowledge of the Torah form the focus of discourse treat study of the Torah as contingent and merely instrumental. Time and again, knowledge of the Torah forms a way-station on a path to a more distant, more central goal: attaining *zekhut*, here translated as "the heritage of virtue and its consequent entitlements."

Torah-study is one means of attaining access to that heritage, of gaining *zekhut*. There are other equally suitable means, and, not only so, but the merit gained by Torah-study is no different from the merit gained by any and all other types of acts of supererogatory grace. And still more astonishing, a single remarkable action may produce *zekhut* of the same order as a lifetime of devotion to Torah-study, and a simple ass-driver through a noteworthy act of selfless behavior may attain the same level of *zekhut* as a learned sage.

Were such stories as these located other than in the Talmud, one might find tempting the thesis that they represented an anti-rabbinic viewpoint. But rabbis told these stories, preserved them, and placed them on exhibition to expose the finest virtue they could imagine. That is why we turn for our integrating conception to that final reversal and revision of the given: just as scarce resources are made abundant, legitimate power deemed only weakness, and facts displaced by revealed truth, so the one-time moment at which *zekhut* is attained from Heaven outweighs a lifetime of Torah-learning. *Zekhut* formed the foundation for the Yerushalmi's conception of political economy for the social order of Israel. It and not Torah defined the whole, of which economics and a politics comprised mere details. It set forth and accounts for an economics and a politics that made powerlessness into power, disinheritance into wealth. How in fact does *zekhut* function?

Zekhut is gained for a person by an act of renunciation and self-abnegation, such that Heaven responds with an act of grace. Works of supererogation, which Heaven cannot compel but highly prizes, *zekhut* defines the very opposite of coercion. It is an act that no one could anticipate or demand, but an act of such remarkable selflessness that Heaven finds itself constrained to respond. That is why the systemic center is formed by an act, on Heaven's part, of responsive grace, meaning, grace one by definition cannot demand or compel, but only provoke. When we make ourselves less, Heaven makes us more; but we cannot force our will upon Heaven. When we ask about the feminization of Judaism, our attention rests upon this fact: the right relationship between Israel and God is the relationship that is not coerced, not manipulated, not one defined by a dominant party upon a subordinated one. It is a relationship of mutuality, negotiation, response to what is freely given through what cannot be demanded but only volunteered. The relationship, in other words, is a feminine, not a masculine, one, when measured by the prevailing, conventional stereotypes.

It is where Heaven cannot force its will upon us that *zekhut* intervenes. It is that exquisite balance between our will and Heaven's will that, in the end, brings to its perfect balance and entire fulfillment the exploration of the conflict of God's will and our will that began with Adam and Eve at their last hour in Eden, and our first hour on earth. And, in context, the fact that we may inherit a treasury of *zekhut* from our ancestors logically follows: just as we inherit the human condition of the freedom to practice rebellion against God's word, so we inherit, from former generations, the results of another dimension of the human condition: our power to give willingly what none, even God, can by right or rule compel.

That is why the structure of Israel's political economy rested upon divine response to acts of will consisting of submission, on one's own, to the will of Heaven; these acts endowed Israel with a lien and entitlement upon Heaven. What we cannot by our own will impose, we can by act of renunciation of our own will evoke. What we cannot accomplish through coercion, we can achieve through submission. God will do for us what we cannot do for ourselves, when we do for God what God cannot make us do. And that means, in a wholly concrete and tangible sense, love God with all the heart, the soul, the might, we have. God then stands above the rules of the created world, because God will respond not to what we do in conformity to the rules alone, but also to what we do beyond the requirement of the rules. God is above the rules, and we can gain a response from God when, on some one, unique occasion, we too do more than obey—but love, spontaneously and all at once, with the whole of our being. That is the conception of God that *zekhut*, as a conception of power in Heaven and power in humanity, contains. In the relationship between God and humanity expressed in the conception of *zekhut*, we reach the understanding of what the Torah means when it tells us that we are in God's image and after God's likeness: we are then, "in our image," the very mirror-image of God. God's will forms the mirror-image of ours: when we are humble, God responds: when we demand, God withdraws.

It must follow that *zekhut*, not Torah, in a single word defines the generative myth, the critical symbol of the successor-Judaism. The signal that the study of the

Torah formed a mere component in a system that transcended Torah-study and divined its structure in some way other than by appeal to the symbol and activity of the Torah comes from a simple fact. Ordinary folk, not disciples of sages, have access to *zekhut* entirely outside of study of the Torah. In stories not told about rabbis, a single remarkable deed, exemplary for its deep humanity, sufficed to win for a ordinary person the *zekhut*—"the heritage of virtue and its consequent entitlements"—that elicits the same marks of supernatural favor enjoyed by some rabbis on account of their Torah-study.

Accordingly, the systemic centrality of *zekhut* in the structure, the critical importance of the heritage of virtue together with its supernatural entitlements—these emerge in a striking claim. It is framed in extreme form—another mark of the unique place of *zekhut* within the system. Even though a man was degraded, one action sufficed to win for him that heavenly glory to which rabbis in lives of Torah-study aspired. The mark of the system's integration around *zekhut* lies in its insistence that all Israelites, not only sages, could gain *zekhut* for themselves (and their descendants). A single remarkable deed, exemplary for its deep humanity, sufficed to win for an ordinary person the *zekhut* that elicits supernatural favor enjoyed by some rabbis on account of their Torah-study. The centrality of *zekhut* in the systemic structure, the critical importance of the heritage of virtue together with its supernatural entitlements therefore emerge in a striking claim. Even though a man was degraded, one action sufficed to win for him that heavenly glory to which rabbis in general aspired. The rabbinical storyteller whose writing we shall consider assuredly identifies with this lesson, since it is the point of his story and its climax.

When we come to the way in which *zekhut* is set forth, we find ourselves in a set of narratives of a rather special order. What is special about them is that women play a critical role, appear as heroines, win the attention and respect of the reader or listener. It is difficult to locate in Rabbinic literature before the Talmud of the Land of Israel—the Mishnah, the Tosefta, Sifra, for instance—stories in which women figure at all. So to take up a whole series of stories in which women are key-players comes as a surprise. But there is more. The story-teller on the surface makes the man the hero; he is the center of the narrative. And yet a second glance at what is coming shows us that the woman precipitates the tale, and her action, not the man's, represents the gift that cannot be compelled but only given; she is the one who freely sacrifices, and she also is represented as the source of wisdom. So our systemic reversal—something above the Torah and the study of the Torah takes priority—is matched by a still-less-predictable shift in narrative quality, with women portrayed as principal actors.

In all three instances that follow and define what the individual must do to gain *zekhut*, the point is that the deeds of the heroes of the story make them worthy of having their prayers answered, which is a mark of the working of *zekhut*. It is supererogatory, uncoerced deeds, those well beyond the strict requirements of the

Torah, and even the limits of the law altogether, that transform the hero into a holy man, whose holiness served just like that of a sage marked as such by knowledge of the Torah. The following stories should not be understood as expressions of mere sentimentality of the clerks concerning the lower orders, for they deny in favor of a single action of surpassing power sages' lifelong devotion to what the sages held to be the highest value, knowledge of the Torah:

> F.   A certain man came before one of the relatives of R. Yannai. He said to him, "Rabbi, attain *zekhut* through me [by giving me charity]."
> G.   He said to him, "And didn't your father leave you money?"
> H.   He said to him, "No."
> I.   He said to him, "Go and collect what your father left in deposit with others."
> J.   He said to him, "I have heard concerning property my father deposited with others that it was gained by violence [so I don't want it]."
> K.   He said to him, "You are worthy of praying and having your prayers answered."
>
> **y. Ta'anit 1:4.I**

The point of K, of course, is self-evidently a reference to the possession of entitlement to supernatural favor, and it is gained, we see, through deeds that the law of Torah cannot require but must favor: what one does on one's own volition, beyond the measure of the law. Here is the opposite of sin. A sin is what one has done by one's own volition beyond all limits of the law. So an act that generates *zekhut* for the individual is the counterpart and opposite: what one does by one's own volition that also is beyond all requirements of the law.

In the continuation of these stories, we should not miss an odd fact. The story tells about the *zekhut* attained by a humble, poor, ignorant man. It is narrated to underline what he has done. But what provokes the event is an act of self-abnegation far greater than that willingly performed by the male hero, which is, the woman's readiness to sell herself into prostitution to save her husband. That is not a focus of the story but the given. But nothing has compelled the women to surrender her body to save her husband; to the contrary, the marital obligations of a woman concern only conventional deeds, which indeed the Mishnah's law maintains may be coerced; failure to do these deeds may result in financial penalties inflicted on the woman in the settlement of her marriage-contract. So the story of the uncoerced act of selflessness is told about a man, but occasioned by a woman, and both actors in the story exhibit one and the same virtue.

When Torah-stories are told, by contrast, the point is, a man attains *zekhut* by study of the Torah, and a woman attains *zekhut* by sending her sons and her husband off to study the Torah and sitting home alone—not exactly commensurate action. Only *zekhut*-stories represent the act of the woman as the counterpart and equivalent to the act of the man; and, in fact, even here, the fact that the woman's uncoerced gift is far greater than the man's—her body, merely his ass—should not go unnoticed. Once more, we find ourselves at the systemic center, where everything is reversed:

> L.   A certain ass driver appeared before the rabbis [the context requires: in a dream] and prayed, and rain came. The rabbis sent and brought him and said to him, "What is your trade?"
> M.   He said to them, "I am an ass driver."
> N.   They said to him, "And how do you conduct your business?"
> O.   He said to them, "One time I rented my ass to a certain woman, and she was weeping on the way, and I said to her, 'What's with you?' and she said to me, 'The husband of that woman [me] is in prison [for debt], and I wanted to see what I can do to free him.' So I sold my ass and I gave her the proceeds, and I said to her, 'Here is your money, free your husband, but do not sin [by becoming a prostitute to raise the necessary funds.].' "

The ass-driver clearly has a powerful lien on Heaven, so that his prayers are answered, even while those of others are not. What he did to get that entitlement? He did what no law could demand: impoverished himself to save the woman from a "fate worse than death."

> Q.   In a dream of R. Abbahu, Mr. Pentakaka ["Five sins"] appeared, who prayed that rain would come, and it rained. R. Abbahu sent and summoned him. He said to him, "What is your trade?"
> R.   He said to him, "Five sins does that man [I] do every day, [for I am a pimp:] hiring whores, cleaning up the theater, bringing home their garments for washing, dancing, and performing before them."
> S.   He said to him, "And what sort of decent thing have you ever done?"
> T.   He said to him, "One day that man [I] was cleaning the theater, and a woman came and stood behind a pillar and cried. I said to her, 'What's with you?' And she said to me, 'That woman's [my] husband is in prison, and I wanted to see what I can do to free him,' so I sold my bed and cover, and I gave the proceeds to her. I said to her, 'Here is your money, free your husband, but do not sin.' "
> U.   He said to him, "You are worthy of praying and having your prayers answered."

Q moves us still further, since the named man has done everything sinful that one can do, and, more to the point, he does it every day. So the singularity of the act of *zekhut*, which suffices if done only one time, encompasses its power to outweigh a life of sin—again, an act of *zekhut* as the mirror-image and opposite of sin. Here again, the single act of saving a woman from a "fate worse than death" has sufficed.

> V.   A pious man from Kefar Imi appeared [in a dream] to the rabbis. He prayed for rain and it rained. The rabbis went up to him. His householders told them that he

was sitting on a hill. They went out to him, saying to him, "Greetings," but he did not answer them.

W.   He was sitting and eating, and he did not say to them, "You break bread too."

X.   When he went back home, he made a bundle of faggots and put his cloak on top of the bundle [instead of on his shoulder].

Y.   When he came home, he said to his household [wife], "These rabbis are here [because] they want me to pray for rain. If I pray and it rains, it is a disgrace for them, and if not, it is a profanation of the Name of Heaven. But come, you and I will go up [to the roof] and pray. If it rains, we shall tell them, 'We are not worthy to pray and have our prayers answered."

Z.   They went up and prayed and it rained.

AA. They came down to them [and asked], "Why have the rabbis troubled themselves to come here today?"

BB. They said to him, "We wanted you to pray so that it would rain."

CC. He said to them, "Now do you really need my prayers? Heaven already has done its miracle."

DD. They said to him, "Why, when you were on the hill, did we say hello to you, and you did not reply?"

EE. He said to them, "I was then doing my job. Should I then interrupt my concentration [to my work]?"

FF. They said to him, "And why, when you sat down to eat, did you not say to us, 'You break bread too'?"

GG. He said to them, "Because I had only my small ration of bread. Why would I have invited you to eat by way of mere flattery [when I knew I could not give you anything at all]?"

HH. They said to him, "And why when you came to go down, did you put your cloak on top of the bundle?"

II.   He said to them, "Because the cloak was not mine. It was borrowed for use at prayer. I did not want to tear it."

JJ.   They said to him, "And why, when you were on the hill, did your wife wear dirty clothes, but when you came down from the mountain, did she put on clean clothes?"

KK. He said to them, "When I was on the hill, she put on dirty clothes, so that no one would gaze at her. But when I came home from the hill, she put on clean clothes, so that I would not gaze on any other woman."

LL. They said to him, "It is well that you pray and have your prayers answered."

Here the woman is at least an equal player; her actions, as much as her husband's, prove exemplary and illustrate the ultimate wisdom. The pious man of V, finally, enjoys the recognition of the sages by reason of his lien upon Heaven, able as he is to pray and bring rain. What has so endowed him with *zekhut*? Acts of punctiliousness of a moral order: concentrating on his work, avoiding an act of dissimulation, integrity in the disposition of a borrowed object, his wife's concern not to attract other men and her equal concern to make herself attractive to her husband.

We note that, at the systemic center, women find entire equality with men; with no role whatever in the study of the Torah and no possibility of attaining political sagacity, women find a critical place in the sequence of actions that elicit from Heaven the admiring response that *zekhut* embodies. Indeed, a second reading of the stories shows that the hero is second to the heroine; it is the woman who, in each case, precipitates the occasion for the man's attainment of *zekhut*, and she, not he, exemplifies the highest pinnacle of selfless virtue. It follows, once more, that those reversals that signal the systemic center culminate in the (for so male a system as this one) ultimate reversal: woman at the height. Just as Torah-learning is subordinated, so man is subordinated; *zekhut*, the gift that can be given but not compelled, like love, in an unerring sense must be called the female virtue that sets atop a male system and structure.

The system here speaks to everybody, Jew and gentile, past and present and future; *zekhut* therefore defines the structure of the cosmic social order and explains how it is supposed to function. It is the encompassing quality of *zekhut*, its pertinence to past and future, high and low, rich and poor, gifted and ordinary, that marks as the systemic statement the message of *zekhut*, now fully revealed as the conception of reciprocal response between Heaven and Israel on earth, to acts of devotion beyond the requirements of the Torah but defined all the same by the Torah. As Scripture had said, God responds to the faith of the ancient generations by supernatural acts to which, on their own account, the moderns are not entitled, hence a heritage of entitlement. But those acts, now fully defined for us, can and ought to be done, also, by the living generation. And, as a matter of fact, no one today, at the time of the system-builders, is exempt from the systemic message and its demands: even steadfastness in accomplishing the humble work of the everyday and the here and now.

The ultimate goal of the Torah and transcending the Torah, *zekhut* speaks of relationship, function, the interplay of humanity and God. One's store of *zekhut* derives from a relationship, that is, from one's forebears. What sort of relationship does *zekhut*, as the opposite of sin, then posit? It is not one of coercion, for Heaven cannot force us to do those types of deeds that yield *zekhut*, and that, story after story suggests, is the definition of a deed that generates *zekhut*: doing what we ought to do but do not have to do. But then, we cannot coerce Heaven to do what we want done either, for example, by carrying out the commandments. These are obligatory, but do not obligate Heaven. Whence then the lien on Heaven? To recapitulate: it is through deeds of a supererogatory character—to which Heaven responds by deeds of a supererogatory character: supernatural favor to this one, who through deeds of ingratiation of the other or self-abnegation or restraint exhibits the attitude that in Heaven precipitates a counterpart attitude, hence generating *zekhut*, rather than to that one, who does not. The simple fact that rabbis cannot pray and bring rain, but a simple ass-driver can, tells the whole story.

The relationship measured by *zekhut*—Heaven's response by an act of uncoerced favor to a person's uncoerced gift, e.g., act of gentility, restraint, or self-abnegation —contains an element of unpredictability for which appeal to the *zekhut* inherited from ancestors accounts. So while one cannot coerce heaven, he or she—for women as much as men enjoy full access to *zekhut*, though they do not to the study of the Torah—can through *zekhut* gain acts of favor from Heaven, and that is by doing what Heaven cannot require of me. Heaven then responds to one's attitude in carrying out his or her duties—and more than those duties. That act of pure disinterest—giving the woman one's means of livelihood—is the one that gains for me Heaven's deepest interest.

When Christianity speaks of the crucified Messiah, the power of weakness, the glory of surrender, it finds counterpart language with *zekhut*. Here we find the ultimate reversal, which the moves from the legitimacy of power to the legitimacy of weakness, in perspective are shown merely to adumbrate. "Make God's wishes yours, so that God will make your wishes his. . . . Anyone from whom people take pleasure, God takes pleasure" (*Abot* 2:4). These two statements hold together the two principal elements of the conception of the relationship to God that in a single word *zekhut* conveys. Give up, please others, do not impose your will but give way to the will of the other, and Heaven will respond by giving a lien that is not coerced but evoked. By the rationality of discipline within, we have the power to form rational relationships beyond ourselves, with Heaven; and that is how the system expands the boundaries of the social order to encompass not only the natural but also the supernatural world.

A life in accord with the rules—even a life spent in the study of the Torah—in Heaven's view is outweighed by a single moment, a gesture that violates the norm, extending the outer limits of the rule, for instance, of virtue. And who but a God who, like us, feels, not only thinks, responds to impulse and sentiment, can be portrayed in such a way as this?

> So I sold my ass and I gave her the proceeds, and I said to her, 'Here is your money, free your husband, but do not sin [by becoming a prostitute to raise the necessary funds].' "
>
> They said to him, "You are worthy of praying and having your prayers answered."

No rule exhaustively describes a world such as this. Here the law of love is transcended, for love itself is not surpassed. Beyond love is the willing, uncoerced sacrifice of self: love of the other more than the love of self, love of the Other most of all. Feminine Judaism relates to God as lovers relate to one another: giving not in order to receive, receiving only in order to give.

Life in conformity with the rule, obligatory but merely conventional, did not evoke the special interest of Heaven. Why should it? The rules describe the ordinary. But (in language used only in a later document) "the All-Merciful really wants the heart," and that is not an ordinary thing. Nor was the power to bring rain or hold up a tottering house gained through a life of merely ordinary sanctity. Special favor responded to extraordinary actions, in the analogy of special disfavor, misfortune deemed to punish sin. And just as culpable sin, as distinct from mere error, required an act of will, specifically, arrogance, so an act of extraordinary character requires an act of will. But, as mirror image of sin, the act would reveal in a concrete way an attitude of restraint, forbearance, gentility, and self-abnegation. A sinful act, provoking Heaven, was one done deliberately to defy Heaven. Then an act that would evoke Heaven's favor, so imposing upon Heaven a lien that Heaven freely gave, was one that, equally deliberately and concretely, displayed humility.

Zekhut was the power of the powerless, the riches of the disinherited, the valuation and valorization of the will of those who have no right to will. *Zekhut* arms Israel with the weapons of woman: the strength of weakness, the power of patience and endurance, the coercion that comes about through surviving, come what may. This feminine Judaism's Israel a family, its God a lover and beloved, its virtue uncoerced, its wisdom uncompelled,—this Judaism served for those long centuries in which Judaism addressed a people that could not dominate, but only reason; that could not manipulate, but only hope; that could not guarantee results, but only trust in what would be. In the context of Christian Palestine, Jews found themselves on the defensive. Their ancestry called into question, their supernatural standing thrown into doubt, their future denied, they called themselves "Israel," and the land, "the Land of Israel." But what power did they possess, legitimately, if need be through violence, to assert their claim to form "Israel"? And, with the holy land passing into the hands of others, what scarce resource did they own and manage to take the place of that measure of value that now no longer was subjected to their rationality? Asserting a politics in which all violence was illegitimate, an economics in which nothing tangible, even real property in the Holy Land, had value, the system through its counterpart-categories made a single, simple, and sufficient statement.

Endnote

[1]Ingolf Dalferth, "The Stuff of Revelation: Austin Farrer's Doctrine of Inspired Images," in *Hermeneutics, the Bible, and Literary Criticism*, ed. Ann Loades and Michael McLain (London: MacMillan, 1992) 71.

Part One
Revelation

Chapter 2

Revelation

Shalom Rosenberg

Before we can speak of the Torah, meaning, the dual Torah, or even torah with a small t, meaning, "law, teaching, instruction," we have to address an issue of common intelligibility. Since Torah in Judaism is the gift of God, we have first of all to take up the issue of revelation, the category, in general knowledge, into which the Torah fits. For when, in the native speech of Judaism, we wish to say, "revelation," we have to say, "God gives the Torah," or "the giving of the Torah." The language bears its own sense, namely, the Torah comes to Israel from God, in Protestant Christian language, the Torah is God's word. Exactly what is meant by "revelation" in the setting of Judaism requires spelling out. Revelation comes to eternal Israel in specific words, in the document, the Torah, in its two media, written and oral. The Torah is given at Sinai, a statement of not historical but much more profound, religious meaning: in these words, God has told us what God commands, our part of the covenant that, through obedience to the Torah, we fulfill. When, describing Judaism, Protestant theologians speak of "covenantal nomism," meaning, carrying out works of the law as acts in loyalty and obedience to the covenant, they formulate in their terms what Judaism says in the simple word, "Torah." It follows that translating the word "Torah" as "law" is partly right, since the Torah contains laws; but it is then entirely misleading, since Torah does not contain only commandments but also God's self-manifestation: it is how we know God, as much as how we serve God, through the Torah that we mean by "Torah." In this chapter, we follow the ways in which Judaic theologians spelled out the meaning of revelation; what is important is that there is no discussing "revelation" in general without shifting immediately to the Torah, in particular.

***

The term *revelation* has a twofold meaning in English as well as in other languages—like, for example, *Offenbarung* in German. The first meaning denotes the hidden God's revelation of himself; the second denotes the God who reveals not himself but rather "the Torah from heaven" (*Torah min ha-shamayim*)—the God who communicates information or commands. Revelation in this second sense is expressed in the realm of language, whereas revelation in the first sense goes beyond the linguistic sphere to indicate a fact—the encounter between God and man. This distinction between the two meanings of the term parallels the distinction between propositional and nonpropositional conceptions of revelation in modern theology. However, this parallel is applicable only with certain restrictions. Any discussion of revelation in the framework of Judaism requires us to concern ourselves not only with revelation whose content is the Torah, that is, with the revelation of some information about God, man, or the world, but also with revelation whose content is religious commandments, namely, a system of norms and laws. If we understand *proposition* in this broader sense, which includes commands, then the parallel is valid.

The study of the history of this distinction in the framework of Jewish thought leads us to the work of Salomon Ludwig Steinheim, who lucidly described both meanings in his book on revelation according to the teachings of Judaism.[1] Nathan Rotenstreich summed up his position as follows: "According to Steinheim, revelation is theory. That is, it belongs in the realm of propositions for inquiry and cognition and not in the realm of concrete reality and its various levels."[2] Steinheim also expressed, symbolically, the distinction between the two concepts by comparing them to the differing functions of the eye and ear in revelation. This distinction was later to become more accepted in the form expressed by Heinrich Graetz in one of his early works:

This fundamental difference in the conception of the divine can be developed still further. To the pagan, the divine appears within nature as something observable to the eye. He becomes conscious of it as something seen. In contrast, to the Jew who knows that the divine exists beyond, outside of, and prior to nature, God reveals Himself through demonstration of His will, through the medium of the ear. The human subject becomes conscious of the divine through hearing and obeying. Paganism sees its god, Judaism hears Him; that is, it hears the commandments of His will.[3]

Over against the Christian incarnation, Judaism places "the divinely given Torah." The incarnation is unquestionably foreign to Jewish thought, but it is certainly possible to extend the concept of the revelation of various entities from hypostases of divine attributes to angels and supernatural messengers. The concept of revelation can be broadened to encompass a very great variety indeed of mystical phenomena, from the revealing of the *Shekhinah* (the divine Presence) to the revealing of the prophet Elijah. Yet broadening this concept, however necessary, creates a new problem—where to draw the boundaries between the meanings. For example, one might well ask which kind of revelation the intuition of ideas constitutes.

Broadening the second meaning of revelation makes continuity between the two meanings possible, but then we are faced once again with the necessity of drawing the precise boundaries between revelation as an event belonging to the real, concrete world and revelation in the realm of language.

However, we should be very cautious in our use of this formulation. A study of the writings in the various branches of classical Jewish thought does not permit any limitation of the medium of revelation to the sphere of language in the ordinary sense of the term. We must also allow for revelation via things and events that are by no means linguistic creations but are nonetheless revealed as symbols of another reality. Such a view is based upon the approach to prophecy found in the main currents of medieval Jewish philosophy. In a vision, some form of reality is revealed to the prophet, although that reality is nothing but the result of the joint action of rational and imaginative faculties. Accordingly, in the words of Hasdai Crescas, the vision is simply a transformation of "a spiritual and cognitive overflow from God to man, either directly or. . . ."[4]

This passage shows how problematical was the early attempt to define the difference between the meanings of revelation. Of course, this observation cannot obscure the fundamental distinction between the meanings; it can only make us aware of the doubts that arise in many cases, and not necessarily borderline cases at that. Hence we perceive a need to broaden the concept of the language revelation employs and to establish clear boundaries between concrete and symbolic revelation.

The distinction between concrete and symbolic revelation is blurred when we come to the teachings of the kabbalah. In the kabbalistic framework, both the Torah and all of concrete reality are symbols of a higher reality. The symbolic essence of the Torah is expressed in the statement that the Torah is nothing but a tissue of the names of God. The words of the Torah are not only linguistic creations consisting of information about God and the world, but also concrete objects—"names." This identity of symbols and reality leads to an understanding of the sacredness of the Torah as well as to consciousness of its divine status. An extreme instance of this view is found in the teachings of Hayyim ben Isaac of Volozhin, who considered the Torah itself to be a part of the worlds of the Infinite (the kabbalistic conception of God before his self-revelation through finite creation).[5]

In consonance with the symbolic conception of revelation, Steinheim considered revelation as Torah.[6] In this sense, Steinheim considered himself close to Moses Mendelssohn. The difference between them parallels the possible changes in the understanding of Torah. According to Mendelssohn, the content of revelation is commandments. According to Steinheim, its content is theology, that is, truths that mankind could not have acquired on its own.

In the twentieth century, Franz Rosenzweig subjected the concept of revelation to a new systematic discussion in which he placed the concept in the framework of a conceptual triangle consisting of creation, revelation, and redemption. This framework is fruitful and important, particularly because of its insistence upon a fundamental pluralism in reality in which the various entities cannot be juxtaposed. Relying on Rosenzweig, Buber shows that it is Christianity "which fused the essentials of revelation and the essentials of redemption in Christ."[7] The conflation of the two, Buber underscores, is indicative of the concrete conception of revelation.

The work of modern thinkers on this issue raises such fundamental questions as: Does the concept of concrete revelation exist in classical Jewish philosophy? Can we find in the latter any characteristic features of the former, such as the separation between creation and redemption?

We shall demonstrate the difficulty of giving unequivocal answers to these questions by quoting a number of passages from kabbalistic and philosophical literature, without regard for chronological or systematic order. The first example is taken from Moses Ḥayyim Luzzatto's commentary on the Lurianic kabbalah, *Kela ḥ Pit ḥ ei Ḥokhmah* (chap. 4):

> The *Ein Sof* [the Infinite], blessed be He, wanted to bestow the perfect good, and thus deemed to reveal manifestly his full unity. Accordingly, he set down this governance, the Torah, by which he governs and by virtue of which evil will be restored to good.

In this passage, Luzzatto interweaves two motifs. According to the first, the creation itself represents an act of revelation: "God's purpose in creating the world is to bestow goodness in accordance with his passionate love of the ultimate good" (ibid., chap. 3). According to the second, redemption is revelation, "the revealed unity." The first motif is the classical one, although innumerable changes in the basic scheme are conceivable. Thus, for example, in Ḥayyim Vital's *E z Ḥayyim*[8] dots the creation is explained as God's compulsion, so to speak, to expend

> his activities and powers by means of actions and products [because otherwise] He could not, so to speak, be called *Shalem* [whole] . . . because He is [also] called the Lord, and the meaning of lordship is having servants over whom one is the lord, and if He did not have creations, He could not be called the Lord.[9]

In these different versions there is an element of revelation or even of self-revelation in the very act of the creation.

The second motif, which appears in the passage from Luzzatto cited above —namely, the revealing that is linked to redemption—also contains the possibility of nuances that would be suited to the changing content of the concept of redemption.

In *Kela ḥ Pit ḥ ei Ḥokhmah*, revelation is cosmic. An instance of individual revelation is that of the *Shekhinah* to the righteous *(ha- ẓ addikim)* during their lifetimes or after their deaths.

So far we have seen the concept of revelation as a fundamental component of creation and redemption. However, between creation and redemption there extends the sequence of time on the stage of history. According to Buber, the fact that the elements of creation, revelation, and redemption exist without being identical creates a place for "the essence of time, which was closely allied to the essence of our spirit . . . time which distinguishes between past, present, and future." However, Buber adds, we must qualify the temporal distinction: "From the point of view of the Bible, revelation is, as it were, focused in the middle, creation in the beginning, redemption in the end."[10]

What does "revelation . . . in the middle" mean? Can it be translated in the terms of classical Jewish thought into a concept in its own right whose systematic function parallels such a use of revelation?

To judge from the context, this concept is surprisingly close to that of providence *(hashga ḥ ah)*. Of course, providence should not be identified with any dogmatic teaching about reward and punishment. Providence is expressed in God's attitude to man, his "interest" in the activities of flesh and blood. The category of divine knowledge also expresses this attitude, but from the standpoint of God. Providence is a reflection of this attitude from the perspective of man, and accordingly it is the revelation of divine knowledge to man and the world.

I have underscored this aspect of the issue in order to stress that the classical parallel of the concept of revelation in the sense of uncovering does not exist in the concept of "the divinely given Torah," but rather sometimes in the doctrine of providence, which represents, to a certain extent, a philosophical transformation of "the revealing of the *Shekhinah*." An instance of the linkage between the concept of revelation in modern thought and the classical doctrine of providence may be found in Moses Maimonides' writings on God's revelation to Moses in the cleaving of the rock (Exod 33:12-23). In his commentary on these verses, Maimonides suggests several fundamental principles that determine the framework for the classical Jewish understanding of the revealed Torah:

> Know that the master of those who know, *Moses our Master,* peace be on him, made two requests and received an answer to both of them. One request consisted in his asking Him, may He be exalted, to let him know His essence and true reality. The second request, which he put first, was that He should let him know His attributes. The answer to the two requests that He, may He be exalted, gave him consisted in His promising him to let him know all His attributes, making it known to him that they are His actions, and teaching him that His essence cannot be grasped as it really is. *(Guide, 1:54)*

Although Maimonides is referring to the doctrine of attributes, his ideas may be translated into the concepts of the doctrine of revelation. The "essence and true reality" of God go beyond his watching over man, beyond his self-revelation. Only God's attributes are within human comprehension—but what are these attributes?

> His request regarding the knowledge of God's attributes is conveyed in his saying: "Show me now Thy ways, that I may know Thee, and so on" (Exod 33:13]. Consider the wondrous notions contained in this dictum, For his saying, "Show me now Thy ways, that I may know Thee," indicates that God, may He be exalted, is known through His attributive qualifications, for when he would know the *ways*, he would know Him.
>
> *(ibid.)*

The knowledge of God is simply the knowledge of his ways. God's self-revelation is the revealing of his ways. And in fact the doctrine of revelation is no more than the doctrine of providence.

The parallel between revelation and providence is more than a purely formal one. Medieval Jewish thinkers were greatly exercised by the dilemma of personal versus general providence. These two possibilities actually delimit what may be called in the realm of revelation nature and history. Revelation is universal by its very nature, whereas historical revelation possesses a particular essence like that of the personal providence of classical Jewish philosophy. If we do not simplistically identify providence with the doctrine of reward and punishment, then this concept comes closer to the search for a metahistorical layer, for a God beyond nature, for a reality that behaves according to its wont—in short, the search for the hidden God.

The concept of the divinely given Torah, which is unquestionably a close parallel of the propositional meaning of revelation, became ever more central in the late Middle Ages. This phenomenon seems absurd in view of the centrality of the Torah to every Jewish philosophy. Nonetheless, a change did come about that was more than merely semantic. Earlier this concept had constituted a branch of the prophetic doctrine, which also determined the method by which it was derived. As a branch of the prophetic doctrine, the differentiation of the concept assumes the existence of a philosophical theoretical system on the basis of whose assumptions the possibility of revelation may be proved. This system is the Torah that God gave Moses. But inasmuch as this was a historical, not a metaphysical, affair, it must be studied by means of an essentially historical method. This reservation notwithstanding, we shall attempt to explain the doctrine of revelation within the framework of the given theological method.

An example of the renewed discussion of revelation is to be found in the teaching of Hasdai Crescas, whose innovative approach influenced the formulation of the principles of faith. According to Crescas, the classical discussion of the doctrine of the principles of faith, precisely because it is anchored in various philosophical systems, is unsystematic. The new systematic method that Crescas employs is a transcendental deduction based upon the existence of the Torah. This starting point may be phrased as a question. "How can the Torah exist?" The answer is to be found in the Jewish system of principles. Crescas calls these transcendental principles "Toraic fundaments," in order to distinguish them from the true beliefs originating in revelation.

> Concerning the fundaments [*pinnot*] of the Torah, that is, the foundations and pillars upon which the house of the Lord shall be established [cf., Isa 2:2] and by virtue of their existence the existence of the Torah, as given by God, becomes conceivable. And if one of these fundaments were missing, the Torah in its entirety would fall, God forbid. (*Or Adonai* 2, preface)

The belief in the existence of God is the root that lies even beyond the transcendental principles. The fundaments are "one, God's knowledge of existing things; two, His providence over them; three, His power; four, prophecy; five, [man's power of] choice; six, the purpose of the Torah" [ibid.]. Although we may disagree on the contents of this list of principles, it nonetheless provides us with a stratification, since it is the "divinely given Torah" that is the main principle. Before it comes the first root, which is "the beginning of all the beliefs in the Torah and is the belief in the existence of God, blessed be He," and the "fundaments," which elucidate the concept of revelation and make possible the existence of the Torah and the religious commandments.

The term *divinely given Torah* and its parallels enable us to understand the sharp distinction between the different meanings of the concept of revelation. This distinction applies also to classical Jewish thought, although we should note one exception that unified the different concepts through the use of a single term. I am referring to Judah Halevi's concept of the "divine cause," which is prophecy (*The Kuzari* 1:43, 95) connected with concrete evidence "which will bring down to them the cause of God so that they may see it and receive it as they received the pillar of smoke and the pillar of fire in the Exodus from Egypt" (1:97) or that "His light seen through them [the Jews] is the same as that seen in heaven" (2:50). The term *divine cause* certainly gives the reader the impression of an impersonal entity, as if it were a power that performs purely mechanical actions. The term is borrowed from Islamic philosophy, but Halevi identifies it with the *Shekhinah*: "because you will experience, with [the help of] My *Shekhinah*, the best of your land" (1:109). The adherence to the divine cause is identified with the revealing of the *Shekhinah*. Thus we have come full circle.

In the teaching of Judah Halevi, the commandments are a preparation for receiving the divine cause (1:84), and man cannot reach the divine cause except by the word of the Lord, that is, "according to God's commands" (1:98). So the goal of observing the Torah, the ultimate reward, is the sight of the supernal world, the hearing of the speech of the Lord (1:103), "the closeness of the Lord" (1:109, 115). This is the accepted interpretation of Halevi's view of the purpose of the commandments. However, this interpretation is incomplete. For the purpose of the commandments is not merely to prepare man for receiving the divine cause. Rather they represent, at least in part, a portion of the bond to the divine: "We still hold a connection with the Divine Influence through the laws which He has placed as a link, a covenant (*brit*) between us and Him. This is the circumcision . . . and the Sabbath" (2:34). The covenant is simply revelation, which is an encounter, and the commandments of the covenant are our steps toward this encounter.

Halevi's view requires us to examine another instance of a possible transition between the different meanings of revelation. Indeed, modern thought has pursued this line, producing a reduction that converts the revealed into a byproduct of the encounter. Revelation is conceived of as an "encounter," and the Bible, formerly a means or an organ of revelation, now becomes human testimony to the occurrence of revelation. The essence of the liberal interpretation is that it shifts the nature of revelation from its content, that is, "divinely given Torah," to the formal meaning. This interpretation is a function of the decline or even the total negation of the place of halakhah (religious law) in Jewish thought. When this approach does devote any attention to halakhah, it takes the form of a reinterpretation of the meaning of religious law as a human response to the experience of the encounter with the divine.

We find this linkage in Buber's attempt to remove the law from the revelatory encounter. Encounter is not in itself a process, but sets off, as it were, a process that is completed in the law. This process is nothing but the revelation of man to himself. The Torah exists within man, to be awakened where there is a call.[11]

Is this reduction of the concept of revelation legitimate? Any answer to this question must perforce involve one's personal theological commitments, so in fact no purely objective answer is possible. I should nonetheless like to examine one issue that will be encountered in any attempt at answering this question. Maimonides considered the binding of Isaac as evidence of prophecy, and as revelation, noting that like Abraham

> the prophets consider as true that which comes to them from God in a prophetic revelation. For it should not be thought that what they hear or what appears to them in a parable is not certain or is commingled with illusion just because it comes about *in a dream and in a vision.* Accordingly [Scripture] wished to make it known to us that all that is seen by a prophet in *a vision of prophecy* is, in the opinion of the prophet, a certain truth, that the prophet has no doubts in any way concerning anything in it, and that in his opinion its status is the same as that of all existent things that are apprehended through the senses or through the intellect.
>
> (*Guide* 3:24)

This approach to the binding of Isaac may be understood in the framework of Maimonides' interpretation, which views every test as a kind of drama. Though the protagonists are unaware that they are merely actors, this is a type of play in which the various events, that is, the commands, facts, and actions, are not directed at the personalities directly involved, but rather at the audience that hears or reads:

> The purpose of the test of a person performing a certain act is not the act itself but rather the purpose is that it should be an example to learn and follow.
>
> (ibid.)

If we draw the proper conclusions from Maimonides' position, then the binding of Isaac expresses two assumptions that lie at the heart of biblical prophecy. The first is explicit in Maimonides' interpretation. Although the prophetic vision is a phenomenon that may be termed subjective, it is no illusion. The binding of Isaac proves that prophecy must contain the criterion for its own verification, namely, the element of self-evidence. The second assumption, which Maimonides does not formulate explicitly but which is implicit in his interpretation, underscores the principle that prophetic revelation is the divine revealing of a "content" and not merely a call for a human response. The test of the binding is meaningless unless the command given to Abraham was a divine one. Thus, if revelation is only an encounter and the commandment merely man's response to it, then the binding is blasphemy and sacrilege. To my mind, the tragedy of the binding is that it points up two conflicts in the human condition. The first is that which usually exists between personal interest, inclinations, natural urges, and religious commandments. The second is the conflict between the various commandments that sometimes confront man in a concrete human situation.

However, conflict is created in the wake of the revelation, and the test is meaningless unless the revelation explicitly includes the implication of "divinely given Torah." Any teaching that views revelation as an encounter, and what is revealed as a response, will interpret the binding of Isaac as a mere illustration of the difficulties of ethical monotheism in educating man.[12] But it will be blind to the tormenting struggle between the religious and the moral, which testify to the existence of the Ineffable who bursts in upon us "from the Heavens" to reveal the Torah.

Endnotes

[1]*Die Offenbarung nach dem Lehrbegriffe der Synagoge.* 4 vols. (1835–1865).

[2]Nathan Rotenstreich, *Modern Jewish Thought* (1950), 169ff.

[3]Heinrich Graetz, *The Structure of Jewish History*, trans. and ed. Ismar Schorch, (1975) 68.

[4]*Or Adonai* , Vienna ed., bk. 2, pt. 4, 41a.

[5]See Nachum Lamm, *Torah le-Shmah* (1972) 77-83.

[6]Rotenstreich, 167. For a discussion of the concept of revelation in the teaching of Steinhem see ibid., 180.

[7]Martin Buber, "The Man of Today and the Jewish Bible," in Buber, *On the Bible: Eighteen Studies*, ed. N. N. Glatzer (1968) 7.

[8]Hayyim Vital, *Heikhal Adam Kadmon*, chap. 1, para. 1.

[9]According to Vital, this passage is based upon the *Zohar*, "The Portion of Pinchas" (257b): "Before He created the world He was called by all these titles because of the creatures that were to be created."

[10]Buber, "The Man of Today and the Jewish Bible," 7-8.

[11]Martin Buber, *Israel and the World* (1948) 114. See also the exhaustive bibliography in Benny Kraut, "The Approach to Jewish Law of Martin Buber and Franz Rosenweig," in *Tradition*, 12:3-4 (1972) 49-71, and Emil Fackenheim, "Martin Buber's Concept of Revelation," in *The Philosophy of Martin Buber*, ed. P. A. Schilpp and M. Friedman (1967) 288-90.

[12]Cf., for example, J. H. Gumbiner, "Existentialism and Father Abraham," in *Commentary* (1948).

Bibliography

Joshua Haberman, "Salomon Ludwig Steinheim's Doctrine of Revelation," in *Judaism* 17 (1968).

Shlomo Pines, "Spinoza's Tractatus Theologico-Politicus, Maimonides, and Kant," in *Scripta Hierosolymitana* 20 (1968).

Shalom Rosenberg, "Hitgalut Mitmedet," in Moshe Halamish and Moshe Schwartz, eds., *Hitgalut, Emunah ve-Daat* (1980).

Chapter 3

Understanding Revelation

Abraham J. Heschel

From a description of ideas associated with revelation in general and Torah in particular, we turn to a much more profound statement of not facts of what has been said but conviction concerning what is true. Here we ask why people reject the idea of revelation, on the one side, and how people should think about revelation, on the other. The important point is the answer to the question, "is revelation necessary?" Here we take up the kinds of knowledge that we possess, the various ways in which we find things out. Heschel takes up experiences that are common in human existence: the mystery of living, the sense of awe, wonder, or fear: "The root of religion is the question what to do with the feeling of the mystery of living, what to do with awe, wonder, or fear." Taking this question as the starting point, with the human situation as the centerpiece, Heschel works his way toward a fresh understanding of the conception of revelation. Notice that he addresses people in general, not eternal Israel in particular; that comes later. He speaks not of the Torah but of the Bible. In this way, Christians may derive religious understanding from the encounter with God and the word of God that Judaism invokes.

***

We have never been the same since that day on which Abraham crushed his father's precious symbols, since the day on which the Voice of God overwhelmed us at Sinai. It is forever impossible for us to retreat into an age that predates the Sinaitic event. Something unprecedented happened. God revealed His name to us, and we are named after Him. There are two Hebrew names for Jew: *Yehudi*, the first three letters of which are the first three letters of the Ineffable Name, and *Israel*, the end of which, *el* means in Hebrew God.

If other religions may be characterized as a relation between man and God, Judaism must be described as a relation between *man with Torah* and God. The Jew is never alone in the face of God. The Torah is always within him. A Jew without the Torah is obsolete.

The Torah is not the wisdom but the destiny of Israel; not our literature but our essence. It was produced neither by way of speculation nor by way of poetic inspiration but by way of revelation. But what is revelation?

*From To Grow in Wisdom: An Anthology of Abraham Joshua Heschel. Edited by Jacob Neusner and Noam M. M. Neuser. Copyright © 1990. Reprinted by permission of Madison Books, a subsidiary of University Press of America.

The Mistaken Notion

Many people reject the Bible because of a mistaken notion that revelation has proved to be scientifically impossible. It is all so very simple: there is no source of thought other than the human mind. The Bible is a book like any other book, and the prophets had no access to sources inaccessible to us. 'The Bible is the national literature of the Jewish people.' To the average mind, therefore, revelation is a sort of mental outcast, not qualified to be an issue for debate. At best, it is regarded as a fairytale, on a par with the conception that lightning and thunder are signs of anger of sundry gods and demons, rather than the result of a sudden expansion of the air in the path of an electric discharge. Indeed, has not the issue been settled long ago by psychology and anthropology as primitive man's mistaking an illusion for a supernatural event?

We Forgot the Question

The most serious obstacle, however, which we encounter in entering a discussion about revelation does not arise from our doubts, whether the accounts of the prophets about their experiences are authentic; the most critical vindication of these accounts, even if it were possible, would be of little relevance. The most serious obstacle is *the absence of the problem.* An answer, to be meaningful, presupposes the awareness of a question, but the climate in which we live today is not genial to the growth of questions which have taken centuries to bloom. The Bible is an answer to the supreme question: What does God demand of us? Yet the question has gone out of the world. God is portrayed as a mass of vagueness behind a veil of enigmas, and His voice has become alien to our minds, to our hearts, to our souls. We have learned to listen to every ego except the 'I' of God. The man of our time may proudly declare: nothing animal is alien to me but everything divine is. This is the status of the Bible in modern life: it is a great answer, but we do not know the question any more. Unless we recover the question, there is no hope of understanding the Bible.

Is It a Meaningful Problem?

Revelation is a complex issue, presupposing first of all certain assumptions about the existence and nature of God who communicates His will to man. Even granting the existence of a Supreme Power, the modern man, with his aloofness to what God means, would find it preposterous to assume that the Infinite Spirit should come down to commune with the feeble, finite mind of man, that man could be an ear to God. With the concept of the Absolute so far removed from the grasp of his mind, man is, at best, bewildered at the claim of the prophets like an animal when confronted with the spectacle of human power. With his relative sense of values, with his mind conditioned by circumstances and reduced to the grasp of the piecemeal, constantly stumbling in his efforts to establish a system of universally integrated ideas, how can it be conceived that man was ever able to grasp the unconditioned?

The first thing, therefore, we ought to do is to find out whether, as many of us seem to think, revelation is an absurdity, whether the prophetic claim is an intellectual savagery.

Is It a Meaningful Question?

Is it meaningful to ask: Did God address Himself to man? Indeed, unless God is real and beyond definitions that confine Him; unless He is unfettered by such distinctions as transcendence and immanence; unless we feel that we are driven and pursued by His question, there is little meaning in starting our inquiry. But those who know that this life of ours takes place in a world that is not all to be explained in human terms; that every moment is a carefully concealed act of His creation, cannot but ask: Is there any event wherein His voice is not suppressed? Is there any moment wherein His presence is not concealed?

True, the claim of the prophets is staggering and almost incredible. But to us, living in this horribly beautiful world, God's thick silence is incomparably more staggering and totally incredible.

Why Study the Problem?

Is it historical curiosity that excites our interest in the problem of revelation? As an event of the past that subsequently affected the course of civilization, revelation would not engage the modern mind any more than the battle of Marathon or the Congress of Vienna. However, it concerns us not because of the impact it had upon past generations, but as something which may or may not be of perpetual, unabating relevance. Thus, in entering this discourse, we do not conjure up the shadow of an archaic phenomenon, but attempt to debate the question whether to believe that there is a voice in the world that pleads with man at all times or at some times in the name of God.

It is not only a personal issue, but one that concerns the history of all men from the beginning of time to the end of days. No one who has, at least once in his life, sensed the terrifying seriousness of human history or the earnestness of individual existence can afford to ignore the problem. He must decide, he must choose between Yes and No.

Is Revelation Necessary?

In thinking about the world, we cannot proceed without guidance, supplied by logic and scientific method. Thinking about the ultimate, climbing toward the Invisible, leads along a path on which there are countless chasms and very few ledges. Faith, helping us take the first steps, is full of ardour but also blind; we are easily lost with our faith in misgivings which we cannot fully dispel. What could counteract the apprehension that it is utter futility to crave for contact with God?

Man in his spontaneity may reach out for the hidden God and with his mind try to pierce the darkness of His distance. But how will he know whether it is God he is reaching out for or some value personified? How will he know where or when God is found: in the ivory-tower of space or at some distant moment in the future?

The certainty of being exposed to a Presence which is not the world's is a fact of human existence. But such certainty does not result in esthetic indulgence in meditation; it stirs with a demand to live in a way which is worthy of that Presence.

The beginning of faith is not a feeling for the mystery of living or a sense of awe, wonder or fear. The root of religion is the question what to do with the feeling for the mystery of living, what to do with awe, wonder or fear. Religion, the end of isolation, begins with a consciousness that something is asked of us. It is in that tense, eternal asking in which the soul is caught and in which man's answer is elicited.[1] Who will tell us how to find a knowledge of the way? How do we know that the way we choose is the way He wants to pursue?

What a sculptor does to a block of marble, the Bible does to our finest intuitions. It is like raising the dead to life.

Metaphysical Loneliness

The ideals we strive after, the values we try to fulfill, have they any significance in the realm of natural events? The sun spends its rays upon the just and the wicked, upon flowers and snakes alike. The heart beats normally within those who torture and kill. Is all goodness and striving for veracity but a fiction of the mind to which nothing corresponds in reality? Where are the spirit's values valid? Within the inner life of man? But the spirit is a stranger in the soul. A demand such as 'love thy neighbour as thyself' is not at home in the self.

We have all a terrible loneliness in common. Day after day a question goes up desperately in our minds: Are we *alone* in the wilderness of the self, alone in this silent universe, of which we are a part, and in which we also feel like strangers?

It is such a situation that makes us ready to search for the voice of God in the world of man: the taste of utter loneliness; the discovery that unless the world is porous, the life of the spirit is a freak; that the world is a torso crying for its head; that the mind is insufficient to itself.

Saying No to Man

Modern man used to think that the acceptance of revelation was an effrontery to the mind. Man must live by his intelligence alone; he is capable of both finding and attaining the aim of his existence. That man is not in need of superhuman authority or guidance was a major argument of the Deists against accepting the idea of prophecy. Social reforms, it was thought, would cure the ills and eliminate the evils from our world. Yet, we have finally discovered what prophets and saints have always known: bread and beauty will not save humanity. There is a passion and drive for cruel deeds, which only fear of God can soothe; there is a suffocating sensuality in man, which only holiness can ventilate.

It is, indeed, hard for the mind to believe that any member of a species which can organize or even witness the murder of millions and feel no regret should ever be endowed with the ability to receive a word of God. If man can remain callous to a horror as infinite as God, if man can be bloodstained and self-righteous, distort what the conscience tells, make soap of human flesh, then how did it happen that nations did not exterminate each other centuries ago?

Man rarely comprehends how dangerously great he is. The more power he attains, the greater his need for an ability to master his power. Unless a new source of spiritual energy is discovered commensurate with the source of atomic energy, a few men may throw all men into final disaster.

What stands in the way of accepting revelation is our refusal to accept its authority. Liberty is our security and to accept the word of the prophets is to accept the sovereignty of God. Yet our understanding of man and his liberty has undergone a serious change in our time. The problem of man is more grave than we were able to realize a generation ago. What we used to sense in our worst fears turned out to have been a utopia compared with what has happened in our own days. We have discovered that reason may be perverse, that liberty is no security. Now we must learn that there is no liberty except the freedom bestowed upon us by God; that there is no liberty without sanctity.

Unless history is a vagary of nonsense, there must be a counterpart to the immense power of man to destroy, there must be a voice that says NO to man, a voice not vague, faint and inward, like qualms of conscience, but equal in spiritual might to man's power to destroy.

From time to time the turbulent drama is interrupted by a voice that says 'NO' to the recklessness of heart.

The Voice speaks to the spirit of prophetic men in singular moments of their lives and cries to the masses through the horror of history. The prophets respond, the masses despair.

The Bible, speaking in the name of a Being that combines justice with omnipotence, is the never-ceasing outcry of 'No' to humanity. In the midst of our applauding the feats of civilization, the Bible flings itself like a knife slashing our complacency, reminding us that God, too, has a voice in history. Only those who are satisfied with the state of affairs or those who choose the easy path of escaping from society rather than of staying within it and keeping themselves clean of the mud of vicious glories will resent its attack on human independence.

How did Abraham arrive at his certainty that there is a God who is concerned with the world? Said Rabbi Isaac: "Abraham may be compared to a man who was travelling from place to place when he saw a *palace in flames.* 'Is it possible that there is no one who cares for the palace?' he wondered. Until the owner of the building looked out and said, 'I am the owner of the palace.' Similarly, Abraham our father wondered, 'Is it conceivable that the world is without a guide?' The Holy One, blessed be he, looked out and said, 'I am the Guide, the Sovereign of the world.' "[2]

The world is in flames, consumed by evil. Is it possible that there is no one who cares?

Is God Concerned?

There is an abyss of not knowing God in many minds, with a rumor floating over it about an ultimate Being, of which they only know: it is an immense unconscious mass of mystery. It is from the perspective of such knowledge that the prophets' claim seems preposterous.

Let us examine that perspective. By attributing immense mysteriousness to that Ultimate Being, we definitely claim to know it. Thus, the Ultimate Being is not an unknown but a known God. In other words: a God whom we know but one who does not know, the great Unknower. We proclaim the ignorance of God as well as our knowledge of His being ignorant!

This seems to be a part of our pagan heritage: to say, the Supreme Being is a total mystery, and even having accepted the Biblical God of creation we still cling to the assumption: He who has the power to create a world is never able to utter a word. Yet why should we assume that the endless is forever imprisoned in silence? Why should we *a priori* exclude the power of expression from the Absolute Being? If the world is the work of God, isn't it conceivable that there would be within His work signs of His expression?

The idea of revelation remains an absurdity as long as we are unable to comprehend the impact with which the reality of God is pursuing man. Yet, as those moments in which the fate of mankind is in the balance, even those who have never sensed how God turns to man, suddenly realize that man—who has the power to devise both culture and crime, who is able to be a proxy for divine justice—is important enough to be the recipient of spiritual light at the rare dawns of his history.

Endnotes

[1] *Man Is Not Alone*, 1:68f.
[2] *Genesis Rabba*, chap. 39.

Part Two
Torah

Chapter 4

Celebrating the Revelation at Sinai

Eugene B. Borowitz

It is one thing to set forth Scripture's message. It is another to interpret that message in terms and language that contemporaries can grasp. That is the achievement of the great Reform Judaic theologian, Eugene Borowitz, and his co-workers since World War II. They were the ones to move theology of Judaism beyond the limits of philosophy of religion, to make theology out of apologetics. Certainly the premier among them speaks here. Borowitz begins with the Festival of Havuit, "weeks," referring in English to Pentecost (fifty days beyond Passover, in May of the year), which celebrates the giving of the Torah at Sinai. Without a Torah at Sinai, there also is nothing to celebrate, and on that hook he hangs his tale. Borowitz asks the questions of non-belief in order to set forth the imperatives of the faith: "even in the moments of which I can say I have been closest and most intimate with God, I have not found him speaking words." Then what is the sense of "revelation" that permits the celebration of Sinai on Shavuot? Borowitz finds in the covenant of Sinai the occasion for celebration, and for him, the Torah stands for that covenant, and, through worship on Shavuot, they celebrate Sinai in the here and now: "They discover what was ever theirs. They gain what they always had."

***

The problem of the continuing observance of Shavuot, the Feast of Weeks, is both the Biblical story itself and the legal discipline that claims to derive from it. The question is hardly whether the mountain was on fire, a horn sounded, or the people "saw" thunder.[1] The Bible reports and the holiday service celebrates God's giving words of instruction to his people. Some he himself said for all the people to hear; the rest he spoke to Moses to say to them. The rabbinic tradition authorized itself by saying that God also gave Moses either in principle or in detail the teaching which was to be handed down orally but authoritatively from generation to generation by the teachers of the law. Shavuot celebrates God's giving of the words of the Torah, both written and oral, and I cannot believe that. With all the love and respect I have for the Jewish tradition and its wisdom, which regularly far surpasses my own, I cannot believe that God reveals himself in words. My reasons do not fully explain the reality of my faith as I try to live it, but two critical considerations affect me. Even in the moments of which I can say I have been closest and most intimate with God, I have not found him speaking words—though that may only prove what I well know, that I am no prophet. When I consider the words that others have heard which they said were God's own (though of course put in human terms), it seems far more consistent with everything else I at this point know of man's history and God's nature that these are men's own words in response to God, not his dictation.

In my opinion, the most characteristic theological assertion of liberal Judaism is that such knowledge as men have of God is subjective, a human response to him, rather than objective human reception of his formulations.[2] It is this personal grounding of revelation which makes for the fundamental liberalism of modern Judaism, that is, its effort to maximize religious freedom of choice and its trust in the responsible individual. Theoreticians may disagree to what extent God is actively involved in the process of man's coming to know Him, arguing in humanistic versions that religious knowledge is really self-knowledge for which "revelation" is hardly an appropriate term. Because I believe God still has an active role in such human experience, I still want to speak of revelation, though I do not believe in verbal revelation. Regardless of the term used and its special nuances, the liberal Jewish thinkers, almost without exception, are united in their insistence on the subjectivity of man's knowledge of God.

If Shavuot is traditionally the great Jewish commemoration of God's objective revelation, how can those who affirm its subjectivity celebrate Shavuot?

It will help to begin with some phenomenological observations, with the reality of the given situation. It has the advantage of preventing the continuing regress to basic assumptions which soon undercuts every attempt to analyze a complex, synthesizing theological symbol such as Sinai. To be sure, the phenomenological basis chosen will necessarily seem arbitrary to some and may therefore appear to provide a skewed or perverted sample of experience to be analyzed. Such subjectivity is not to be avoided, and with that recognition the following observations are the foundation for this discussion: (1) Liberal Jews celebrate the Festival of Shavuot essentially in a communal, liturgical manner, and though its observance does not resolve all their questions concerning the Festival, they know it is expressive of their relation to God. (2) They observe Shavuot in their way as a continuation of a traditional observance of the Jewish people. They did not originate this day; neither have they rejected it as they did certain other Jewish practices. (3) At the same time, it is a Reform innovation in the commemoration, the confirmation ceremony, which makes the day most meaningful.

Analysis of so rich a human experience should be undertaken with a certain humility. The past century and a half of liberal expositions of the meaning of Jewish practice should have demonstrated that observances remain more meaningful than analyses of them can disclose. Liturgy and ritual are a creative language of their own and not merely a primitive substitute for the philosopher or social scientist or theologian's self-consciousness. The validation of the observance comes in the practice itself, not in its abstract discussion. Yet the elucidation of the meanings implicit in religious activity has an important place in religion: men are morally obligated to know what they can and thus increase the responsibility of their decisions. Such knowledge may shape even if it does not determine a man's deeds as he seeks to live his faith. This discussion, then, does not seek to exhaust the meanings of Shavuot or to validate it but in accordance with this heuristic understanding of the theology of ritual, to make plain some of the meaning that seems to continue to move Jews.

It will also save some needless argument to clarify what Jews are not required to celebrate on Shavuot day, namely, the legendary associations of the revelation at Sinai. Here the tradition was already quite clear. The halachic regimen for the observance of Shavuot does not obligate the Jew to affirm the historicity of every rabbinic hyperbole on the giving of the Torah, e.g., that the whole world was silent or that the Decalogue was heard in seventy different languages around the world when God spoke.[3] The authority of the halachah does not extend to such details despite the occasional efforts of zealots to turn *aggada* into dogma. Such midrashic allusions occur only in the liturgical poetry and not even in all of it, for these hymns are far more concerned to stress the greatness of the Ten Commandments and the Torah than the legends that surround the day.[4] Since such legendary material as does occur is limited to this poetic context, it should be clear that it need not be taken literally. Liberal Jews, whose passion for the chronological is well developed, should have little difficulty distinguishing rabbinic elaboration from Biblical account.

Yet the fundamental difficulties involved in the reconciliation required here have in no way been eased. Before undertaking such an enterprise it will also help to set forth the historical-intellectual frame in which it is offered. One advantage of the many varieties of liberal Jewish thought over the past century and a half is that they have explored a number of available alternatives. By exposing the consequences implicit in various theological perspectives, they have made it easier for succeeding thinkers to know which assumptions deny or require the sort of Jewish religious existence that they somehow know to be true for them. This is particularly true in that most perplexing of all liberal Jewish theological problems: What does God still require Jews to do? A typology of the answers given thus far would find them clustering around two poles. The one set seeks to derive practice largely from a conception of God. The other speaks more of the peculiar practice of the people of Israel.

The earlier views see religious practice as a celebration and rehearsal of the unity of God—most often as eternal ethical principles derived from the acknowledgement of his overarching oneness. Shavuot thus celebrates the supreme ethical discovery and commitment of the Jewish people. True monotheism (the first three commandments) is the necessary foundation for all true morality (the last six commandments). The difficulty with all such theories is the logical inconsistency of seeking to justify particular actions by universal values. They can never satisfactorily explain why, now that the universal values are known in a truly universal way, anyone need bother to practice them in a highly particular fashion, e.g., on the sixth of Sivan, which falls on a Friday (as in 5729, 1969). The answers attempted have never been convincing. Some have argued that the Jewish idea of God was unique, or that Jewish ethics were unique, or that Jewish ethical monotheism was unique and required the Jewish people to make it manifest in history.[5] Yet if God and ethics are truly universal, they cannot be especially Jewish, except by accident of discovery. Hegel, the unwitting source of the concept that most connects universal ideas with a particular people (and its celebrations), already provides its refutation. Now that the ideas have risen to the state of full, self-conscious, philosophic reflection, their religious elaboration, less pure and less universal, is superseded effectively. Since one knows, one need not celebrate. Pragmatic arguments (the help religious observances give in opening man to ethical monotheism or keeping him faithful to it) will not help much. Try justifying the Fourth Commandment this way! The Sabbath is not directly an ethical activity, and surely one could get more direct aid for one's ethical aspirations in contemporary society by Sunday rather than by Saturday observance, and by recreation and education rather than by liturgy and sanctification, though all non-Orthodoxy has steadfastly called for the primacy of the latter. The argument is even weaker with a Shavuot that falls on a Friday. The theological reasoning the average Jew derives from this universalist, God-centered view is impeccable; if he believes in the one God and does the right thing, isn't he really a good Jew though he doesn't come to temple or observe Shavuot? The liberals taught him well, unfortunately, and must bear intellectual responsibility for his minimal observance.

The counterargument seeks to emphasize the ethnic element in Jewish existence and, by authorizing the particular group, to motivate the Jewish form of observing. This position is even less satisfactory to the American Jew whose sociological strivings to be an equal reinforce his intellectual insistence on validation in terms of universals or autonomy. The ethnicists are led either into chauvinism, social determinism, or social utilitarianism. So one hears that Jews have a racial talent for religion, or that one is required by the laws of sociology to express one's religion through one's people, or that it is best for one's mental health not to reject one's group; or that it will be a way to enrich one's cultural existence by amplifying it with these old folk functions.[6] An individual might well derive some personal satisfactions from joining his people's folk festivals, though I doubt that one would get very far with a Friday Shavuot by such reasoning. Moreover, why unless God is somehow real and present to this people, should they make his formal worship the focus of their late-spring festivities? After all, the holiday traditionally celebrates his doing more than the Jewish people's being, and it gives them little positive to do other than to pray to God and to rehearse his goodness toward them.

Contrasting these ideas vis-á-vis Jewish practice (a good Jewish way of pursuing this unaccustomed intellectual enterprise), one may learn that any theology of Jewish observance which does not include both a real and present God and some sort of special relationship between him and the people of Israel will not result in any meaningful continuation of traditional practices. If there is no God, Jews can at best celebrate themselves or be that antiquarian-minded remnant of humanity which still takes time out (on a Friday morning?) to remember one interesting day in an Arabian peninsula (though rationally they should free themselves of this cultural laggardness and give over their limited celebration time to more directly significant events in man's self-understanding, i.e., Freud's discovery of the unconscious). At the same time, if Israel does not have some special link with God, then Jews might just as well celebrate their individual belief all by themselves. Private celebration will be not only more convenient but less fraught with the risks of boredom and personal irritation which are the steady threat of public worship. Because many are not willing to face up to what they believe about God, many a Shavuot celebration quietly substitutes the aesthetic experience for the liturgical, the impressive dramatic reading for the communal reliving of what God did at Sinai. And because others—though far fewer, I think, than once was true—are not clear about the corporate nature of the Jew's relation to God, such liturgies as are created for the confirmands sound, except for a few Hebrew sentences and modes, more like public high school baccalaureate exercises than the people of Israel renewing its Covenant and its task. Thus a Jewish theology that will be adequate to the religious realities of the continuing observance of Shavuot must somehow know a real God and a significantly unique bond between him and the congregation of Israel. And that experience/knowledge is the framework within which I seek to clarify what I solemnize at Shavuot.

Though I cannot commemorate the giving of the Torah in the objective sense that traditional Judaism understood it, I celebrate the establishment and the continual reestablishment of the relationship between God and Israel. I rejoice in *kiyum brit*, the inauguration of the full Covenant with the Israelite people rather than *matan torah*, the giving of the body of law and instruction by which it was to be lived. The one is basic to the other. I accept the fundamental God-Israel relationship. So do those who go beyond it to accept also its verbal quality and accompanying rabbinic interpretation. As one who affirms that Covenant as the foundation of his existence, I too acknowledge that I stand under the law. Only for me the law is not identical with the written or the oral law of tradition. Rather, it is that living discipline which flows from the consciousness of standing in direct personal relationship with God, not merely as a private self, but as one of the community with whom he has covenanted. Although I cannot agree that the pact between God and Israel established at Sinai was fixed then in immutable, contractual terms (together with the principles of their extension and elaboration over the generations), I know that a relationship is meaningful only insofar as it results in action, that Covenant without responsibility, faith without deed, is meaningless. My sense of obligation under the Covenant is more dynamic and less institutional than the traditional, but it too rests on what happened at Sinai and was recapitulated in later generations, as today on Shavuot. So establishing the relationship is my equivalent to "the giving of the law."

This understanding clarifies, it seems to me, the nature of my observance.

I celebrate the traditional holiday, on the traditional date, with liturgical forms that are substantially traditional. The Covenant did not begin with me. I came into it when I was born; it was, so to speak, there waiting for me. It belongs to history. If it depended on me and my abilities to initiate such a covenant from the human side, I do not think there would be a covenant. I know I am not what Father Abraham was; but because he was, I can try to emulate him.

The Covenant is not carried through history or renewed by me alone. It did not remain the possession of one family for long. Indeed, the first man of the Covenant was promised that he would become a father of nations, a mighty people. He had to be in order to enter and survive and transform human history. Sinai is the culmination of the Covenant with Abraham, the inception of its full form, not a Covenant with Moses, but one with all the Household of Israel. So I, who affirm that relationship, am not free to choose a private date or time to celebrate the establishment of my people's relationship with God. I celebrate it on our day, in their midst, and, essentially by liturgy, for our relationship is with Him, the real and present God, the living God. We rejoice not simply with one another, but with him, for what we celebrate is that we know him and continue to serve him, and that of all human communities ours has been permitted to have had this intimate and continuing experience of him.

The traditional Jew, looking at my observance, will find many of its features strange. He will be particularly perplexed that I interpret *brit* in personal rather than legal terms.[7] But he should be able to recognize (and that is increasingly my experience) that what unites him and me is greater than what separates us. We stand as part of the same Jewish people united in the same basic relationship with the same God. (Because one does not need to define someone to have an authentic relationship with him, the issues of the identity of our concepts of God is as irrelevant to this dimension of the discussion as to the traditional *aggada*.) We both believe that this Covenant relationship authorizes and requires communal and individual action. We differ only—though it is a great Jewish "only"—on what constitutes that required action, its substance, hierarchy, and religious weight.

Because the partners of the relationship have remained substantially the same over the centuries, though the terms used to describe them have differed, the sort of action that derives from the relationship will remain recognizably continuous with what went before. However, new social circumstances and intellectual insights may make it possible to enrich and enhance, as they may require Jews to modify or to reject, the old patterns of living the Covenant. The confirmation ceremony is an excellent example because its proper practice is already its justification.

The tradition knows no such group rite:[8] for girls as well as for boys; at the conclusion of a prescribed course of study; at an age well past thirteen; as part of the Shavuot liturgy; climaxed by an act of dedication on the children's part. Reform Jews may have dropped the celebration of the second day, the *musaf*, the additional festival liturgy, and the customary *piyyutim*, the religious poetry. They may have modified the *birchat hashashar*, the opening prayers, and condensed the *shacharit*, the regular morning service. None of these touches the heart of the relationship to God nor deprives the congregation of the central means of sanctifying the day. To the contrary, the reality of that Covenant relationship comes alive for moderns precisely because its ancient feel is conveyed in the modern mode by an air of serious attention, harmonic music, understandable prayers, family seating—and, most of all, by the confirmation ceremony itself.

What is being done with these young people? They cannot now be inducted into the congregation of Israel and its millennial responsibilities since they have been part of it from birth. That was imposed upon them, a necessity, so to speak, of being born to just this family. Now, however, they may turn destiny into personal choice. At confirmation they are welcomed to conscious, individual affirmation of God's Covenant with Israel. That is why they had to study before they ascended the pulpit; they had to know what history had bequeathed to them so that they could know what burdens they must carry. That is why they had to be of a more mature age than thirteen, so that their understanding could be fuller and their affirmation more responsible. (Why not at the end of high school, an even more mature and critical time?) So girls as well as boys are included, for the Covenant relationship is as real with women as it is with men. So, too, the ceremony involves a group of young people, in the presence of a great and numerous congregation, for the Covenant is no private matter but one which binds private souls to the people of Israel's pact. That is why it takes place on Shavuot day, for that is the day when the Israelite folk itself had to decide whether to accept God's Covenant relationship. Now each year the Sinai day rolls round and the faithfulness of Israel to that ancient pledge is once more tested (as in so many other ways) and—how surprisingly for this stiff-necked folk—once again renewed. The confirmation children join all the Children of Israel in their rededication, only they do so publicly, formally, in a way that therefore marks a turning point in their Jewish development. They may soon not care, or rebel, or quietly turn to things that are more fun. It is their privilege, to use their freedom for good or ill. Yet the people of Israel did its duty by them and by their God in helping them to know that precious, sacred history and by inviting them to personal appropriation of that untiring messianic task.

That is why the congregation is so moved by the ceremony. Of course, it is sentiment mixed with guilt, the consciousness of aging fused with the illusions associated with the children. Yet these are not base emotions, unworthy of bearing God's truth or sensitizing men to his presence. The worshipers may not have been the Jews they ought to have been, the Jews their parents or grandparents or rabbis wished them to be. They may have failed the children often as they sought to guide them, and they hide from rather than acknowledge what they have repaid God for his benefits. But on Shavuot day, in the sanctuary, seeing the children on his altar, this Sinai, hearing them affirm and avow and depose and declare, they know they have not been altogether faithless. By bringing them to confirmation, they have confirmed their loyalty, and confirming them, the adults are confirmed as well. That is true not only for the parents of the confirmands but for every Jew who identifies himself with the Jewish community and shares in its mutual responsibility for the education of all Jewish children. The confirmands are the Jews' children, the next necessary step in the people's purposeful history, the hope that the Covenant effort will continue yet farther into history, working and waiting for the Kingdom of God.

Traditional Judaism knew no such ceremony as confirmation, but if Shavuot day celebrates the establishment of God's Covenant with Israel, what act could be more relevant? Indeed, it illuminates and upholds the rest, for at least Jews still love their children, though they find it difficult to understand, much less practice, the love of God. (That is why some Shavuot services are exercises in the manipulation of congregational emotions rather than an openness to confrontation with the covenanting God.)

There remains one last question, the most crucial of all. Its several forms are one: Did God really make a Covenant with Israel? Is it true that God has a special relationship with Israel? How do you know? How can you believe this? "Really . . . true . . . know . . . believe . . . how," these are the words that chart the regress of every theological assertion back to ontology, epistemology, and beyond, to those fundamental assertions which turn the chaos of the fully open mind into the creation called premises or assumptions. To answer requires a radical return to the first questions of theological methodology and thence a gradual working out of these initial principles until they reach Sinai and thus Shavuot. That is, no less, the demand for a systematic Jewish theology. Yet the question cannot altogether be set aside here, for if nothing really happened at Sinai, if nothing could have happened at Sinai, then for all its intellectual utility, the Covenant theory is meaningless.

Without seeking to duplicate in Jewish circles the debate that Rudolf Bultmann's radical rejection of historicity continues to evoke among Protestants, this much may be said: what "really" happened at Sinai lies outside the sphere of the modern academic discipline known as history.[9] The historian, as historian, can tell us something about the records and traditions of the Sinaitic Covenant. He will want to have his say in the continuing argument over the likely date of the exodus and how many of the Hebrew tribes were involved in the Egyptian experience. He may even be able to contribute something about how the events described as taking place at Sinai compare with similar events in the history of other peoples. What he cannot suggest, as long as he sticks strictly to historic evidence, is whether God and Israel did in fact make such a Covenant. This question involves fundamental metaphysical questions to which his historical evidence is irrelevant: Is there a God? Does he act? Does he make covenants? Normally, historians are reticent about their implicit metaphysics, admitting that what they offer is an imaginative reconstruction of the past which is as valid as their premises about what "really" powers and shapes history. The latter, being a metaphysical matter, they generally do not argue but accept as a matter of modern methodology or good academic discipline. What is vital to this discussion is that good modern methodology involves leaving God out as an active factor in history. It is one thing to state this as a methodological procedure. It is quite another to claim it as a statement of reality. A modern historian cannot say much about what happened at Sinai because his very methodology prevents him from knowing a God who acts in history, but because he cannot detect this reality with his specialized instruments does not yet mean that what the texts say took place did not take place.[10]

The same is true of the contributions of the psychologist, the anthropologist, and other social scientists. They may disclose much about religious behavior; what they cannot assess is whether religion is true. Their very methodology (since it is rigidly empirical) prevents them from knowing God and hence they are incompetent to deal with the most vital of all religious questions. They do not know what is real because they cannot know it until they forsake scientific method for metaphysics.

Philosophy then stands between me and the Shavuot services. In recent Jewish history, philosophy was less a menace than a friend.[11] Neo-Kantian ethicism and post-Hegelian historicism seemed ideal means of expressing ancient Jewish themes in modern tones. They could do this because each in its own way could show what then seemed rational access to metaphysical reality. Kant knew no metaphysics of the natural order, but he clearly asserted the validity of the noumenal order reached via ethics. Hegel saw the one absolute spirit making itself manifest in the zigzag of historic development. Religion therefore could be substantiated by philosophy and yet remain reasonably true to its own personal and historic genius.

Contemporary philosophy is nowhere nearly so hospitable to religion. If anything, its antimetaphysical compulsions make it downright hostile. Linguistic analysis is generally as atheistic as its parent, logical positivism. Phenomenology and existentialism are resolute in their rejection of the claims that there is a God. Such occasional metaphysical assertion as is still heard labors mightily to bring forth some sense of ultimate reality, but does so under the handicap that most modern philosophers consider that task, much less their results, well outside the limits of the acceptable use of the term "rational."

These metaphysical issues are not to be dismissed. They are not trivial. If what religion is speaking about is to be made meaningful, it must somehow come to terms with modern philosophic idiom, even if that means to fight, refine, or even break modern philosophy's constricted sense of what can be real. Although the average man or the educated man who comes to the service is unaware of this technical philosophical discussion, he nonetheless reflects it in the covert metaphysics upon which, quite unwittingly, he builds his life. Religion cannot altogether ignore the issues posed by contemporary philosophy even though they seem in our day, as against what they were in another generation of liberal Judaism, to reject the possibility of meaningful religion.

Now, however, as I begin to ponder these questions for the hundredth time, I realize that the fifth of Sivan is drawing to a close. Shavuot is upon me with its claim for observance. I will not have time to resolve these metaphysical problems before the holiday is here. If I insist on doing so I shall almost certainly never observe the Festival this year. My insistence on clarifying all the premises of religion before I move on to religious practice will, in effect, be the equivalent of denying belief in God and the Covenant he entered into with Israel at Sinai.

To affirm the Covenant, however, need not mean one has resolved all the metaphysical issues inherent in that belief. I have not. The question of my response to the coming of the sixth of Sivan hinges rather on whether, despite all my doubts and difficulties, I still manage to believe enough that I can accept the advent of the Festival; whether my sense of what is finally real in the universe is such that I can still go to meet my God as one of his covenanted people.

I do not go to Shavuot services out of dogmatic security, but despite my unanswered questions and unresolved conflicts, out of a knowledge of what has happened to me there before, and not just on this festival but day by day as I have tried to live under the Covenant. And I am grateful to have discovered that, though some of my problems with Judaism deepen as the years go by, the question of whether I possess sufficient affirmation to attend to this observance, as to many others, has grown less difficult to answer positively.

If I am to lead the service, this knowledge that the service justifies itself imposes special responsibilities upon me. It cannot today be only a fulfillment of the previously existing Jewish piety; it must be an experience in Jewish rediscovery and reaffirmation. It cannot simply count on what the modern, secularized congregation brings with it; it must reach out to them so that they know as they can in so few other ways truly know, that God and Israel still stand bound in Covenant.

The leader must manage the service. But if his mind is on the organist's cues, the undependable microphone, the inattentive ushers, or the nervous confirmation class, he will never bring to bear the personal *kavvannah*, the devotion, which will mold sound and music, silence and movement, reading and response, into living liturgy. No wonder Roman Catholic tradition prescribes a master of ceremonies to stand beside the officiant and guide him through the intricate order of the special mass so that he may concentrate on the meaning of what he is doing rather than on keeping order! The Jewish prayer leader cannot shirk his responsibility in transforming an audience into a congregation, but only as he transcends techniques and leads the praying will the congregation come jointly to face its God.

That too is why the service itself is not time for metaphysical reflection. Precise meanings and integrated intellectual structures will have to wait for later. Now is the time to say what can be said and see what happens. Of course, one phrase or another may stick in the throat or be rejected by the mind as an honest expression of the whole self. Sometimes a whole paragraph may seem unsayable —though I am inclined to believe that many people so enjoy the posture of complaining about the prayer book that they cannot pray what, if they stopped posing, they could pray. Even to interrupt the service with many comments about the prayers, their meaning or origin, is to objectify the mood and shatter the developmental integrity of the service, thereby defeating the hope of making the festival worship a personal experience of Israel's communal Covenant reality. Thinking is no less present to the person for being subordinated now to what the whole man finds himself in this congregation at this moment able to say.

Yet any possibility of accomplishing this small liturgical miracle depends on what happens in the prayer leader himself. Jewish worshipers may once have been far more self-sufficient. Today modern calls for decorum have made them highly dependent on the man who stands before them. Most of the time his person will establish the context of what may happen at the service. He cannot not know this. In part, what attracted him to the rabbinate or cantorate was that he might be the focus of this community. Now he will read or sing or bless or speak and they will attend to him—and there will be many, many watching, listening, in a special mood of attention. If he does not gratify himself on this occasion, he will surely not be able to give to it the fullness of self on which all else hinges. But if he does so only to gratify himself, he has required his people to covenant with him rather than with God. True, he cannot deny his ego and its needs. Yet he can and must find a way in this vortex of institutional, intellectual, and emotional demands to be a transparent witness to the reality of the Covenant which binds this people to its God. Standing beyond drive and mind and ego, he must serve God with a whole heart.

Such accomplishment is not credible. The Household of Israel is too impious, the synagogue too bourgeois, the rabbi too human, God too distant. That is all true—and yet it happens. It has happened in the past—were the vessels of God's covenanting inhumanly saintly in Biblical times? And it has happened to many Jews on and off who found themselves one Sabbath, one holy day, one weekday, entering the service just people and becoming in it once again the people of his Covenant.

I cannot know whether it will happen once again this sixth of Sivan. I cannot tell what difference it will make if nothing special happens. Nevertheless, I know that if without tears or tongues or thrills or sparks something does happen, I shall probably recognize it as something old and familiar. It will not be altogether new and strange. When the service comes alive, Jews are not converted, only returned, restored, renewed. They discover what was ever theirs. They gain what they always had.

Endnotes

[1]Exod 20:18. Note the characteristic difference of interpretation between Ishmael and Akiba in *Mechilta Bachodesh* (Lauterbach ed., Philadelphia: The Jewish Publication Society of America, 1933) chap. 9, lines 1-5.

[2]Gunther Plaut's insistence on the reality of revelation to the early Reformers is not in any way a contradiction of what is being asserted here, as the excerpts he gives demonstrate (*The Rise of Reform Judaism* [World Union for Progressive Judaism, 1963] 125).

[3]For a typical collection, see Louis Ginzberg, *The Legends of the Jews* (Philadelphia: The Jewish Publication Society of American, 1913) 3:90ff., and 6:35, n. 198.

[4]A complete list with brief description is given by Abraham Idelsohn, *Jewish Liturgy* (New York: Henry Holt & Company, Inc., 1932), in Appendix C. See especially 336-37. It is noteworthy that the Hertz and Birnbaum prayer books for the entire year and the Rabbinical Council of America prayer book for Sabbath and Festivals consider only the *Akdamut* of sufficient importance to warrant inclusion in their volumes. It contains no legendary material.

[5]The Pittsburgh Platform in its very first article asserts the superiority of Israel's God-idea and then goes on in Articles 3 and 4 to set up universal ethics as the criterion of religious practice. David Philipson, *The Reform Movement in Judaism* (New York: The Macmillan Company, 1907) 491. Despite Ahad Ha'am's championing of the idea of a unique Jewish ethical understanding and the many Reform Jewish Neo-Kantians who have placed great stress on Jewish ethics, no work since that of Moritz Lazarus has appeared which would seek to define those ethics or to indicate their unique approach. For the latter view, see Leo Baeck, *The Essence of Judaism*, 1st English trans. (New York: The Macmillan Company, 1936) 281ff., and the entire first book of *This People Israel* (New York: Holt, Rinehart & Winston, Inc., 1964).

[6]So Geiger and Kohler are racialists, though they used the term far more loosely than we do. *Jewish Theology* (Riverdale Press, 1943) 325ff. See the justified attacks by Mordecai M. Kaplan in *Judaism as a Civilization* (Toronto: The Macmillan Company, 1934) 119, and his return to the attack over two decades later, as if the idea were still widespread, in *The Greater Judaism in the Making* (Reconstructionist Press, 1960) 291ff. Kaplan's own position is a mixture of the last two views, that one cannot fight social necessity and that one can benefit by accepting it. See *Judaism as a Civilization*, 48, 184, 261.

[7]In biblical usage it often carries the connotation of specified law rather than relationship, e.g., Ps 25:10 as contrasted with Ps 44:17.

[8]Although in 1831 a prominent Orthodox rabbi had already begun conducting regular confirmation ceremonies for classes of boys and girls ("Confirmation," *The Jewish Encyclopedia*, IV:219 f.).

[9]For a survey of the question, see James M. Robinson, *A New Quest of the Historical Jesus* (London: SCM Press, Ltd., 1959), particularly 1-25. For a Jewish reaction, see Lou Silberman, "The New Quest for the Historical Jesus," *Judaism* 2/3 (Summer, 1962).

[10]The many problems relative to the creation of a philosophy of history can only be noted here. For a good brief summary of the range of issues from the standpoint of philosophy of religion, see John A Hutchison, *Faith, Reason, and Existence* (New York: Oxford University Press, 1956) 167ff. A review of the problem, which sketches the history of philosophy and theology of history from the earliest time to the present, is Alan Richardson, *History, Sacred and Profane* (Philadelphia: The Westminster Press, 1964).

[11]This theme is discussed in greater detail in my *Layman's Introduction to Religious Existentialism* (Philadelphia: The Westminster Press, 1965) 69ff.

Chapter 5

Not by Bread Alone

Jakob J. Petuchowski

Another way of setting forth in terms contemporaries can grasp the imperatives of Sinai, the concept of revelation, the category "the Torah," seeks in a metaphor for language and images that serve. People find no difficulty in the concept of "grace," a blessing over food before eating it that says, "Blessed are You, Lord our God, king of the world, who brings forth bread from the earth." Yet they know that bread comes from the earth not through an act of God but through the labor of workers of many kinds and at many stages. All of this people can easily hold together with the notion that God makes bread possible: all that we have and are come from an act of God's grace and love. Here that fact is turned to the service of the comparable and complementary conception, expressed in the theological phrase by which, in Judaism, we speak of revelation, "Torah from heaven." For the phrase, "bread from the earth" has its counterpart in the matching language, "Torah from heaven." This is how another Reform Judaic theologian finds it possible to translate into terms and language that make sense for contemporary Reform Jews the conception of revelation.

***

Bread, the "staff of life," the staple of man's sustenance in symbol and in fact, is regarded in the Jewish Tradition as a gift from God. Partaking of it, the pious Jew engages in what is quite consciously seen to be an imitation of a sacrificial act. His hands must have been washed so that he breaks bread in a state of ritual purity similar to that demanded of the priests in the Jerusalem Temple. He says a prayer before breaking bread, and prior to eating it, he dips his slice of bread in salt—even as salt was an absolute prerequisite in the ancient sacrificial cult.[1] A lengthy grace concludes those of his meals during which bread is eaten. And even after the meal, bread continues to be treated with respect. A pious Jew will guard the leftovers and crumbs from willful destruction almost with the same care which a Roman Catholic priest bestows upon the leftovers of the eucharistic wafer.

While the Talmud recognizes the validity of even a simple doxology like "Praised be the Merciful One, the Master of this bread,"[2] the standard form of the Jewish "Grace before Meals" has long been the following: "Praised art Thou, O Lord our God, Ruler of the Universe, who bringest forth bread from the earth." The idea that it is God who brings forth bread from the earth is one at which even liberal religious Jews do not take umbrage. They do not suspect it of primitive anthropomorphism. They do not feel that their knowledge of the natural sciences has taught them better. And why should there be any objection to this simple prayer? Were not the Jews who first uttered it themselves engaged in agricultural pursuits, knowing full well man's own share in the production of bread? God was indeed the Heavenly Provider, but man had to do the plowing, the reaping, the grinding, and the baking. Man may even have to spread manure over his fields before they will yield their produce! And yet, there is the recognition of what moderns might call man's dependence on natural processes, and of what the ancients more readily saw as man's dependence on Nature's God.

When, therefore, it became known, some years ago, that in some of the Israeli settlements they had substituted for the old prayer the phrase, "Praised be the farmer who brings forth bread from the earth," there was a feeling of annoyance by no means confined to Orthodox circles. No, with all his knowledge of the workings of Nature, the modern liberal Jew can still share his ancestors' gratitude to God "who brings forth bread from the earth."

What the liberal religious Jew finds difficult, if not impossible, to do is to share his ancestors' conviction that the God who brings forth bread from the earth also brings forth His Torah from Heaven. Now, it may seem curious that we should have introduced a discussion of the doctrine of Revelation with a brief disquisition on the Jewish attitude toward bread. But the two subjects happen to be more closely related than might appear at first sight.

Grammatically, the phrase, "bread from the earth" (*lechem min ha-aretz*), has the same structure as the traditional name for Revelation (*torah min hashamayim*, literally: "Torah from Heaven"); and there is a beautiful symmetry in the thought that the God who supplies our material needs from the earth also nourishes our spiritual needs from above. It may, of course, be argued that the word "Heaven" is merely a metonym for God Himself. As such, it does, in fact, frequently occur in Rabbinic literature.[3] There is, then, ample support for David Hoffmann's view[4] that, when the *Mishnah*[5] denies a share in the World-to-Come to him who says that "the Torah is not from Heaven," it is thinking of one who claims that "the Torah is not from God." On the other hand, "Heaven" was surely not understood as a mere metonym for God in that version of the "Blessing over the Torah" which is recorded in the Tractate *Sopherim*,[6] and which reads:

> Praised are Thou, O Lord,
> Who hast given us a Torah from Heaven
> And eternal life on high.
> Praised art Thou, O Lord, Giver of the Torah.

To say to God in a direct address: "Thou hast given us a Torah from God" is not a very likely liturgical phrase; nor, were we to accept such an interpretation, would the poetic parallelism be preserved that matches the "Torah from Heaven" with the "eternal life on high." Besides, the idea that God reveals Himself "from Heaven" is certainly a biblical one![7] Nevertheless, while admitting that the parallel presented by *torah min hashamayim* to *lechem min ha-aretz* first inspired these meditations, we do not want to press the point too far nor wish it to be regarded as the crux of our argument.

We are on firmer ground in drawing attention to the *halakhic* (i.e., legal) relation between the blessing over bread and that over the Torah. The Rabbis were aware of the fact that the only blessing explicitly commanded in the Torah itself is the "Grace after Meals." It is found in Deuteronomy 8:10, "And thou shalt eat, and thou shalt be satisfied, and thou shalt bless the Lord thy God for the good land which He hath given thee." The Torah does not explicitly prescribe a blessing to be recited before or after the reading of the Torah. But in the words, "He hath given thee," in the law relating to the "Grace after Meals" the *Tosephta*[8] sees a reference to the blessing to be recited over the Torah and the performance of the commandments. This is based on the fact that the same word, "give" occurs in Exodus 24:12, where God says to Moses: "Come up to Me into the mount, and be there; *and I will give thee* the tables of stone, and the law and the commandment, which I have written, that thou mayest teach them." Similar arguments occur in other parts of Rabbinic literature."[9]

Perhaps the most detailed form of the argument deriving the obligation to recite a blessing over the Torah from the biblical commandment to say "Grace after Meals" is to be found in Karaite literature. Rejecting the Rabbinic hermeneutics, the Karaites were forced to employ their own, above all the *kiyyas* (the argument by analogy), in all cases where they wished to retain a Rabbinic observance and had to find their own support for it in the Bible. Thus we find Anan, the founder of the sect, reasoning as follows, in his *Sepher Ha-Mitzwoth*:[10]

Scripture commands the blessing over food in Deuteronomy 8:10. In Ezekiel 3:1 we read about the Prophet's being bidden to "eat this scroll." Now, "this scroll" could only have been the Torah, which is further proved by Ezekiel's report (3:3) that "it was in my mouth as honey for sweetness," seeing that, in Psalm 19:11, the Torah itself is described as "sweeter also than honey." With this analogy between eating and Torah study thus established, it follows, of course, that Torah reading must be accompanied by benedictions just as eating is. No doubt, Anan was more "Rabbinical" here than he would have cared to admit!

The modern mind will find the Rabbinic and the Karaite arguments equally strange, and will wonder whether the venerable institution of thanking God for the Torah really has nothing more solid to rest on than farfetched analogies between Torah reading and eating. Such skepticism is wholesome. We would indeed be doing the ancient Rabbis an injustice were we to imagine them as meditating on the words of Deuteronomy 8:10, and suddenly coming up with the discovery that what is implied here is a blessing over the Torah. It is much more likely that the blessing over the Torah was instituted on its own merits,[11] and that only afterward did the Rabbis look for a "proof-text" in the Bible.

Yet, if the sequence was indeed such as we have tried to indicate, and as the modern reader would naturally be inclined to assume, if, that is to say, we are in a position to look above and beyond the mere formal structure of Rabbinic hermeneutics, there is still a question to which an answer must be attempted. Supposing that the Rabbis were looking for a biblical basis for the blessing over the Torah, why, of all things, did they go to the "Grace after Meals"? Surely, they should not have found it too difficult to come across something more apropos, something more explicitly and intrinsically related to the institution of the Torah blessing which they were trying to promote!

In other words, we suspect that, over and above the merely formal analogy they discovered between the eating of bread and the reading of the Torah, they were aware of a deeper underlying connection. Could it have been the verse in Deuteronomy 8:3, "Man doth not live by bread alone, but by everything that proceedeth out of the mouth of the Lord doth man live"? Or take the beginning of the fifty-fifth chapter of the book of Isaiah:

> Ho, every one that thirsteth, come ye for water,
> And he that hath no money;
> Come ye, buy and eat;
> Yea, come, buy wine and milk
> Without money and without price.
> Wherefore do ye spend money for that which is not bread?
> And your grain for that which satisfieth not?
> Hearken diligently unto Me, and eat ye that which is good,
> And let your soul delight itself in fatness.

Not only are the traditional Jewish commentators unanimous in regarding this as an invitation to the people to avail itself of *spiritual* sustenance, but, in the light of the context, it is hard to assume that the Prophet could have meant anything else. The hunger and the thirst he had in mind was that, as Amos had asserted before him,[12] "of hearing the words of the Lord."

It is, therefore, not simply a matter of an arid legalism if the Rabbis established a relationship between bread and Torah. It was part of Israel's Prophetic tradition. It was also implied in the Festival of *Shavu'oth*, with its twofold aspect of harvest festival and feast of Revelation. As Theodor H. Gaster aptly remarks, "If, in the primitive agricultural rite, man offers God two loaves of the new bread as a symbol of cooperation, in the historical counterpart—by a fine and inspired inversion—God offers to man the two tablets of the Law."[13]

The connection between bread and Torah is of more than historical interest to us. In it may be found the solution of a very modern theological problem. We have already noted that the modern liberal Jew is not deterred by his knowledge of natural processes and agricultural "know-how" from regarding God as the One "who brings forth bread from the earth." But, when it comes to the old doctrine of "Torah from Heaven," the modern liberal Jew balks.

Having been made aware of the human element which went into the composition of the Bible, having learned to prefer the laborious process of *Quellenscheidung* (separation of the various sources and strata) to the "naïve" belief in a Sinaitic Revelation which was *einmalig* (once and for all time), he feels that he can no longer accept the "primitive" dogma of *torah min hashamayim.* Perhaps the responsibility is not altogether his own. He may have been driven to this position by Orthodox intolerance. The Orthodox rabbinate of the nineteenth century was apt to see in the slightest demand for external reforms an evidence of apostasy, a denial of fundamental Jewish dogma. Of course, according to the Rabbinic interpretation of Numbers 15:31, the slightest reservation about the complete divine origin of the entire Torah was sufficient to place one in the category of those who "despise the word of the Lord." And this includes him who believes in the divine origin of the whole Torah, but has reservations about certain laws not explicitly stated there, but merely derived from the text by means of one or another of the Rabbinic hermeneutic rules.[14]

The anti-Sadducean point of such remarks is very obvious, and though such an extremist interpretation of the divine origin of the Torah may have been justified in its time, it is, to say the least, questionable whether it should have been pressed against the Reformers of the nineteenth century. The effect was what in Rabbinic idiom might be described as "a thrusting away with both hands" and as a "closing of the door in front of the potential penitents." The time was to come when the Reformers would accept the Orthodox accusations—and feel proud of them!

That, however, is only one side of the coin. The other has to do with the inner development of the Reform movement itself. Just as in the case of the Rabbinic derivation of the Torah blessing from the law of Deuteronomy 8:10 the practice itself preceded the finding of a basis in Scripture, so, in the case of the Reformers, it will have to be admitted that, by and large, the theological foundations came *after* the practical reforms. In other words, we are not to imagine that an Orthodox Jew studied the Prophets and, on that basis alone, came to the conclusion that the dietary laws were of no religious consequence—whereupon he bit into a ham sandwich. Rather was it the man, already lax in ritual observance, who found support for his deviations from Tradition in what he called "Prophetic Religion."

Seen in this light, the incorporation of the Higher Criticism of the Bible into the theological foundations of Reform Judaism in the twentieth century (though, be it noted, not before, and not by the original apostles of Classical Reform!) becomes intelligible as a kind of "Occam's Razor" for the purpose of dealing with Judaism's adjustment to the practical problems of modern life. Instead of arguing *within* the framework of the traditional *Halakhah* (Jewish Law), which is not always easy, and which, as Conservative Jews well know, always invites the fierce opposition of the Orthodox who can play at the same game, Reform cut the Gordian knot by denying the very premise on which *Halakhah* is predicated, namely the doctrine of "Torah from Heaven."

The Bible became a human, instead of a divine, document. It was read as a record of man's quest for God, rather than as a statement of God's demands on man. In this manner, the detection of the human element became synonymous with disproving the divine authorship.

"For the basis of the old legalism has crumbled away," wrote Claude G. Montefiore.[15] "We no longer believe in the Mosaic and divine origin of the *whole* Pentateuchal law; we no longer believe that all the ordinances date from the same period, and that they are *all* perfect, immutable, and divine. Some of the ceremonial laws may be, in their ultimate origin, much older than Moses, resting as they do upon primordial conceptions, and even upon superstitions or taboos, which have wholly passed away, while others of the ceremonial laws are undoubtedly much later than Moses."

Yet the late Claude G. Montefiore would hardly have approved of the following statement: "For the basis of the old *motzi* [blessing over the bread] has crumbled away. We no longer believe that God is personally concerned with the production of each and every slice of bread, so that the very sandwich we eat could be thought of as a direct gift from God. Some of the ideas behind the *motzi* may be, in their ultimate origin, much older than Judaism, resting as they do upon primordial conceptions, and even upon superstitions and remnants of animism and the worship of fertility gods, which have wholly passed away, while, unlike the ancient Israelite, the modern Jew is fully aware of the processes from gestation through packaging which bring the bread upon his table." Claude G. Montefiore would not have approved of this because, as a deeply religious soul, he was able to perceive the hand of the Creator behind the physical aspects of His creation.

We suggest that a similar view could be taken of the doctrine of "Torah from Heaven"—even by those who feel quite confident that they are able to determine precisely who wrote what, and when, in the post-Mosaic literary history of the so-called Law of Moses. As Franz Rosenzweig wrote to Jakob Rosenheim:

> Even if Wellhausen would turn out to be right in all his theories, . . . it would not make the slightest difference to our faith. . . . We, too, translate the Torah as *one* book. For us, too, it is the work of *one* spirit. We do not know who it was; that it was Moses we cannot believe. Among ourselves we call him by the sign which the Higher Criticism uses to designate the final redactor assumed by it, "R." But we resolve this sign not into "Redactor," but into *"Rabbenu"* [Our Teacher]. For,

whoever he was, and whatever sources he might have utilized, he is our Teacher, and his theology is our Teaching.[16]

The time is past when the mere denial of the doctrine of "Torah from Heaven" was deemed capable of solving all the practical problems of Reform Judaism. The assumption of the existence of various strata in the composition of the Pentateuch is no longer such a novelty. Many Conservative Jews share it; and the Protestants, who had originally discovered it, have long since proceeded to listen again for the "Word," and to transcend, though not to ignore, the multifarious stratification of sources in a higher "unity of the Bible."

It is, of course, very likely that a modern interpretation of the doctrine of "Torah from Heaven" is going to make somewhat less sweeping demands than the Rabbinic interpretation of Numbers 15:31, which we discussed above. On the other hand, a doctrine of "progressive revelation"—as preached by Reform Judaism—which does not confine the Word of God to the Written Text might not, after all, be so adverse to finding Revelation in the Oral Torah as well. At any rate, the time may well have come when the doctrine of "Torah from Heaven" should be taken seriously again.

Taking "Torah from Heaven" seriously may not be easy for the modern liberal Jew, but it is not impossible. At least, it is not impossible as long as his rationalism does not prevent him from thanking God for bringing forth bread from the earth. For unless this tribute to Nature's God merely covers up for an apotheosis of Nature herself, the Jew who believes in God's power to produce bread from the soil cannot very well remain deaf to the admonition that "man doth not live by bread alone, but by every thing that proceedeth out of the mouth of the Lord doth man live."

Endnotes

[1]Cf. Leviticus 2:13.

[2]*b. Berakot* 40b.

[3]Cf. A. Marmorstein, *The Old Rabbinic Doctrine of God* (London, 1927) I:105ff.

[4]David Hoffmann, ed., *Mischnaiot, Seder Nesikin* (Berlin, 1898) 189, n. 9.

[5]*Mishnah Sanhedrin* 10:1.

[6]*Sopherim* 13:8 (ed. Mueller, xxii).

[7]Cf., for example, Deuteronomy 4:36.

[8]*t. Berakot* 7:2 (ed. Zuckermandel, 15f.).

[9]Cf. *y. Berakot*, chap. VII (11a, b); and *Abudraham*, beginning of chap. III.

[10]*Sepher Hamitzvoth*, in *Likkuté Kadmonioth*, ed. Harkavy (St. Petersburg, 1903) II:17.

[11]Cf. the blessing before the reading from the Torah as described in Nehemiah 8:5-8.

[12]Amos 8:11.

[13]Theodor H. Gaster, *Festivals of the Jewish Year* (New York, 1953) 63.

[14]*b. Sanhedrin* 99a; and cf. *Sipre* to Numbers 15:31 (ed. Friedmann, 33a).

[15]Claude G. Montefiore, *Outlines of Liberal Judaism* (London, 1912) 218f.

[16]Franz Rosenzweig, *Briefe* (Berlin, 1935) 581f. [My translation from the German.]

Part Three
Commandments

Chapter 6

Commandments

Yeshayahu Leibowitz

What is given through the Torah is not only knowledge of God, made manifest in the Torah, but also a body of commandments, which are concrete and specific. The entire holy way of life that Judaism prescribes derives from the Torah of Sinai and is meant to spell out in deed and gesture, in discipline and restraint, in moral action and humble circumstance alike, what God has told eternal Israel to do and not to do. What does Judaism understand by "commandments" and why do these form the central definition of the way of life of holy Israel? Judaism finds its definition, its spiritual content, in the commandments of the Torah. There is no understanding what has happened in Judaic theology from Auschwitz without a grasp of how and why the life of faith found its most vivid reaffirmation, beyond catastrophe, in the renewal of the life under the law that forms the heart and soul of the Torah, of Judaism. In the account at hand, we find how the commandments of Sinai define the faith, with emphasis upon the faith not of theologians or prophets but everybody, ordinary people living commonplace lives. Protestant Christian critiques of Judaism always insist on the inferiority of a religion of works, which Judaism assuredly is, as against a religion of faith. Judaism is represented as a religion for robots or bookkeepers, drawing an antithesis—in Liebowitz's words—"between the intense religious experience and the formalism of mi z vot [commandments]." But it is through the commandments that eternal Israel meets God, and the religious life never comes to an end, never reaches closure, until death. Then, and only then, is the yoke of the commandments lifted from the shoulders of the faithful Judaist.

***

The *mi z vot*, or ritual commandments, enjoined by the Torah are to be regarded first and foremost as religious praxis. As such the *mi z vot* are the ground of the living religious reality known as Judaism. The *mi z vot* are thus to be understood not in terms of their so-called philosophical "reasons" but rather as the matrix of Judaism as one lives it and is capable of living it in the here and now, in the everyday life of the believing Jew who has bound his life to the rule of God's Torah. As a religion of *mi z vot* Judaism is an institutional religion; its institutions, viz., the *mi z vot*—not its dogmas and values—define its spiritual content. Accordingly, Judaism is not an abstract or confessional faith, but is rather an emphatically concrete faith grounded in a complex of well-defined religious deeds and ritual practices.

To be sure, there is a vital interdependence between the institutional reality of religion and its values and beliefs. The nature of this relationship often depends, however, on the spiritual disposition of the individual. Thus there are religious individuals for whom faith is prior to their religious praxis and others for whom religious praxis is prior to their faith. There are individuals who from a world of abstract values—dogmas and feelings of obligation—seek the realization of these values in a specific form of life; and there are others who come to a world of values through having accepted a specific form of life and religious praxis—the yoke of institutional religion, which, in turn, also leads them to faith. Whoever has a basically religious temperament will attain religious values and faith only through institutional religion. Hence, it may be said that a Jew is one who attains religious values and faith by virtue of the *mi z vot*, which bear not only Judaism's values but also its categories of religious knowledge and feeling.

The primary features of Judaism qua a religion of *mi z vot* is that it is primarily a religion of the ordinary, unexceptional individual who is not necessarily blessed with a spiritual disposition. In consonance with this fact, Judaism is also a realistic religion: It apprehends the individual in his concrete, everyday existence and regards him in light of this reality, and not in terms of a "vision" of an ideal reality. Judaism is concerned with the individual's tasks, obligations, and responsibilities in his concrete, mundane existence, and renders it impossible for him to evade his responsibilities through the deception of attaining a different, "higher" reality. Indeed, halakhic religion considers the person strictly from the standpoint of his trivial, quotidian reality. *Mi z vot* are norms for this humdrum existence, the real and constant reality of man: Halakhic religion is not enthusiastic about the ecstatic, unusual episodes of one's spiritual life, the "holiday" moments of life, so transient and momentary; *mi z vot* relate essentially to the general and constant, not the exceptional, which is by definition only occasional and ephemeral. Grounded in *mi z vot*, Judaism renders religion the prose of life, a religion of mundanity. This is the very strength of Judaism. There is no intention here to denigrate the poetry of life, the episodic occasions when an individual rises above his or her daily existence, achieving blissful moments of ecstasy and enthusiasm; on the contrary, it may well be that ordinary existence pales in significance beside those episodes; nonetheless, the basis and continuity of human existence are not those moments of rare poetic elevation, but rather the even keel of prose. At the age of forty or more, Monsieur Jourdain of Moliére's *Le bourgeois gentilhomme* suddenly discovered that all along he had been speaking prose. Had Monsieur Jourdain been a poet, he would never have sung his verse unawares; a person recites poetry only intentionally, in extraordinary moments of his life. A religion that primarily seeks to promote spiritual exaltation and even ecstasy is a religion of poetry, a religion that is principally an ornament to life. The religion of *mi ẓ vot* is the religion of life itself.

It is the nature of halakhic Judaism to be antirhetorical, antipathetic, antivisionary, and, above all, to oppose all self-deception: It does not permit one to believe that reality is different from what it actually is and it prevents him from trying to escape from his responsibilities and obligations in this terrestrial world to an imaginary, ideal world that is all good, beautiful, and sublime. It is not by chance that a very large portion of the *mi ẓ vot* have to do with a person's body—conception and birth, eating and drinking, sexual intercourse, illness and death. The largest division in the basic formulation of the halakhah, the Mishnah, is the tractate *Taharot* (Purity), which deals with all the "filthy" aspects of one's biological existence, from which there is no escape.

The most characteristic quality of the life of *mi ẓ vot* is its nonpathetic nature. The life of *mi ẓ vot* does not rely upon the awakening of religious feelings and does not grant importance to a special spiritual impulse prompting unusual experience and actions. It constantly strives to establish the religious act—even in its more sublime manifestations—as a fixed pattern of fulfilled obligation: "Greater is he who is commanded and does, than he who is not commanded and does" (*b. Qidd.* 31a). And precisely this very nonpathetic tendency manifests a tremendous pathos. How vain and empty is the vaunted antithesis between the intense religious experience and the formalism of *mi ẓ vot*, an antithesis often advanced by opponents of traditional Judaism.

Hence, in contrast to Judaism, directed to human existence as it is, there are religions that seek to redeem man from his mundane existence and transpose him spiritually to another order of existence in which utterly different tasks and obligations obtain. Christianity is clearly a religion of the latter type. The Christian who accepts that Jesus Christ died for his sins is said to be redeemed; that is to say, the basis of his spiritual existence is ontologically changed—among other things, he is free from the *mi z vot*. Needless to say, halakhic Judaism does not recognize such redemption. The obligation it places on a person is permanent and eternal, and no religious achievement can be deemed as so absolute that one acquires a dispensation from any further obligation. The fulfillment of the Torah and its *mi z vot* is only a preparation to continue to fulfill the Torah and *mi z vot*. The existential stance of the Jew and the tasks that follow from it are not changed one iota through any external religious event or internal religious achievement.

A symbolic exemplification of this is to be found in the great moment of the conclusion of the Yom Kippur service. After this day of atonement, prayer, and fasting, through which Jews are "purified"—"and before Whom do they purify themselves and Who purifies them?" as Rabbi Akiva rhetorically asks in the very last sentence of the Mishnah *Yoma*—there comes the *Neilah*, the closing prayer of the service in which the Shema is recited by the entire congregation and the *shofar* is awesomely sounded. But this is immediately followed by the opening prayer from the daily evening liturgy: "And He the merciful One will forgive our sins." That is to say, the situation of the individual at the conclusion of the Yom Kippur service is exactly as it was before the afternoon prayer of the day before Yom Kippur. His achievement is no more than just his religious effort on that great day, and he must begin forthwith to prepare for the next Yom Kippur, a process that repeats itself until the end of his days. Similarly, devotion to the study of Torah is not a means to attain a specific goal but a toil that is a goal unto itself. As Maimonides comments, "Until when must one learn? Until the days of one's death" (*MT Hil. Talmud Torah* 1:10).

As a religion that opposes all forms of self-deception, halakhic Judaism surely does not delight a person envisioning religious life as the attainment of a goal. The life of *mi z vot*, which obligates a person from earliest maturity to death, is not affected whatsoever by any spiritual achievement one may attain. The fulfillment of the *mi z vot* is the way leading a person toward his God, an infinite way whose goal is never attained and is, in fact, unattainable. Indeed, it is incumbent upon the Jew to realize that the way is eternal. He embarks on this way and is always at the same point. The realization that the religious task placed on one is infinite and that one can never reach the goal—this is the religious faith realized in the fixity, continuity, and permanence of the *mi z vot*. The circle of the *mi z vot* always returns to its beginning: "Every day should be as new in your eyes" (Rashi, ad loc., Exod 19:1), because after every performance of the *mi z vot* one's position remains as it had been before. A person cannot attain the goal of nearness to God, who is infinitely removed from Him: "For God is in heaven and you are on earth" (Eccl 5:1). And yet the meaning of the *mi z vot* lies precisely in the very effort one expends in reaching the paradoxically unattainable goal.

Mi z vot as a way of life, as a fixed and permanent form of human existence, preserve religion as a goal in itself and prevent it from turning into a means for attaining a goal. Indeed, most of the *mi z vot* have no sense unless we regard them in this manner, as an expression of selfless divine service. Most of the *mi z vot* have no instrumental or utilitarian value and cannot be construed as helping a person fulfill his earthly or spiritual needs. A person would not undertake this way of life unless he sees divine service as a goal in itself, not as a means to achieve any other purpose. Therefore, the halakhah directs its attention to one's duties and not to one's feelings.

If *mi z vot* are service to God and not service to man, they do not have to be intended or directed to man's needs. Every reason given for the *mi z vot* that bases itself on human needs—be they intellectual, ethical, social, or national—voids the *mi z vot* of all religious meaning. For if the *mi z vot* are the expression of philosophic knowledge, or if they have any ethical content, or if they are meant to benefit society, or if they are meant to maintain the Jewish people, then he who performs them serves not God but himself, his society, or his people. He does not serve God but uses the Torah of God for human benefit and as a means to satisfy human needs.

Therefore, the so-called "reasons for the *mi z vot* " (*taamei ha-mi z vot* are a theological construct and not a fact of religious faith. The only genuine reason for the *mi z vot* is the worship of God, and not the satisfaction of a human need or interest. If, for example, the meaning of the Sabbath were social or national, it would be completely superfluous: The secretary of the labor union takes care of the workers" need for rest. The divine Presence did not descend upon Mount Sinai to fulfill that function. If the Sabbath does not have the meaning of holiness—and holiness is a concept utterly devoid of humanistic and anthropocentric meaning— then it has no meaning at all.

The same evaluation can be applied to the ethical meaning that the secularists seek to attribute to the Torah and its *mi z vot* . Ethics as an intrinsic value is indubitably an atheistic category. Accordingly, only he who sees man as an end unto himself and as a supreme value—that is to say, puts man in the place of God—can be an ethical person. He who looks upon man as one creature within creation and recalls the verse "I am ever mindful of the Lord's presence" (Ps 16:8) cannot accept ethics so conceived as the criterion and touchstone of his behavior before God. Ethics has only one of two meanings: (1) directing a person's will according to his rational recognition of the truths of nature—namely, the ethics of Socrates, Plato, Aristotle, the Epicureans, and the Stoics (especially the latter), and in modern philosophy Spinoza; or (2) directing a person's will according to his recognition of rational, ergo human, obligation—namely, the ethics promoted by Kant and German idealism. In contradistinction to both these conceptions of ethics, the Shema declares, "So that you do not follow your heart and eyes" (Num 15:39), "do not follow your heart," in effect a negation of Kant's concept of ethical autonomy; "do not follow your eyes" is the negation of Socrates" conception of ethics. The Torah gives us immediately the reason for this double negation: "I the Lord am your God" (Num 15:41). The Torah does not recognize ethical commandments whose source is in the recognition of natural reality or the recognition of man's obligation to man; it recognizes only *mi z vot.* The Torah and the prophets never appeal to man's conscience, for such an appeal is always suspected a possible expression of idolatry. In fact, the term *conscience* is not to be found in the Hebrew Bible. The guidance of conscience is an atheistic, indeed, an idolatrous concept; "The god in one's heart" whose standard is raised by humanistic ethical teachers is a foreign god. The halakhah as religious instruction does not tolerate the concept of ethics, and needless to say it does not tolerate any utilitarian criteria for behavior, whether its benefit is to accrue to the individual, nation, or society. "Love your neighbor as yourself" (Lev 19:18) is the great principle of the Torah not because it is an idea beyond the formalism of the law and above the specification of the *mi z vot,* but precisely because it is one of the 613 *mi z vot.* The principle to "love your neighbor as yourself" is not unique to Judaism; similar teachings were propounded by sages and thinkers who were not at all influenced by Judaism and never heard of it, the sages of China, India, and Greece. Moreover, the verse "You shall love your neighbor as yourself—I am the Lord" (Lev 19:18) The duty of loving one's neighbor does not derive from the status of a person as a person but from his status before God. "You shall, . . ." without the conclusion "I am the Lord" is, in fact, the great principle of the atheist Immanuel Kant. The novelty and greatness of this noble principle in the Torah is in its position within the framework of the *mi z vot,* namely in its inclusion in the long list of *mi z vot* the portion of the Hebrew Bible known as *Kedoshim* (lit., "sanctified actions"; Lev 19-20) along with such *mi z vot* as reverence for father and mother; the Sabbath, prohibition of idolatry, rules of sacrificial offerings; the prohibition against reaping the edges or gleanings of one's fields (which must be left for the poor to gather); the prohibition of theft, fraud, false oath, and the delay in paying for a worker's labor; the prohibition of mixed seeds and garments of linen and wool; the law of an indentured female servant; the prohibition of eating from a tree during its first three years. In this context, "You shall love . . ." ceases to be merely good advice, a pious wish, a noble striving and sublime idealism and becomes something real, a law to which a person must relate seriously and solemnly, like the laws of a state. Let not the laws of the state be regarded contemptuously, for it was the talmudic sage Rabbi

Johanan ben Zakkai who addressed his pupils before his death: "May it be God's will that the fear of God be as real for you as the fear of a human being" (*b. Qidd.* 28b). Similar to the misleading effect of the partial citation of "You shall love . . ." is the falsifying quotation "And you shall do the good and the upright," for the verse states, "Do what is right and good in the sight of the Lord" (Deut 6:18).

What does the religious person attain from the fulfillment of the *mi z vot*? This is clarified by the last of the biblical prophets: "And you shall come to see the difference between . . . him who has served the Lord and him who has not served Him" (Mal 3:18). The *mi z vot* are means by which one serves God, and only through them can one actually assume the yoke of the kingdom of heaven. For as long as one's religious life expresses only one's personal understanding, conscience, ethics, and values, one's religious acts are merely self-serving, and hence tantamount to rebellion against the kingdom of heaven. There is an absolute opposition between service to God through the Torah and its *mi z vot* and the service of "the God in the heart" or "the conscience" of humanistic religion, which ultimately can be nothing but service to man. This latter form of religion is the idolatry referred to in the verse "so that you do not follow your heart" (Num 15:39). Every action through which one satisfies his own needs, whether physical or spiritual, is a service to himself and not service to God. If one attributes to such an action a religious meaning, it means in the final analysis that one makes one's god a means and an instrument for oneself. One serves God only when one takes it upon oneself to fulfill *mi z vot* that are an expression of God's will and not a means to satisfy one's physical or spiritual needs. Therefore, in Judaism an expression of genuine service to God is, for example, the donning of *tefillin* (phylacteries) in accordance with all the detailed requirements of the Torah. There is absolutely no instrumental incentive for undertaking this act, nor can there be any other incentive except to do the will of God, who commanded this rite of donning the *tefillin*. Similarly, the observance of the Sabbath with all its strange laws—laws that have no discernible significance for man's physiological, social, or psychological life—is service to God. Sabbath-prohibited work is not in the least determined by the amount of energy invested in particular types of prohibited labor or the toil this labor may entail, but rather by the very principles of halakhah itself. The only genuine meaning of the Sabbath is its holiness—to submit a seventh of one's life to the rule of a special regimen, not stemming from one's nature, inclinations, and needs but only from one's decision to accept the yoke of the kingdom of heaven and concomitantly to submit to a way of life that is diametrically different from the natural way of life. Indeed, the very laws of the Sabbath emphasize and highlight this difference: "It shall be a sign for all time between Me and the people of Israel" (Exod 31:17). Hence, the Sabbath loses all its pristine religious meaning should its laws be adjusted to human inclination and convenience. Similarly, the laws of family purity or the dietary laws, which contrary to some "modern" interpretations have no physiological reason, are meant only to subdue human nature of the service of the divine creator.

Having no physiological, philosophical, or sociological reasons and being required neither by man's reason nor by his feelings, *mi z vot* are to be understood in the light of the problem of freedom. For of the person who takes upon himself Torah and *mi z vot*, it may be asked whether he has forfeited his autonomy. It is well known that many argue—and many are the arguments—that a person who has assumed the yoke of Torah and *mi z vot*, has enslaved himself. Both the concept of enslavement and that of freedom, however, require careful semantic analysis. "The world pursues its natural course" (*b. 'Abod. Zar.* 54b). That is to say, there is a lawfulness to the world of natural happenings; there are fixed functional connections between events. The very recognition of this fixed, lawful pattern in accordance with which man must live and act is of great religious significance, and, moreover, is the basis upon which the life of halakhah is structured—in contradistinction to a faith in repeated interventions from above. If there is a fixed pattern and lawfulness in the world, man is a part of it and is necessarily subject to the whole system of natural reality that includes not only his body but also his soul. Man is subject to the natural order both physiologically and psychologically. (Although it is of concern to metaphysics, the purported division of body and soul is irrelevant and superfluous from the standpoint of religious faith. From a religious point of view, the dividing line is not between "matter" and "spirit" but between the creator and the created, that is, between God and the world. Creation—the world, nature—includes everything material and spiritual apprehended by man.) From this perspective, freedom is then the acceptance of a way of life that does not stem from man's nature. To be sure, there are many definitions of human freedom. Philosophically, the most profound conception is that of Spinoza, who holds that freedom is acting from the necessity of one's own nature. Does man, however, truly have his own nature? As a natural being he is only a part of nature as a whole, and his nature is only a link in a causal chain of inanimate nature and biological reality that acts on and through him. Further, human psychology is only an expression of these forces. Where, then, is man's vaunted autonomy? Man activated by his "own" nature is actually only a puppet activated by the forces of nature, just like an animal pasturing in the field, which is also free of Torah and *mi z vot*, that is to say, from every law externally imposed. In the Talmud, Rava says, "All bodies are sheaths, happy is he who has been privileged to be a sheath for the Torah" (*b. Sanh.* 99b). A person is never completely of "his own"; he is always a receptacle for something not "his own." To be sure, he may regard himself as being free from every external command, acting according to a Spinozistic freedom, guided by his nature alone, but his nature is an expression of all the blind forces of nature in general, as well as man's psychological nature—his wishes, inclinations, and desires. From a religious point of view there is no place for the threefold division of nature-spirit-God. There are, as noted, really only two basic entities: nature, which includes man's spiritual aspects, and God. There is only one way man may liberate himself from subjugation to the forces of nature, namely by attachment to God. Concretely, this means doing God's will and not that of man, since man's will is intrinsically a fact of nature.

Contrary to the modern atheistic perversion of the Hebrew Bible, it is necessary to emphasize that it does not recognize man's spirit as antithetical to matter. The famous verse, so often distorted and falsified by modern commentators, does not set human spirit against matter but rather against the spirit of God: "Not by might nor by power, but with My spirit" (Zech. 4:6)—the spirit of man belongs to "might" and "strength." Hence, there is no freedom from the chains of nature except through accepting the yoke of the Torah and *mi z vot*, a yoke not imposed by nature. This is the meaning of the rabbinic saying, "The only free person is he who is concerned with Torah" (*m. 'Abot* 6:2). Such an individual is free from enslavement to nature, precisely because he lives a life contrary to nature. Therefore, there is no need—from either a religious or a philosophic perspective—to submit the world of *mi z vot* to the world of human concepts and interests; in the very "strangeness" of the *mi z vot* lies hidden their strength. Attempts to rationalize the *mi z vot* and to delineate their "reasons" are religiously and philosophically meaningless and have but trivial theological or psychological interest.

Genuine human freedom is thus attained only through the religion of *mi z vot*. Yet some have criticized this religion as being mechanical, for by the very testimony of the Hebrew Scripture itself such a religion is the "commandment of men learned by rote" (Isa 29:13). After all, the critics argue, even the rabbis realized that "the Merciful One demands the heart" (*Sanh* 106b) and that every deed should be determined by the heart's intention. Therefore, the critics ask, what is the value of a religion whose main theme is a way of life attained by habitual practice till it becomes second nature? However, the "commandment of men learned by rote" is not necessarily a flaw in religious behavior, just as it is not a flaw in obedient citizenship. Only a very small minority of people actually determine their conduct of life upon the basis of a conscious decision, and even such individuals determine their conduct on the basis of conscious, intentional decisions only in special moments of life—the moments of poetic exaltation, which occasionally punctuate the overwhelmingly dominant prosaic flow of one's life. In the prose of life one acts according to habit, upon the basis of practices and conventions to which one is accustomed and which direct one's conduct quite unawares. Let us not hold such habitual action, "the commandment of men," in contempt, for it—and not the rare personal decision and intention—is the main shield against barbarism. If certain human societies attained a social order in which there was a basic minimum of human decency and civility and became societies of law-abiding citizens, they did not attain this because their citizens struggled with all the perplexities considered by the imprisoned Socrates until like him they recognized that a person must obey the laws of his state even if they run counter to his personal interests, but simply because as citizens they had become habituated to civilized behavior. "It is not the practice of our place" (Gen 29:26)—this is the classic expression of the "commandment of men." The contempt poured upon "social superstitions," "meaningless habitual behavior," "empty conventions"—this contempt loosens the social bonds, removes the restraining reins, and lets loose dark, violent forces that had been controlled only by "commandments."

Our generation more than any previous one has with untold pain learned that most people are incapable of living as human beings on the basis of their own "autonomous" decisions and personal responsibility. The same principle applies to the sphere of religion: Only the prophet Isaiah, whose eyes saw the king, lord of hosts, was permitted to despise the "commandments of men learned by rote" and to deem it as religiously inadequate. As for us ordinary mortals, would that we be privileged to stamp upon our lives the seal of a bond to God through the habitual and disciplined norms of *mi z vot*. After we have been privileged to attain the religious level of life of the "commandments of men," inculcated by the regimen delineated in the *S h ulhan Arukh* that the proponents of purified religion so despise, we will strive to advance further toward a religious existence in full consonance with the proper intentionality and spiritual awareness. The champions of spiritual spontaneity who scorn religion that restrains experience with laws and disciplined mores and concomitantly celebrate the unbounded expression of experience have often been the cause of the greatest atrocities. How powerful was the religious feeling and how mighty the religious experience of the idolaters who sacrificed their sons to Molech and surrendered their daughters to the sacred prostitution of Ashtoreth (cf. Lev 18:21; 20:3-5). The Torah, however, utterly rejects such free, spontaneous, and natural religiosity, which it deems tantamount to idolatry. The Torah unabashedly confines one in the "prison" of *mi z vot* and is not at all daunted by the danger of becoming a religion of commandments "learned by rote."

The molding of one's life on the basis of divine commandments means creating a sphere of deeds endowed with holiness. In Judaism, holiness—which in the religious sense of the term is to be clearly distinguished from its intemperate secular uses—is achieved only by the performance of the *mi ẓ vot*, those precepts specifically intended as service to God. Every other type of action, whether it is deemed good or bad, that a person does for his pleasure or to satisfy a physical or spiritual need is in the last analysis service to himself and as such is intrinsically secular. The distinction between the sacred and the secular is a primary religious category; moreover, it is a basic feature of institutional religion, the religion of *mi ẓ vot*. To conceive of the sacred as an immanent quality of specific things—be they persons, places, institutions, objects, events—is a fundamentally mystical, even magical view, and smacks of idolatry. There is no holiness except in the divine sphere—that is, the realm of human deed formed not by human values but through the *mi ẓ vot* of God, in which man acts for the sake of God alone: "The Holy One, blessed be He, possesses in His world only the four cubits of halakhah" (*b. Ber.* 8a). There is nothing in the world that is intrinsically holy, there is only that which is "holy *to* God," that is, deeds sanctified to God through the specific purpose of service to God. Halakhic Judaism knows only this concept of holiness. Indeed, the biblical declaration "You shall be holy" (Lev 19:2) introduces a passage dealing largely with specific *mi ẓ vot*, and the words "for you are a holy nation" (Deut 7:1) prefaces a passage devoted exclusively to specific *mi ẓ vot*.

One of the shrewdest stratagems of anthropocentric secularism, which hides behind the mask of pure religion, is to proclaim the cancellation of the separation between the holy and the profane and to spread a mantle of holiness over natural functions and human values. If holiness is present in the elements of natural reality in and of itself, or if the forces and drives of man himself are holy, there is no place for "the Holy God" transcendent to natural reality, for this reality itself is divinity and man himself is God. The abolition of the specific category of religious holiness and the enthronement of human functions and psychic drives as holy is a most dangerous phenomenon, not only from a religious point of view but also from a communal, educational, and ethical perspective. Our generation—more than all preceding generations—has been witness to what has been done for the sake of and in the name of the homeland, the nation, honor, freedom, equality, and every human value rendered holy as a consequence of man's having forgotten the basic truth that holiness exists only in a world beyond human values. In the light of the grievous confounding of the holy and the profane, we might better appreciate the extraordinary educational importance of the *mi z vot*. Grounded in the transcendent sphere of holiness, the *mi z vot* constitute by their very existence a constant demonstration and announcement that everything outside their framework is not holy and cannot be authentically exalted as holy—and, alas, there is nothing that our generation needs to be daily reminded of more than this.

It may be asked whether the creation of a sphere of holiness through the *mi z vot* is indeed the goal of religion. One must reply both yes and no. On the one hand, there is no doubt that the religious goal that the prophets call "knowledge of God" and the psalmist "closeness to God" is not merely a matter of one's conduct. As Maimonides observed, "Man's perfection is not found in actions or ethical qualities but in knowledge" (*Guide*, 3:52). The goal of religious life is then spiritual perfection, spiritual knowledge, and worthiness. Accordingly, Maimonides, it would seem, places the *mi z vot* not in the realm of the preparatory and the educational. In this sense the *mi z vot* are not the religious goal itself, but only a means and method.

However, in the profound dialectic of Maimonides" philosophic outlook, the preparatory position of the *mi z vot* is transformed into the goal of the religion: "Know that all the practices of the worship, such as reading the Torah, prayer and the performance of the other *mi z vot*, have only the end of training you to occupy yourself with His *mi z vot*, may He be exalted, rather than with matters pertaining to this world; you should act as if you were occupied with Him and not with that which is other than He" (*Guide*, 3:51). So we find, after nine chapters (26-34) that deal with the "intention of the Torah," that is, the intention of its *mi z vot* , in general, and fifteen chapters (35-49) of specific reasons for *mi z vot* , emphasizing their usefulness in improving man and society, that Maimonides reveals to us the secret that the performance of the *mi z vot*, which is nominally presented to us as an educational means, has as its goal to train a person to recognize that the knowledge of God and drawing close to him are these very same *mi z vot*. And this is also the meaning of his summarizing remarks in his *Commentary on the Mishnah* (Intro. to Sanh. 10:1, ch. *"Ḥelek"*): "The purpose of truth is only to know that it is true; and the Torah is true, and the purpose of knowing it—to fulfill it."

On the other hand, religious perfection can never be actually realized; it always remains as an eternal guidepost, pointing toward the right direction as an infinite road. A person cannot fulfill the Torah perfectly—because it is divine, not human. Even the perfect individual cannot cling to God, because, as Maimonides puts it, he can never remove the last barrier separating him—"being an intelligence grounded in matter"—from God (*Commentary on the Mishnah*,

Shmoneh Perakim, chap. 7). Therefore, the act of "fulfilling the Torah" can be only the eternal striving to fulfill it.

The eternal striving toward the religious goal that is never attained is embodied in the performance of the *mi z vot*. This performance is never completed, the extent of the task is never diminished no matter how much effort is invested in it, and the goal draws no closer despite the amount of ground the person has covered in moving toward it. Every morning a person has to arise to the service of the creator, that very service that he performed yesterday, and at the conclusion of the Yom Kippur service—after the great realization of *teshuvah* (return) and forgiveness—there begins again the yearly cycle of the daily *mi z vot* toward the coming Yom Kippur, and so on eternally. It turns out, therefore, that the *mi z vot*, even though they are only a means toward an intrinsically unattainable goal of religious perfection, are from man's standpoint the final goal of religious perfection that he is able to attain.

Gotthold Ephraim Lessing, a leading spokesman of the Enlightenment, said that if God were to give him the choice between the pure truth and the eternal search after the truth he would choose the latter, "for the pure truth is for God alone."[1] A great Jewish leader of the socialist movement, Eduard Bernstein, expressed himself in a similar vein: "The movement itself is everything, the goal is nothing."[2] So, too, will a proponent of the "religion of *mi z vot*" say to a proponent of "pure religion": "The eternal striving toward the religious goal through the constant performance of religious acts—that is the true goal of religion for man." Or in the concluding words of Ecclesiastes (12:13): "The sum of the matter when all is said and done; Revere God and observe His *mi z vot*! For this applies to all mankind." The final goal is one of God's secrets. And so we find Abraham Isaac Kook saying: "If man is always liable to go astray . . . this does not spoil his perfection, for the essential basis of this perfection is the striving and fixed desire to attain perfection" (*Orot ha-Teshuvah*, chap. 5). One of his pupils, Yaakov Moshe Harlap, expands on these remarks in the actual language of Lessing—whose work he certainly did not know, and of whose statement he surely never heard: "The endeavor is more than the actual attainment, and particularly according to Maimonides" explanation that there is no goal in the world other than God alone, so that the essence of the endeavor is only the striving for the goal . . . We must give precedence to the search for wisdom over the attainment of wisdom" (*Mei Marom*, chap. 7).

Endnotes

[1] Gotthold Ephraim Lessing, "Eine Duplik," in *Werke*, ed. Fritz Fischer 6 (1965) 297.

[2]Eduard Bernstein, *Evolutionary Socialism: A Criticism and Affirmation*, trans. Edith C. Harvey (1970) 202.

Bibliography

Eduard Bernstein, *Evolutionary Socialism: A Criticism and Affirmation*, trans. Edith C. Harvey (1970).

Yitzhak Heinemann, *Taamei ha-mi z vot* be-Sifrut Yisrael, 2 vols. (1942–1957).

Gotthold Ephraim Lessing, "Eine Duplik," in *Werke*, ed. Fritz Fischer 6 (1965).

Joseph B. Soloveitchik, *Halakhic Man*, trans. Lawrence Kaplan (1983).

Efraim E. Urbach, *The Sages: Their Concepts and Beliefs*, trans. Israel Abrahams 1 (1979) chaps. 1 and 2.

Chapter 7

Torah and Law

Emanuel Rackman

Any picture of revelation and the Torah proves incomplete without an account of how the law of the Torah takes into account the life of ordinary people. The issue of God's will in competition with human freedom is played out in the life under the law. Humanity is God's partner in the Torah, including its law, and it is the task of humanity to find life in the commandments. The law adjusts itself to the requirements of the affirmation of life, which means that the law contains within itself occasions for its own suspension or remission. Any picture of the law of the Torah as unchanging and brutal, disregarding the human situation, distorts the facts, as Rackman here explains in great detail. The law evolves in response to its own imperatives and in accord with its own rules. Here we move from the theoretical to the practical and see precisely how an entire community—the community formed by eternal, holy Israel, in the here and now of organized Jewish affairs—governed itself in accord with the Torah, and at the same time in the context of on-going historical existence.

***

Fundamental in Judaism are God's attributes as Creator and Legislator. Biblical passages are explicit on this point. Less explicit is the notion that man is God's partner in the exercise of both functions. However, Judaism does assign that role to man. As he joins God in Creation he has many questions involving the how and the why. But he is encouraged to explore the universe, conquer its resources, and search for purpose and meanings. In his role as God's partner in the development of God's law, he is encouraged to study it, to master its mandates and their corollaries, revealed and hidden, and to be preoccupied with their viability at all times, despite their presumed immutability because God had promulgated them. Man's imitation of God is thus fulfilled in two spheres—that of nature and that of human society.

If man had not been honored to share with God a creative function in nature, how would he dare to arrogate unto himself the privilege of frustrating God's will when God strikes with illness or other misfortunes? How would he focus on the emancipation of the enslaved and the enrichment of the impoverished? If he was meant to be inert with regard to all such evil simply because God had caused the sufferer to suffer and consequently no one should interfere, then the Bible would not have mandated the healing of the sick and support of the poor. True, not all religions adopted the authentic Jewish point of view. Indeed, neither did all Jews. However, the overwhelming majority did and they relied on verses, explicit and implicit, to justify their involvement in that which God had ordained—hopefully for the better, but, alas, ofttimes for the worse.

God had ordered man to "conquer" the earth (Gen 1:28). Moreover, a verse in the second chapter describes all that God created as having been created "to continue functioning" (*ibid.*, 2:3). This implied that nature would be dynamic and man was authorized to respond to that dynamism. One verse specifically approves of attention to the ailing with an eye to curing them (Exod 21:19) while another prohibits the wanton waste of natural resources which God had given (Deut 20:19).

Less clear, however, is the authority to tamper with the Law. In this connection one asks first: Why did God reveal a Law which is less than perfect and inadequate for eternity without man's participation in its development? The Psalmist did sing that God's law was perfect. However, it was inevitable that as the conditions of man in nature and in society change—in great measure precisely because of man's partnership with God in contributing to the world's dynamism—the Law too would require innovation. That man was endowed with free will and a penchant for evil played an important role in necessitating that creativity. And that creativity was the function of the "Doctors of the Law" obedience to whom was mandated by the Law itself.

Consequently, one finds that as God made man His partner in a continuously changing universe so He made man His partner in the continuous flowering of the Law which represents His abiding will. He presumably endowed that Law with the potential to cope with all that may come to pass but with unrelenting commitment to its value system and parameters.

Yet one question remains. In the absence of a specific grant of authority to tamper with the Law itself, how did the rabbis justify their arrogance in making themselves God's partners in the sphere of law as in the sphere of nature? What were the verses on which they relied and what were the exegeses employed to make the Law cope with more than three thousand years of political, social and economic change? It is to these questions that this paper purports to make reply.

In connection with man's partnership with God in the flowering of the Law, the masters and custodians of the Oral Law were able to legitimize what they were doing on the basis of at least two texts in the Pentateuch. These two texts were crucial for man's role in making the revealed Law viable forever.

The simplest one is the statement in Leviticus (17:5) that the laws were given that the Jewish people shall "live by them." This statement ruled out any possibility of interpreting the Law as requiring martyrdom. Jews were to live by it and not die because of it (B.T. Yoma 85b). It was for this reason, for example, that it was deemed permissible to wage a defensive war on the Sabbath.

The second text in Deuteronomy (17:8-12) assumes that there will be need to resolve questions that will arise in the future and authority was vested in the judges of every age to engage in their resolution. The Jews were ordered to respect and obey the authority of these judges. Despite the fact that their competence may vary from generation to generation, Jews owed obedience to the judges of their day.

A third text is found in the Psalms. The Psalms are not as authoritative a source of the Law as is the Pentateuch. But in Psalm 119:126 the order is: "When the time comes to act for the Lord, violate the Law given you." In circumstances when a higher purpose for God's sake warrants ignoring the Law, do so. In at least two situations the Oral Law, because of this verse, based its permission to violate strict rules. First was the permission granted to commit the Oral Law to writing. And second was permission to Jews to use God's name as they greeted each other—which is in fact mentioning His name in vain.

Still other verses in the Bible supported resort to creativity and will be referred to hereafter in connection with specific areas of the law.

I

One area in which there had to be greater accommodation to the realistic requirements of the social order in many periods of Jewish history was the area of public law—the criminal law and the law of war.

But the Written and Oral law contained many directives for each of these subjects. Indeed, much of the humanization of the laws of crime and war, is due to the influence of the Jewish tradition. Recently even the Supreme Court of the United States cited Talmudic sources to support opposition to capital punishment. However, it appears that especially ancient and medieval society required a stronger hand for the authorities charged with the maintenance of public order and safety. For example, the biblical rules of evidence, too, often made possible the avoidance of prosecution and punishment. Consequently, there was resort to what was virtually a parallel system of law.

Professor Arnold N. Enker developed this theses in a brilliant essay[1] in whose summary he writes: "Jewish criminal law for Jews functions on two tracks. One, which for want of a better term might be called the purely exclusive jurisdiction in this area. Special procedures and unusual rules of evidence and of substantive law apply in these cases and serve to limit punishment of offenders to the most serious and brazen acts of open defiance of God's will. The second track involves the day-to-day concerns of law enforcement and the protection of the social order. On this track, which is administered apparently primarily by the king's courts, although the religious courts also have such jurisdiction, the courts are mostly free to apply whatever rules of practice and evidence that they see fit, to evaluate the evidence free of restraint by formal rules and to punish the defendant as seems to them appropriate to accomplish the protection and preservation of the social order.

"There is biblical foundation for approaching the violation of God's law in these two ways. The earliest biblical chapters contain two stories describing man's sins. In the Garden of Eden story, Adam violates God's law by eating the fruit of the tree of life. In the second story, Cain murders his brother and fellow-man Abel. The law forbidding eating fruit has no apparent social significance. Its behavioral content is not part of those norms of conduct essential to the social welfare. Note that God duly warned Adam that he may not eat the fruit of the tree and that the punishment for this offense will be death, but the Bible contains no record of God having warned Cain that he is forbidden to murder his brother. The essence of Adam's sin is disobedience to God's command, rebellion against His will. In contrast, Cain's sin is murder, which is most destructive of civilized society.

"There are several common themes running through both stories. Most strikingly, the punishment is the same in both—banishment and the cursing of the earth which will no longer give forth its fruit as readily as before. These two stories are essentially one, their object being to explore two aspects of sin. On the one level, the essence of sin is disobedience, rebellion against God's will. But in its second aspect, sin is the violation of that order which is beneficial to society, the infliction of harm on others. In some cases one aspect is dominant, in others, the second aspect is more apparent, but both are present to some degree, and this division of criminal law into two tracks, one administered by the religious courts and concerned primarily with the aspect of rebellion against God, the other administered by the king, i.e., the civil authority, and concerned with protection of the Jewish law's primary sources.

This parallel system of law called "The King's Law" was based on a verse in the book of Joshua (1:18). The verse states that the people invested Joshua with the power to give orders and to impose the death penalty on anyone who defied him. This blanket grant of power later became the basis for many a medieval monarch to claim that his right to rule derived from the people. In the same period Jewish communities in Europe hesitated to arrogate unto themselves the same power. They preferred another biblical source upon which to predicate their power to exercise control over the economy and in this way managed to maintain law and order.

From a verse in the book of Ezra (10:8) the Talmud derived the power of a rabbinical court to expropriate a person and by virtue of the property being ownerless it could then award it to whomsoever it deemed worthy of it. The power was to be exercised judiciously but it was a very effective way both to legislate in matters involving property and also to exact from constituents obedience to new and old regulations.

The people had granted Ezra the power to issue an order disobedience to which would result in the forfeiture of all of the offender's property. This grant of power became the justification for the rule that a duly constituted rabbinical court can declare anyone's property ownerless and also transfer it to another. It was because of this power, one view in the Talmud holds, that Hillel was able to avoid the cancellation of all debts at the end of the sabbatical year. He provided a way for creditors to collect from debtors—in violation of biblical law—which in effect was an expropriation of debtors in favor of creditors. Circumstances warranted his innovation. It was not a capricious ruling. On the other hand, it was for the benefit of debtors—to make credit available in the years preceding the sabbatical year. But, nonetheless, it was revolutionary legislation.

In the Middle Ages this power enabled the Jewish communities—and their councils and judiciary—to govern, to impose taxes and collect them, as well as to punish offenders against all the laws of the community. The combination of the two powers—that of the "King's Law" and that of declaring property ownerless—made it possible for communities to legislate in many areas pertaining to the economy, such as rent control, prohibiting resort by litigants to non-Jewish courts, punishment of informers, etc. In a general way, biblical law pertaining to virtually every area of commerce and industry could be updated to cope with general or local needs.

Another phrase in the Bible also made possible the amelioration of strict law to achieve equity—a higher standard of justice. For example, even in Talmudic times, a debtor who mortgaged his property as security, and lost it to his creditor, could redeem it any time after the foreclosure (*b. Baba Mes* 35b). There was no time limit on this right. Equity required it. And the biblical verse was clear. "One must do the righteous and the good" (Deut 6:18).

Because of this verse, judges in Judaism, were never as bound by precedent as they are in the Anglo-American system. They are to achieve justice as required in each case before them.

Nachmanides" commentary on this verse was also the source for one of the most insightful essays by Rabbi Professor Walter Wurzburger on what he called "Covenantal Imperatives."[2] While many have debated whether Jewish ethics are exclusively heteronomous, Wurzburger clearly shows that Judaism permits a substantial measure of autonomy in resolving ethical issues. The precedents of the Halacha are not always the ultimate source for the resolution of ethical questions. In many a case the Halacha provides the guidelines or parameters within which decisions are made because of the Sinaitic covenant and the overriding mandate "to do the righteous and the good." Moreover, he correctly argues that no Jew should claim the right to be the sole decisor for another. Many try to claim this right but the claim is that of a usurper and not justified by the sources.

"Thus, true to its name, the Halakhah does not serve as the final goal of the Jew, but rather as the way, guiding him in his individuality towards authentic personal decisions in the domain of covenantal imperatives. After all, Jerusalem, so the Sages have told us, was destroyed because our forebears merely abided by the letter of the law. In the final analysis we can properly fulfill our covenantal obligations only when, reaching out beyond the minimum requirements of the law, we respond as free individuals to the summons to an all encompassing service which is issued to us as individuals in our existential subjectivity, uniqueness and particularity by a God who is One and Unique."[3]

II

It is in family law that we find the most extensive innovation or creativity despite the absence in the Written Law of any authority vested in the rabbis to do what they did. They simply posited an unrebuttable presumption that every man who betroths a woman intends that his act shall be subject to the approval of the rabbis. Though they do not mention that the bride's intention is similar, we must assume that she also approves of the same condition because the betrothal would not be valid without her unequivocal agreement (*b. Qidd*, 7A). Thus we have an implied condition in every Halchic marriage that its validity and continuance is based on rabbinic consent. Rabbis have differed as to how extensive the rabbis' power is but there is adequate authority in support of the proposition that it is unlimited. The Jerusalem Talmud goes so far as to approve of the annulment of marriages, ex post facto, if they were consummated in a manner of which the rabbis disapproved. It does not rely on the presumption cited in the Babylonian Talmud.

There is a view that this power is given the rabbis because the groom in the marriage ceremony usually "consecrates" the bride, with her consent, according to the law of Moses and Israel. But this is pure rationalization. The rabbinic power is exercised even if the bride and groom never mention those words.

It has also been suggested in the Talmud that this power of the rabbis is a corollary of the power the rabbis have to declare property ownerless—to divest one person of property and vest it in another (*b. Ketub.* 3A). With this power they can annul marriages by declaring that the gift given the bride by the groom was not his, which is enough to make the marriage a nullity. But as the Talmud asks, what do they do with a marriage consummated by sexual intercourse? The answer is that they can declare the coitus to have been two unattached persons.

In modern times distinguished Halachic authorities have held that a couple that does not arrange for a Halachic marriage under orthodox auspices are not married *ab initio*. This might not apply to couples who live in countries where Halachic marriages are unavailable and, therefore, their failure to seek a Halachic marriage does not necessarily imply the rejection or the negation or intention to enter into one.

Despite the fact that the power is well established in both the Jerusalem and Babylonian Talmuds the source of the power is not indicated. The power may have been well established in the Oral Law from time immemorial but one finds no reference to it in the literature of the Tanaim. It is brought often in the literature of the Amoraim and later authorities.

A search of the literature on the subject does not yield very much with regard to the source or the basis for the exercise of the power. The Bible, however, does recognize the validity of conditional agreements (Num 32:20-24). And at least two medieval commentators have suggested that the Talmud holds that if a man betroths a woman on the condition that her father approves and then the man cohabits with her, the marriage will be a nullity if the father does not consent. On the basis of this analogy the rabbis were given the status of the bride's father. If they withhold consent there is no marriage. The authority to legislate derived from the substitution of the rabbis for the father.

The Jerusalem Talmud appears to have assumed that the rabbis have the power to suspend, and even to ignore a biblical command when circumstances require it. Interesting it is that this was done even in matters that are unequivocally of a religious nature, such as the law pertaining to heave offerings to the priests. And instead of making the presumption that all who wed according to the Halacha condition their deeds on the consent of the rabbinical authorities, the Jerusalem Talmud simply assumes that the rabbis have the authority to legislate even in defiance of biblical rules. The instances in both Talmuds are legion. However, they have not yet been given adequate analysis so that one can form any conclusions as to when this can be done and when not.[4]

Perhaps the main source is the overriding mandate that the Law was given that Jews might live by it and not die because of it.

Some of the situations in family law in which biblical law was ignored are the following:

a. The wife of a Kohen who claimed that she was raped and must be divorced by her husband, has credibility by biblical Law, but is denied it by rabbinic law and continues to be the Kohen's wife in all respects—a flagrant suspension of biblical law which would terminate the relationship.

b. Despite the firm requirement that in all matters of family law two competent witnesses are required, a women whose husband is missing, can rewed upon the testimony of one witness and even on the basis of generally inadmissible hearsay evidence.

However, it was in the extensive use of conditions available to brides and grooms that the law was liberalized so that unhappy developments in the marital relationship were anticipated and provision made in advance to ease their impact.

Thus, for example, provision was made for the marriage to be automatically terminated if the husband died childless and the widow would have to obtain a release (Halitza) from a surviving brother of the husband who was a minor and could not grant the release—a situation causing untold grief in modern Israel especially in a period of war. When the rabbis put an end to conditional marriages this process of liberalization came to an end, but not because of any lack of power but rather because the stability and permanence of marriages were adversely affected.

The ingenuity of the rabbis in solving problems that arose in Jewish family law because of established rules presumably originating in biblical sources is best reflected in an encapsulation of the entire corpus of Jewish family law in the well-known formulation of Sir Henry Maine: "From status to contract." It is submitted that in Jewish family law we have a movement from status to contract, then from contract back to status, and most recently again from status to contract.

III

One area insufficiently explored is that of human rights and how they were derived from biblical sources. One such right is the right to privacy. The area in which one would want maximum protection of the right to privacy is the area of religious thought and religious performance. Yet here one encounters a paradox. On the one hand, Judaism is a faith that prescribes in a most comprehensive fashion what one shall think and what one shall do. Yet, despite that, even in ancient Judaism no attempt was ever made to invade the privacy of Jews by ferreting out information as to what they believed or how they behaved. The Jew was generally on his honor. And God was the sole judge. If the Jew misbehaved in public then he might be punished for his offense against the prevailing norm. However, the Jewish state was never a police state. The faith may pertain to every aspect of life and action. It may also be in a measure authoritarian because it has many dogmas and doctrines, and the active propagation of heresy is proscribed. But there was never surveillance by the state as to what one did in private or what opinions one held.

The very important biblical source for this liberal approach, which is too often overlooked, is found in Leviticus (15:13, 28). Males and females become *temaaim* (ritually unclean) because of certain emissions from their genitals. To be relieved of such a state they must undergo immersion in water, but first they must count clean days. A man must count and a woman must count—there are separate commands for him and for her. And after each command to count there appears an added work meaning "for himself" and "for herself." No one else counts for them. There is no supervision to make sure that they do not cheat and thus accelerate the process of becoming *tahor* (ritually clean). They are on their honor. Thus the Talmud interprets the verses. And in this way it expanded the right to privacy some 2,000 years ago.

Unfortunately, there have been Jewish communities which did not fathom this beautiful feature of the Jewish heritage and in the facilities which they established for the prescribed ritual immersion they kept records that might reveal whether anyone cheated. This is not consonant with the authentic tradition. One ought to rather associate the tradition with the decision of one of New York City's Commissioners of Welfare to respect the mere statement of anyone seeking help that he needed it. There was to be no investigation. An investigation was only made when facts subsequently appeared that created doubts as to the integrity of the claimant.

Otherwise the poor were on their honor, as are the rich with regard to their income tax returns. I do not now pass judgment on New York's policy but I do marvel that so long ago Jewish law was very sensitive with respect to the privacy of males and females in matters of religious observance. Still the theme merits a more extensive analysis.

Can it be perhaps that pragmatic considerations alone account for the failure to monitor the private beliefs and behavior of individuals? One might make a very good case for such a contention. After all, how much could the Jewish state spend on spies and informers? And without evidence how could the state prosecute? The confessions of the accused were never admissible in criminal proceedings conducted according to Jewish Law. Courts required witnesses but there would be no witnesses unless the state provided a cadre of spies. Therefore it might be thought that the state reconciled itself to inaction because inaction was the only sensible, realistic policy to adopt.

Yet this is not altogether correct. Jewish courts could have encouraged informers by rewarding them as did the medieval Church in Europe. What is more, it could have used decoys to trap those who did not believe or behave as required. One must note that Jewish Law recognized this tactic but tolerated it in only one situation. That situation involved a person who sought actively to propagate heresy by influencing others. Because he was a threat to the ideological character of the state, it was permissible to trap him. However, if he did not try to seduce others to share his point of view, decoys could not be used simply to elicit from him what his views were. Thus it appears that Jewish Law simply kept hands off impious beliefs and behavior so long as they were not expressed or performed in public. Only then could they be deemed subversive of the society of the faithful.

That the right to privacy is based on verses related to human sexuality should not be surprising. In the Jewish tradition the value of privacy in sexual relationships between husband and wife became associated with the observation imputed to the non-Jewish prophet Balaam. He noted how goodly were Jewish tents because their openings did not face each other. Couples enjoyed privacy even in the wilderness. They did not cohabit in the presence of other couples. Indeed, this was deemed a hallmark of civilized human behavior as distinguished from that of some animals.

However, concern for privacy in sexual relationship was deemed worthy not only of the dignity of man, it also had a religious dimension. It is in their sexual conduct that men and women are called upon to act on their honor, out of their sense of duty to God and what He mandated. If in matters of sex there was to be no trust then the authorities would have to give up because constant supervision is impossible. Instead, self-control must be cultivated. The ability to exercise self-restraint must be induced; without it civilized life would be impossible. Human society itself would become worse than a jungle. Fathers and mothers, brothers and sisters had to learn to abstain from incest on their honor. And that applied to all illicit relationships.

One of the most specific mandates in the Pentateuch with regard to the right to privacy is the command that a creditor may not enter the home of the debtor to collect the debt due him (Deut 23:11). The Talmud extended the prohibition to include the court's sheriff (*b. Baba Mes.* 113a). However, it seems not to associate this commandment with the right to privacy. Perhaps the rabbis deemed it an extension of the right to property. But the United States Supreme Court (Griswold N. Connecticut, 85 Supreme Court Report 1678) did base the right to privacy in part on the constitutional right to be protected against searches and seizures.

IV

The Talmudic term which comes closest to describing the notion of concern for the dignity and inviolability of the person is *Kavod ha-B'riyot* (Respect for persons). And the context in which it is most fully discussed in the Talmud, involves the obligation of a Jew to undress in public when he discovers that he is wearing a garment made of a combination of materials that Jews are forbidden to wear. The obligation would be based on the general principle that God's will is primary and man must obey even at the sacrifice of his personal dignity. However, the Talmud's conclusions are impressive. First, there are times when God's will can be ignored by failure to act. This is passive disobedience. The Jerusalem Talmud also suggests in one version that if the disobedience would be only for a brief interval so as to allow the person wearing the prohibited garment to remove it privately, he may not need to suffer embarrassment. Second, by a very remote interpretation of a totally unrelated verse the High Priest is permitted to ignore the biblical mandate to avoid contact with a cadaver of a pauper who has no kin to bury him. The High Priest may perform the act of mercy although he thereby flouts an unambiguous biblical prohibition (*b. Ber.* 20a).

One can cite many Talmudic passages that protect the dignity and sanctity of human beings but most of them do not involve any violation of biblical mandates. For the purpose of this study they represent no problem because if the prohibition is rabbinic, and not biblical—and most of the prohibitions of Jewish Law are of that kind—then consideration for the dignity of the person is the paramount consideration. This position is easily rationalized because it is assumed that all rabbinic prohibitions were made initially with the thought that they would not be applicable if the dignity of the human person was endangered.

For this reason many contemporary rabbis feel that this premise can become the basis for many innovations in Jewish life and practice in accordance with the Halacha.

There is still another group of principles which in the past made possible what is in fact rabbinic legislation, and not only revision by judicial interpretation. These are the principles:

1. The requirements of a peaceful society must prevail.
2. The avoidance of evoking hate from Jews and non-Jews.
3. The need for "mending" the world—making life in it better than it was.

Many of the rules pertaining to the rights of persons to dignity, safety, and well-being, derived from these principles, and often property rights had to yield to them.

Moreover, without calling them natural rights the rabbis recognized and enforced rights which were precisely that. For example, when the schools of Shammai and Hillel debated the status of a person who is half slave and half free—owned by one partner and emancipated by the other—the school of Shammai convinced the school of Hillel with an argument from natural law. The school of Hillel had thought that it would be possible for such a person to work for himself one day and for his half owner the next. The rejoinder of the school of Shammai is classic. "You have taken good care of the master but have you taken care of the slave himself?" He cannot marry a female slave because he is half free and he cannot marry a free woman because he is half slave. How will he fulfill God's will to populate the earth?" Needless to say, if his status does not allow him—because of God's law—to populate the earth, then he is under no obligation to do it. It is God's law that stops him. But the school of Shammai was concerned with the slave's natural right, though that term is not used. The slave is not to be denied his humanity.

This controversy clearly indicates that the rabbis reckoned with the existence of natural rights—in this instance, the right to have and raise a family equal in status to that enjoyed by others in that society. It is not simply because God gave the command to be fruitful and multiply to all humans and the slave half slave and half free—is entitled to fulfill that command given to him by God. The fact is that his right is broader. Even in his half slave and half free condition he could procreate. There are women with whom he may cohabit—at the very least women in the same status as he. But what he cannot do is to procreate and have completely free offspring. Yet it is this very right that the rabbis safeguarded for him—a natural right—to be equal to all in his society with regard to having and raising a family.

In a way the right to privacy is a right involving the protection of a person from intrusion by another and the right of the person half slave and half free also required protection from a disability that would radically affect his personal life from limitation by others.

The same generous spirit inspired a very concerned commitment by the rabbis to the reduction, if not the total elimination, of the incidence of bastardy.

The rabbis were aware of the problematic character of the institution. They too queried, "Shall one enjoy the sin and another pay the penalty?" But they realized that the one sanction there was to deter immoral sexual behavior was the threat that the prohibited pleasure might yield a bastard. This threat might induce restraint. And they did not minify the social stigma and the consequence of ostracism involved in illegitimacy. On the other hand, they magnified the horror of such a status. To such an extent did they magnify it that Jews were wont to prefer the death of such a child. One great rabbi—two centuries ago—sanctioned an abortion rather than permit the birth. And in a set of hypothetical cases the Talmud informs us by inference that the stigma attached to illegitimacy was so great that the mothers of illegitimate infants would rather murder than abandon them. If one came upon a foundling whose mother took precautions to ensure the child's survival, though she was then and there abandoning it, the foundling was presumed to be legitimate, for if the child were illegitimate the mother would rather have sought its death. So successfully did the Law induce the dread of illegitimacy!

At the same time, the Law was also very exacting. It made it very difficult to brand anyone a bastard. This was a typical instance of the Law's dialectic—balancing values, creating the threat of hardship, and then virtually eliminating its incidence.

First, it held that children born out of wedlock were legitimate—a radically different definition from that held by most peoples. Even some children born of unlawful marriages were legitimate. Only such were bastards as were the products of incestuous or adulterous relationships in which no lawful marriage could ever be consummated between the parties—for example, a child born because of the cohabitation of a brother and sister. Yet how can one ever prove an incestuous relationship to establish bastardy? One must never overlook the difficulty found in Jewish Law to prove any kind of guilt. And as for an adulterous relationship, that too was virtually impossible to prove in the face of the presumption that every husband is the father of all the children his wife bears—even if he was away from her for years. Perhaps he came on a magic carpet in the dead of night to cohabit with his wife and impregnate her! Perhaps the wife conceived artificially. The mother could not and would not testify against the child's interest. And the Law was quite clear: only those whose illegitimacy is certain are bastards. When there was doubt there was no bastardy.

This paper does not deal with the diversity in the views of the rabbis with regard to problems that exclusively pertain to creed rather than practice. In that area too there was much bold creativity involving the literal meaning of biblical texts. However, it warrants a separate study beyond the scope of this paper which concerns itself not with who God is and what He does but rather with what man does with God's revealed will.

Endnotes

[1]A. N. Enker, "Aspects of Interaction between the Torah law, the King's law, and the Noahide law in Jewish Criminal Law," *Cardozo Law Review* 12 (1990): 1111-30 Yeshiva University, New York.

[2]*Samuel K. Mirsky Memorial Volume*, ed. G. Appel (Sura Institute and Yeshiva University, 1970) 3-12.

[3] *Ibid*, 12.

[4] See "A rabbinical court may decree the abrogation of a precept of the Torah," *Bar-Ilan Annual*, Faculties of Jewish Studies and Humanities, 7-8:5732 (1970): 117-32.

Chapter 8

The Way of the Law: Law and Observance in Jewish Experience

Ernst Simon

The word for "law" in Judaism is not "Torah," we realize. It is "halakhah," meaning, how things are to be done, the rules and ordinances that govern the everyday. Here we come to a description of the halakhah or law, one that spells out in some detail precisely how the Torah's law shapes the community of Judaism. The halakhah of Judaism produces a community marked by an asceticism held in balance, a sobriety, a totality of discipline, a balance between a commanding and demanding faith, which Judaism is, and a despotism, which it is not. All things are open to argument and negotiation, and that is the opposite of the way of the despot. Not only so, but freedom of teaching and diversity of opinion characterize the life of Judaism, and these are protected and valued. An argument represents the ultimate act of affirmation of the other: taking the opinion of the other seriously; an argument is not an affront but the final gesture of respect. Above all, life under the law is marked by what Simon calls "non-utopian messianism," meaning, a Messianism for the here and now. All of these traits in general derive from the details of the observance of the law.

***

Shlomo Alkabetz opens his famous Sabbath hymn, *lekhah dodi* (composed about 1540), with the words *shamor vezakhor bedibbur ehad*, "observe and remember the Sabbath Day—these commandments God caused us to hear in a single utterance." Alkabetz' phrase recapitulates a formulation of the Talmud[1] in which the rabbis seek to explain the discrepancy between the two versions of the fourth Commandment in the Torah—the one in Exodus 20:8 which says, *zakhor et yom hashabbat,* "remember the Sabbath day," the other in Deuteronomy 5:15 which reads, *shamor et yom hashabbat,* "*observe* the Sabbath day." The rabbis of the Talmud felt that both terms belong together. They are "a single utterance" and represent a unity which in turn reflects God's unity and individuality in space and time.

I

Halakhah has several characteristic features which reflect Judaism's distinctive attitude toward life and the world. One of these distinctive features is that halakhah makes a plea for sobriety in religion. Philo, the first Jewish philosopher (ca. 25 B.C.E. to 50 C.E.), who wrote in Greek but is usually quoted in Latin, once spoke of *sobria ebrietas*, "sober drunkenness." A modern scholar, Max Kadushin, refers to the same phenomenon by using the term "normal mysticism."

Both terms describe the spiritual and intellectual climate which halakhah seeks to create—sober drunkenness. We cannot help being drunk when we come near to God. Yet classical Judaism has always insisted that this intoxication be kept within the limits of sobriety.

But how can drunkenness be sober? Is drunkenness not a state in which I seek to gain myself by losing myself? Is mysticism not a posture in which man seeks what the philosophers have called a *unio mystica*, a union with God which can be achieved only by means of ecstatic contemplation and the complete abandonment of the self? In the ecstasy of the mystic experience, the distinction between God and man disappears, and the danger arises that in this experience God will lose His divinity, and man, his humility.

Precisely because the danger of a complete abandonment of self is always present when man seeks to approach God in prayer, Judaism has attempted to "normalize" mysticism. Halakhah is Judaism's means of maintaining the delicate balance between sobriety and God-intoxication. It tempers self-surrender with self-control and preserves the distinction between God and man; man's relationship to God is achieved not in a mystical union but in the fulfillment of God's commandments in the here and now. And unlike mysticism, which restricts the mysterious experience of a union with God to a select few, halakhah obliterates the distinction between the few select who can experience God, and the masses who cannot. Law and observance are a way to God which is open to all without distinction.

II

A second characteristic of halakhah is what I would like to call its nontotalitarian totality. Jewish law is all-embracing. It is total: it governs all aspects of man's life. No province in the kingdom of man and his life is beyond the reach and discipline of Jewish law. In this respect Judaism differs from the philosophy of the Stoics, who maintained that there are *adaiphora*—"things undecided" which are neither good nor bad, neither commanded nor forbidden. The *adiaphoron* represents an area of neutrality and hence of freedom in the moral realm. Classical Judaism hardly knows such a neutral sphere. No things or actions can ever be morally neutral. Halakhah regulates every area of life—eating, drinking, prayer, work, man's relationship to family and fellowman, even his love life, the most intimate sphere of human existence. It is a total system. It aims at the sanctification of every action and moment of man's life.

I find the meaning of halakhah expressed with particular poignancy in the order of worship which requires that the daily evening prayer is to be said immediately upon the conclusion of the Neilah service on Yom Kippur. The Jew has prayed and fasted throughout the entire day. Now the day is ended. Everyone is eager to go home and break the fast. People are rushing out. Yet there is always at least a small group of persons who remain behind to recite the regular daily evening prayer. Having just cleansed and purified themselves, they again pronounce the daily bid for forgiveness. The Jewish year—time—has no pauses. Halakhah governs the totality of man's life and time.

Nevertheless, this totality is nontotalitarian. Halakhah is demanding and commanding but not despotic. It could not become totalitarian because it leaves room for doubts, discussion, disagreement. Its principles and conclusions are not fixed or frozen into immutable finality. The Talmud is not a book but a record, in twenty volumes, of discussions which were going on in Babylonia and Palestine for a period of at least six or seven centuries. It does not mention the year or period when certain things were said. All the generations talked with one another. Every question may become an answer, and many answers turn out to pose new questions.

Yet the Talmud is not only a record of discussion. It can actually be studied only through discussion. A man can read or study every book in world literature by himself except the Talmud. The Talmud can be studied only by the same oral method —the method of discussion—in which it was developed. There are no commas, no question marks, and, only rarely, periods. Questions and answers or the ends of sentences must be indicated by the rise or fall of the speaker's voice. Rashi, the most famous of all Talmud commentators, gives us a clue to this almost hidden treasure. Whenever a sentence or phrase in the text should be read as a question, even though there is no question mark, he says, "*binhuta*," an Aramaic term which means "in a lowered voice." Rashi uses an acoustic notation to describe a nonexisting but desired graphic or visual symbol. The melody of speech has become the melody of learning. Hence the Talmud is not a dry book. It has music. And it could never become totalitarian because it contains the music of discussion, the staccato arguments of debate, the counterpoint of disagreement, and the final harmonization of differing views.

There is a second reason for which this total system is not totalitarian. Since talmudic times, Judaism has had no central religious authorities, no ecclesiastic hierarchy. When I began my career as a high-school teacher in Germany before my *aliyah* to Israel, I asked my principal on the first day of school to permit me to take Shabbat off altogether or at least those morning hours which I needed to attend synagogue services. At first he denied my request. The regulations left him no choice. When I told him that I would neither write nor carry my books on Shabbat, he suggested that I consult my rabbi and ask him to give me permission to do both. There was only one answer I could give him. A rabbi who would give me permission to violate the Sabbath could not be a rabbi for me. Unlike the Roman Catholic church,

Judaism makes no distinction between priesthood and laity. There is no special group of persons who are entitled to perform particular priestly or sacerdotal functions for others. The entire people is to become a "kingdom of priests"; every Jew, be he the Chief Rabbi of Israel or a simple unlearned Jew in the streets of New York City, is required to fulfill the *mitzvot*. Jews may and do differ in the degree of conscientiousness with which they fulfill the religious commandments. Traditional and liberal Jews and their various subdivisions and denominational groupings differ in the way they define the nature and implications of *mitzvah* and law in Judaism. These are legitimate differences of conviction. But to establish a difference in the standards of observance between rabbi and "layman" would be illegitimate. Jews have no ecclesiastical hierarchy or caste of priests ordained to do the job for them. One cannot be a Jew by proxy. Every single Jew bears full responsibility for his own observance of the law.

In talmudic times, the Jewish community had a central authority, the Beit Din Haggadol. It served as a sort of Supreme Court for the Jewish community, and its decisions, proclaimed in a certain place in the sanctuary, were law. Nevertheless, a scholar who disagreed with the pronouncements of the court was still permitted to question the law and to express his disagreement with it when he taught his students in the academy. He was not permitted to advocate that the law be violated, but he retained the freedom of intellectual dissent. The law was not totalitarian.

Still another factor assures the nontotalitarian character of halakhah; the relative freedom of teaching and opinion that exists in rabbinic Judaism. Near the beginning of his famous codification of the law, the *Mishneh Torah*, Maimonides makes the statement that anyone who believes that God has a body like a human being is a sectarian. He is not a good Jew. Maimonides was a rationalist, the leader of the enlightenment of his day. His philosophic training had convinced him that the anthropomorphisms of the Bible could not be taken literally. However, his views did not remain unchallenged. One of his contemporaries, Rabbi Avraham ben David (the RaBaD), dissented sharply: better and wise men than this author believe that God has a body, yet they do not call the people sectarians. The people are entitled to their beliefs, even though they may be erroneous. They have derived their beliefs from the Aggadah and the Midrashim, Judaism's traditional sources. Maimonides' antagonist fought for the freedom of belief of people whose beliefs he himself did not share. Like Maimonides, Avraham ben David was antianthropomorphic and could not accept the belief that God has a body. Yet he insisted that one can be a good Jew and affirm this belief.[2] Judaism regulates man's acts but not his thoughts. No one has the right to read someone else out of Judaism or to consider him a less adequate Jew because their views of God's nature may differ. Judaism must be able to accommodate both views. Both are possible expressions of Jewish tradition and Jewish faith even though they may contradict each other. The unity of the Jewish people is based not on everyone's acceptance of the same dubious results of philosophical speculation but on every single Jew's faithful performance of the *mitzvot*. Man's notions or thoughts may well be mistaken or erroneous. God's nature is beyond our grasp, but His commandments are neither hidden nor far off.[3]

This relative freedom of thought and teaching is one of the characteristic features of rabbinic Judaism. Luther and Zwingli, two of the giants of the Protestant Reformation, were troubled by a question which was similar to that which had troubled Maimonides and Avraham ben David, when they discussed the question whether the host, the consecrated wafer, merely *symbolizes* God's body or actually *is* God's body. If God has a body, why could He not be in this holy bread? When Zwingli insisted that the bread was more than a symbol and that it actually was God's body, Luther broke off the discussion and said to his colleague, *Wir haben nicht denselben Geist*—"ours is not the same spirit." As a result of this disagreement, the Reformation movement was split into two parts—divided by a question which had been settled by Maimonides and the RaBaD through a single side-remark stating their disagreement but accepting both views as authentic. The controversy did not destroy the unity in Judaism, and every reader of the *Mishneh Torah* today can study both views and reach his own conclusions. Halakhah does not impose specific views upon the Jew. It is not a totalitarian system.

III

A third characteristic of rabbinic Judaism is its partial asceticism. In this respect it differs from the Greek world which, with some noteworthy exceptions, was monascetic. According to the Greek view, man realizes his humanity by living out his life to the fullest, physically and intellectually, even though this course of action might involve indulgence and physical excess. This concept became a conspicuous ideal once again in the Renaissance which spoke of *uomo universale*, all-embracing, universal man. The universal man is the person who actualizes his potential of body and mind to the fullest. Man thus obliterates the distinction between virtues and vices; he is less interested in whether an act is good or bad than whether it is an authentic or inauthentic expression of the individual. The same criterion is correctly applied in the realm of aesthetics. Its highest value is authenticity of expression. Shakespeare's Richard III is an authentic person; Shakespeare could never have created him without a deep empathy for authentic evil. What matters is not whether a man's conduct and life are morally good or bad but whether they are an authentic expression of his personality. This is one approach to life. Its most recent form is existentialism.

Christianity advocates the opposite way of life, complete asceticism. Echoing a saying of ancient Greek mysticism that "the body is a tomb," Christianity, with important exceptions, considered the experiences of the senses sinful and insisted that the desires of the body corrupt and destroy the soul. The ideal Christian personality type was not universal man but the monk and the nun, the person who withdraws from family and the world to avoid temptation and to achieve purity from the desires of the body.

Judaism represents a third way. It posits partial asceticism. It rejects uncontrolled indulgence of desire just as vigorously as it objects to complete asceticism. The body is no less the work of God than is the soul, and it can therefore not be inherently evil. Self-negation is not necessarily a virtue. On the contrary, it may well be an evil by destroying a man's ability to experience the fullness of life. According to a rabbinic interpretation, the biblical verse, "Thou shalt rejoice before the Lord thy God,"[4] refers not only to the joys of the spirit—study, worship, and good deeds—but also to the joys of the body, "food and drink, raiment, and fellowship."[5]

According to the Talmud, man is not only not forbidden but actually bidden to enjoy food, drink, love. They are God's gifts. In the last analysis, the complete ascetic who rejects these gifts rejects God.

Jewish tradition posits partial asceticism—a way of life which is neither surrender to unbridled hedonism nor an ascetic withdrawal from the world. It is a way of life that enables the Jew to live in this world, to enjoy it fully and with all his senses. At the same time, it demands that he always remain in control of himself and invest everything he does with *kedushah*, with holiness, with intimations of the divine.

IV

A fourth element which characterizes rabbinic Judaism and is embodied in Jewish law is its nonutopian messianism. Messianism is a pointing to the future. How, then, can Jewish messianism, the Jewish drive for the millennium and its hope for a better future for Israel and mankind, be defined as nonutopian? "Utopia," a Greek term, was coined by Thomas More in 1516 when he wrote his *Utopia* as an answer to Machiavelli's *Principe*. "Utopia" literally means "no place," and More's book describes the ideal society, which exists in no place but which is to serve as a model for the earthly place and society of the man who envisions it. Distant in the realm of space, it is near in the realm of time. Hence all utopian thinking is pseudomessianic: it tries to hasten the end of historical time, to speed the coming of redemption.

Judaism represents a nonutopian messianism. Jews exist today and can continue to define themselves as Jews because their forefathers, in a decisive moment of Jewish history, said no to various utopias, whether it was the utopia of Christianity or that of communism.

In his last work, *Where Judaism Differs*, Abba Hillel Silver made the point that through the *nays* you can hear the *yeas* of the Jewish people. That which is rejected by Judaism often provides a clue to what Judaism affirms. Judaism rejected Christianity. Among the people who rejected Jesus as the Messiah and refused to accept Christianity were probably some of the best as well as some of the worst Jews. The worst were the cynics who rejected the new faith because they could not believe in the possibility of a better future. The best were the believing realists who rejected the promise of utopia in terms of redemption-in-the-making precisely because they saw the world as it was—still unchanged, still incomplete, still in need of fulfillment.

The Jewish attitude is compellingly illustrated by a story of a Hasidic rabbi who had gone to Eretz Yisrael and had made his home near the Mount of Olives. One morning he heard the sound of the shofar, on a day on which the sounding of the shofar is not prescribed by Jewish law. He left his little hut wondering whether the Messiah had come, for, according to an ancient tradition, the arrival of the Messiah would be heralded by the sounding of the shofar. But as he looked around, he responded to what he saw in the streets in just a single sentence, "The world has not changed." The Messiah could not have arrived. And he returned home to pursue his life of study and piety.

The power to resist pseudomessianic movements and promises has made the Jews the people that carries with it the message of *geulah,* of final redemption. Had they fallen victim to one or the other type of utopian messianism, they would today be disappointed Christians or disappointed communists. Their nonutopian messianism has enabled them to remain hopeful, actively hopeful Jews.

V

A fifth and last characteristic of the Jewish posture is a critical identification with a religiously defined nation or people. Associated with this identification is what I consider to be this generation's main task, the building of Eretz Yisrael.

"Critical identification" is a dialectical combination of terms. How can identification be critical? And how can a critic be identified with the cause he criticizes? To paraphrase Pascal's distinction, criticism is a function of the mind, identification is an involvement of the heart. How can the heart become critical and the mind, identified?

The answer can be found in another, more familiar phrase. We sometimes speak of "critical love" in order to characterize a relationship in which love and criticism, attachment and detachment, are fused together indissolubly. Love should not be so blind as to silence criticism, criticism not so detached as to corrode and kill love.

It is possible to remain critical of the Jewish people from without—without love, without identification with our people and the country which once again has become our homeland. In this case, our criticism will remain external and ineffectual. Obversely, we can permit our glowing hearts to become identified with our people's life and work in Israel to such an extent and with such intensity that our love will silence even justified criticism of ourselves and our work. In this case we tend to become chauvinists, and everything we do today may ultimately lose its meaning because the Jewish people and the Jewish state will no longer be and represent what we hoped and worked for in order to stem the danger of collective assimilation in Israel—instead of individual assimilation in the Diaspora—and to make this land the setting for the fulfillment of an age-old dream.

Critical identification is a characteristic of the attitude of rabbinic Judaism and especially of the prophets. No prophet ever dreamed of leaving his people. No prophet ever claimed that everything Jews did was good because it was done by Jews. They criticized their people precisely because they loved them; and they suffered deeply because their concern for their people's welfare and destiny compelled them to silence their love and compassion in order to criticize. The Prophet Jeremiah personified this attitude.[6] Hananiah, who turned out to be a false prophet, stood up in besieged Jerusalem, whose capture and destruction by the Babylonians had been predicted by Jeremiah. Hananiah proclaimed that the yoke and stranglehold of Nebuchadnezzar on Jerusalem would be broken, that the city would be freed and the captives returned. Jeremiah was present when Hananiah spoke. He listened carefully. He wished from the bottom of his heart that Hananiah was right and that his own prophecies of doom were wrong. He loved his people. He did not want them to suffer. Thus he said "Amen" after Hananiah's oration. Yet he also knew that Nebuchadnezzar's yoke would not be broken and that the suffering that lay ahead was God's punishment for the moral corruption and decay of the people and their disobedience to God. He loved his people, yet he had to criticize them. He wanted to comfort them, yet he had to admonish them for the sake of their welfare and their responsibilities under their covenant with God. But he never parted company with them.

His commitment to his people was put to its most severe test when his prophecy came true and Jerusalem was conquered. The victorious king considered Jeremiah a sort of ally and gave him the choice either to accompany him to Babylonia and live there with the highest honors or to remain in the nearly destroyed city in order to help Gedaliah, son of Ahikam, resettle the remainder of the Jews. Jeremiah remained in Jerusalem. Even after Gedaliah's assassination by his rivals, Jeremiah continued to urge his people to remain in the country and to serve as the nucleus for its rebuilding. Only when they once again began to reject the divine truth that spoke through him, did he finally decide to join the pitiful remnants of his people that were led into exile in Egypt.[7]

This is critical identification. One can be the sharpest critic of one's people yet remain fully identified with it and wish to share its life and tasks. At the end of the volume which deals with the destruction of the Second Temple by the Romans in the year 70 C.E., Heinrich Graetz (1817–1891) asked why Jeremiah, who had predicted the destruction of the First Temple, had been accepted by the Jewish people as a true prophet, while Flavius Josephus, who quoted one of Jeremiah's speeches when he was standing among the Roman legions before the walls of Jerusalem that were besieged by Titus and Vespasian, was considered a traitor, despite the fact that his warnings, too, had come true. Graetz's answer was, "Jeremiah spoke from within; Josephus spoke from the tent of the Roman general." Where you stand when you speak—that makes all the difference. It makes either for identification or for lack of it.

VI

Law and observance provide the climate of Jewish life that safeguards and sustains its distinctive features: its emphasis on sobriety in religion, its nontotalitarian though all-embracing character, its partial asceticism, its nonutopian messianism, its demand for critical identification with the Jewish people. Nevertheless, law and observance may also involve certain dangers to the health of Jewish life.

One possible danger is petrification, arrested development. The term *halakhah* is derived from the verb *halokh*, "to walk." Halakhah is a way of life, not a standpoint of life. It involves movement, change, progression, not immobility and standing still. Yet many Jews use the Talmud or the Shulhan Arukh and our other codes as the Sadducees and the Karaites used the Bible. The Karaites rejected the rabbinic tradition and claimed to base their teachings solely on the text of the Bible, disregarding the outer and inner developments that had taken place between the time of the Bible and their own time. Many Jews have become Karaites of the most recent codification of the oral law. They act as if nothing had taken place since it was published. Thus, there exists what can be called an *evolutionary deficit* in halakhah. Orthodoxy does not reject the principle of change as such. But its method of change has become so ineffective and slow that the danger of petrification is very real.

A second danger lies in the *aesthetic deficit* that can be found in Jewish tradition. Visual art was largely neglected in Jewish life. One of the reasons might have been that the Jew met visual art only in the context of pagan worship and idolatrous practices which were often hideously immoral. The aesthetic realm had no autonomous existence in ancient times. Even in Greek civilization, art was intimately related to religious practice, worship, and cult. The Jew rejected visual art because he rejected the religious and moral aberrations of the idolatrous practices for which the artist's handiwork was used.

Whatever the reasons for the absence of a concern with visual art in Jewish life may be—the fact remains that there is an aesthetic deficit in Jewish tradition. It should be reduced. I do not propose that we place aesthetic values at the top of the pyramid of Jewish values or, for that matter, of human values in general. But we must place them higher than we have done in the past.

A third danger which threatens meaningful observance is excessive legalism, an *emotional deficit*, that can occasionally be found among strictly observant Jews. Some years ago, I wrote an article for a Hebrew journal in which I attempted to show that a religious experience encompasses peaks as well as valleys of intensity. We oscillate between moments of greater and lesser emotion in prayer and observance. In the same way, we respond with varying degrees of intensity to different parts of the Torah. There are some ideas and *mitzvot* which we stress more, which we can feel more deeply, and with which we can identify more adequately than with others. A very observant rabbi, in answer to my article, wrote that I was wrong: all parts of the Torah are of equal value and religious importance; we have no right to make a distinction between the *Shema Yisrael*, for instance, and a biblical sentence dealing with the status of a women who was a concubine. In my answer, I pointed out that I had never heard or read that our martyrs, in the Spanish period or in our own time, went to their death proclaiming their faith in a sentence such as *vetimnah hayta pilegesh*—"and Timnah was a concubine";[8] the cry that rose from their lips at the moment of agony was quite another verse: the *Shema Yisrael*. Emotionally and existentially, there is a vast difference between these verses. Yet it is not easy to accept the validity of such a distinction from a purely legalistic, exclusively halakhic point of view.

There is a last danger. It is the danger of chauvinism. There are people, especially in the Diaspora, who claim that a true Jew must be a pacifist—as if Judaism had always identified itself with the unconditional quest for peace. The facts do not support this claim. According to its classical sources, Judaism is neither for peace nor for war. Jewish tradition—the Bible, rabbinic Judaism, even the Rambam and the prayer book—contain notions and events which support both positions. The opening prayer of the *Selihot* service contains a phrase in which the worshipper forgives his enemies and adversaries and asks that no man should suffer or be punished for his sins and the sins committed against him.[9] Yet only a few pages later, the entire congregation joins in a recitation of the *ashrei*, which says, *v'et hareshaim yashmid*, "and the wicked people God will destroy." Jewish sources are often inconsistent. The Jew today must have the courage to face the fact that his definition of the ideas and commitments of Judaism depends on the sources which he uses. Judaism frequently contains strange or contradictory notions, and the decision as to which element of the Jewish heritage to choose or stress depends on each individual's interests and concerns. Only a chauvinist can claim that everything which is recorded in Jewish tradition is good and above criticism and that nothing Jews ever said or did is wrong. Sometimes, when certain parts of the Torah are read in the Sabbath service, I have the fervent wish not to be called upon to recite the blessing over the Torah. I recite the *berakhah* when I am called to the Torah because I am a good soldier who is bound by discipline and, perhaps, do not have enough courage. But I do not always find it easy to reconcile a benediction with the content of the passages which are being read.

VII

Halakhic observance poses certain dangers; but it also possesses a capacity to create and strengthen the distinctive quality of Jewish life which far outweighs these dangers.

Only halakhah gives Jews the possibility of becoming a religious society and not merely remaining unrelated religious individuals. It is difficult to be a religious Jew as an isolated individual, divorced from the community. This is one of the significant differences between Judaism and Christianity. Both religions bear the mark of their native hours. Judaism was born in a collective experience, the experience of an entire people at Mount Sinai. Christianity was born in an individual experience, the experience of one person believed by his believers to be the son of God. Therefore, the believing individual is central to Christianity, while Judaism, be it traditional or Reform Judaism, has always stressed the community. Judaism and Christianity represent two different approaches to the life of faith, and each may conceivably have something to learn from the other. Jews can learn from Christians how to become believing individuals. Christians can try to learn from Jews how to become members of a religious society. One could write a history of Christianity as a sequence of experiments to achieve a religious society. When Christians tried to establish such a society, as Cromwell and other Puritans tried, they took their guiding principles from the Hebrew Bible. The New Testament does not contain those principles of communal life and organization which could serve as a foundation for the establishment of a Christian society. The Hebrew Bible and halakhah do contain these features. The achievement of a genuinely religious society remains an unfulfilled need.

Another aspect of halakhah which contributes to its efficacy is what both the Hebrew poet Bialik and the German rabbi Josef Carlebach called its "obligating prose." Even though Jewish tradition is characterized by an aesthetic deficit, modern Judaism still possesses too much poetry and not enough obligating prose. In religious life, prose is more important than poetry. Poetry addresses itself to the imagination. Prose addresses itself to the will. Poetry can make a claim for the beauty of expression alone. Prose makes a claim upon man. It demands action and sustained effort. Chaim Nachman Bialik, who succeeded in capturing the poetry of the Aggadah and made it accessible to a wide public in his *Sefer Ha'aggadah*, had the courage to say, in his essay "Halakhah v'aggadah," "We have too much *hibah*, too much loving-kindness, and not enough *hovah*, not enough obligation." If I were able to compose prayers, I would perhaps pray, "Give us *mitzvot*; give us obligations."

What "obligating prose" means can be illustrated by two examples from the recent Responsa literature. Jewish Responsa literature contains the answers to halakhic questions which rabbis are asked. Among the volumes recording the questions and answers of our people during the Holocaust is a Hebrew volume by Rabbi Oshri, formerly a Dayan of Kovno, entitled *Me'emek Habakhah*.[10] The book contains the answers which Rabbi Rubinstein and his colleagues of the rabbinic court, among them the author, gave to questions asked by Jews of Kovno during the time of the Nazi occupation and at the height of persecution (e.g., whether it was permissible to eat nonkosher food in order to maintain one's strength, or to break the Shabbat in order to escape death). The questioners were prepared to accept whatever answer the rabbis would give them. They sought guidance. Therefore, the answers were obligating prose, guidelines for conduct in the face of danger and the threat of imminent death. As far as I can remember, there were only two cases in which the rabbis did not grant permission to do what people had asked for. In response to the question whether a young man was permitted to kill himself in order to escape torture and death at the hands of the Nazis, the rabbi answered, "No, my son. We should never do their evil work for them. We have to live to our last moment." Suicide is the ultimate loss and abdication of faith. It means final despair, the conviction that God cannot help any more.

The second case concerned a young girl's question of whether she was permitted to register as a gentile and dress and act like one in order to save her life. Again the answer was in the negative, despite the fact that Maimonides, in his *Iggeret Hashemad*, had given a different answer. The rational and motivation of the rabbinic court—as difficult as their acceptance may be for us—were based on the unshakable conviction that no person should desert the Jewish people, even under extreme stress. Halakhah is obligating prose, up to the last hour.

Still another feature of halakhah is its tenor of religious chastity. I do not mean the chastity of the body, an important concept in rabbinic thought. I mean the chastity of the soul. A person who studies the Talmud will discover that it says relatively little about God. He is rarely mentioned in the really important passages of the Talmud which are studied customarily and with regularity. Unlike the Billy Grahams of today, the rabbis rarely spoke of God, not because they lacked faith, but because their faith was so profound and secure that it did not require discussion or verbalization. God's presence was felt in all they thought and did. A man of tact and sensitivity does not discuss with others his love for his wife. In the same way, the rabbis of the Talmud rarely spoke of their deepest love, their love of God. The atmosphere of the legal parts of halakhic discussion is one of religious chastity.

VIII

Can a modern Jew still find a rationale for the observance of halakhah? Specifically, can a non-Orthodox Jew take a positive stand with regard to halakhah, and on what grounds can he affirm its validity and accept its claims for himself and his community?

I believe such a rationale can be formulated. Halakhah safeguards the identity of the Jewish faith and the Jewish people. Judaism is a religion that is practiced by Jews. Judaism accepts proselytes but does not seek them. Persons who profess a Christian faith cannot be Jews. A Jew who embraces another faith leaves the Jewish people. He may be a deeply moral person, yet his conversion terminates his membership in the Jewish people. There is a relative identity between the faith and the people, and this relative identify can be established and maintained only by a sanctified way of life. Halakhah is our only means to establish and maintain this sanctified way of life.

Above all, however, halakhah can have profound relevance for the modern Jew because it embodies and represents an attitude toward life which emphasizes the need for the restitution of the intellect in a partly anti-intellectual society, for discipline in a partly libertarian world, for orientation and a sense of direction in a chaos of over-information, and for a rational religion in the face of the inroads of mysticism and obscurantism.

Halakhah stresses the use of the intellect and its restitution in a partly anti-intellectual society by virtue of its uncompromising emphasis on study and the life of the intellect as a mode of worship and religious expression. Dr. Robert Hutchins, the former chancellor of the University of Chicago, concluded the fifth of a series of lectures which he delivered in Jerusalem by saying that the Jewish people had always had his unconditional support and admiration because it was the only people he knew which had made learning a religious duty. Hutchins was not wholly correct; the Chinese had a similar emphasis. Nevertheless, he was right in pointing out that halakhah has always and vigorously insisted on the primacy of intellectual activity and concerns over against emotionalism—an emphasis which can serve as a vitally needed antidote to the anti-intellectual trends in contemporary society.

Halakhah calls for the restoration of discipline in a partly libertarian world and for the recovery of a perspective and a sense of direction in the chaos of over-information. To use the title of a well-known book by Professor Wolfgang Koehler, it calls for a "place of values in the world of facts." Halakhah teaches the place of values in a world of facts. We live in a world that lacks equilibrium between too much and not enough information. We know too much, yet, at the same time, too little. We know too many details but do not have sufficient principles to organize them meaningfully. One function of revelation is to provide orientation and direction. When Jews pray, they turn East in order to face Jerusalem. They have a point of reference by which they orient themselves. It gives them direction and helps organize the data of their experiences. Halakhah provides such orientation, occasionally too much so. But it is easier to reduce a surplus than to fill a vacuum.

Lastly, halakhah represents the unceasing demand for relative rationality in religion, for a rational religious way of life in a world challenged, on the one side, by shallow secularism and, on the other side, by religious obscurantism. The concluding verse in the twenty-ninth chapter of Deuteronomy says, "The hidden things belong unto the Lord our God, but the revealed things belong to us and our children for all eternity, that we may fulfill all the words of His Torah."[11] When I spoke at an academic convocation honoring Professor Gershom Scholem, the foremost authority in the field of Jewish mysticism, on the occasion of his sixtieth birthday, I concluded my address with the words, "At a time when the hidden things are being revealed, the revealed things are being hidden."

Halakhah stands not for what is hidden but for what man can know and do. My plea is for the revealed things—to study them and to fulfill them.

Endnotes

[1]*Rosh Hashanah* 27a; cf. *Y. Nedarim* III 5; 37d.

[2]*Mishneh Torah*, Hilkhot Teshuvah 3:7, and RaBaD there.

[3]Deut 30:11.

[4]Deut 12:18; 16:11; 27:7; cf. Lev 23:40.

[5]Milton Steinberg, *Basic Judaism* (New York, 1947) 72.

[6]Jeremiah, chapters 27 and 28.

[7]Ibid., chaps. 40-43.

[8]Gen 36:12.

[9]*Selihot*, The Rabbinical Assembly of America (New York, 1964).

[10]Efraim Oshri, *Divrei Efraim: Hidushei Halakhot Ubiurei Sugyoth Beshas* (with appendix, Me'emek Habakhah; New York, 1949).

[11]Deut 29:28.

Chapter 9

The Concrete Situation and Halakah

Eliezer Berkovits

Halakhah, or law, through which the sacred is made present and concrete, deals with ordinary matters. All the authorities represented here that the law can and does change. What Berkovits contributes is a first-rate example of precisely how that has happened in the past half century of upheaval, catastrophe, but also reconstruction and renewal. Having spelled out that the law does change, he turns to a matter of acute and immediate concern, which is the status of woman within Judaism. He spells out precise and specific legal problems that require correction. The received law simply places women in a disadvantaged position: "There exists . . . a tension between the moral conscience of the tradition . . . and its institutionalization in specific laws." The status of woman in the law today expresses "the climate and mores of a passing day," of antiquity. The laws can be changed, even though the Torah is eternal, because that is what the Torah itself requires.

***

If we wish to meet the crisis of our times and to make fruitful the turning inward towards our own resources of the spirit, we have to put our own house in order. We have to resolve many of the pressing internal problems of the day. While we have found the New Morality utterly inadequate and itself a symptom of the general collapse of value standards, it does raise a valid question. How can "code ethics" deal with each new and unexpected situation?

We recall Sartre's example of the young Frenchman who could not decide between his two duties and who had no code to guide him. Exactly this kind of a problem has confronted Judaism since its inception. Within the framework of Judaism the young man's problem would be formulated in the following manner: Take the case of a Mil h emet *Mitzvah*, a war of aggression against the Jewish people of a kind that the Torah commands that even a "bridegroom has to leave the bridal chamber" in order to join the ranks.[1] One young man is the only support of his old mother, and the Torah commands him, "Honor your father and mother." Which *Mitzvah* should the son follow? Now this is a typical halakhic problem. Indeed, it is in order to meet the challenge of each unexpected new situation on the basis of the teaching of the Torah that the *halakhah* or, as it should be called in its origin, the *Torah SheBe'al Peh*, the oral Torah, had to be placed beside the *Torah SheBikhetav*, the written

Torah. Similarly, the case histories of Bishop Pike, to which we made reference in the third chapter[2] are exactly the kind of questions that are dealt with in the *halakhah*. The woman who was an alcoholic to the extent that, as we would say, *Ḥayyei Ishut*, marital life, became impossible, represents indeed the kind of question that has been discussed in innumerable responses of the rabbis (though the case need not have been alcoholism, but some other affliction having the same results). Judaism has codes but—as with all codes—they do not deal with specific situations that are often unique. However, for very potent reasons—and we have analyzed them above— Judaism does not leave the decision to the husband to act spontaneously, guided only by "the law of love" as he understands the law in the unique situation of assumed incoherence with any previous procedure of a similar nature. There are no codes for specific situations. *Halakhah* is the life of the Torah that renders decisions in the concrete situation in the spirit of the principles and values that are the very heart of the Law.

2

Rabbi Joseph Albo, the fifteenth century Jewish philosopher, was a disciple of Rabbi Ḥasdai Crescas, himself a philosopher and outstanding rabbinic scholar from the school of the great Rabbenu Nissim (*Ran*). His background is well-authenticated. Albo has the following to say for the need of a *Torah SheBe'al Peh*, an Oral Tradition not set out in any code:

> It is impossible that God's Torah should be complete in such a manner that it should provide in advance for all times. The forever emerging new particulars of the law, the affairs of men, in laws, and things enacted, are too numerous to be contained in a book. Therefore, at Sinai Moses received orally general principles, briefly hinted at in the Torah, so that through them teachers in each generation may promulgate the new particulars.[3]

This is a bold statement coming from a spiritual descendant of Rabbenu Nissim. Albo intends to explain why *Torah SheBikhetav* is not enough. The Law, as it is laid down in the Torah, cannot rule in anticipation of every possible new situation. It is for this reason that the *Torah SheBe'al Peh* was needed to guide the teachers by general principles to reach decisions in the concrete situation. This is the very essence of the *halakhah*.

Let us see how *halakhah* functions; what is the work that it does. Let us look at some quite well-known examples, as well at others less well-known. A very famous case of a halakhic problem and its solution is Hillel's *prosbul*. To put it concisely and perhaps not quite accurately, it was the transformation of private debts into public debts. Otherwise, in accordance with the written law of the Bible, these debts would have been forfeited in the *shemittah* year. This was a bold innovation, which Samuel, of a later generation, would have liked to abolish. How and why was it instituted by the great Hillel? He was committed to the law of the *shemittah*. But in his time, this law came into conflict with other valid concerns of Judaism. On the one hand, there was a Torah obligation to protect the interests of the poor who, as the seventh year was approaching, could not obtain any loans for fear that in the *shemittah* year the money would be lost. On the other hand, there was also the important practical consideration for the effective functioning of the economic process within society, which is also a valid concern of Judaism. Rab Hisda expressed the meaning of the term *prosbul* with an etymologically monstrous, yet essentially correct interpretation: *pros bulee ubutee*, an ordinance in the interest of the poor and the rich.[4] Where did Hillel find the authority for his innovation? Where was it written in the Torah? It was, of course, not found in any text, in any code. He found it within himself. There was a clash between equally valid laws, principles and concerns of the Torah. He had to find a resolution to the conflict. There was no text, no *Torah SheBikhetav* to tell him which course to follow. He could find the solution to the problem within his own understanding of the comprehensive ethos of Judaism as he was able to gather it in his own heart and in his own conscience from the totality of the Torah-teaching and the Torah-way of life.

Let us consider another example. According to the written law of the Bible, two witnesses are required in order to establish a fact in court. Yet, in the case of a husband who has disappeared, the teachers of the Talmud accepted the testimony of one witness alone to prove the death of the husband in order to allow the wife to remarry. How could they rule in this manner against an explicit law of the Torah? There are all kinds of interpretations for this bold innovation.[5] However the technicality of the ruling may be explained, the decisive motivation for the ruling was, as it is clearly stated in the Talmud:[6] *mishum agunah akeelu boh rabbanan*, meaning: in order to save the wife from the status of an *agunah*, i.e., from being a woman tied, to the end of her days, to a man who has disappeared, they applied the law leniently in her case. Once again, it is the authentic halakhic problem situation. There is the written law of the Bible, but this time it is in conflict with another obligation of the Torah-true Jew, the care and concern for a woman whose husband has disappeared. Once again, there was no written code to consult. On the basis of the rabbis' understanding of the overriding Torah-purpose formulated nowhere explicitly, but absorbed into their own consciousness as the result of a life of dedication and commitment to Torah and its living realization, they gave the answer, a halakhic solution to a halakhic problem.

The examples are innumerable. For instance, the case of Rabba bar Bar Hana who had hired some workers to carry some barrels of wine. Somehow, the workers broke the barrels and the wine was lost. Whereupon Rabba took away their clothes as a guarantee for, or in lieu of, damages, to which he thought he was entitled. They brought the case for adjudication before Rab, who ruled that the clothes were to be returned to the workers. Asked Rabba: "Is this the law?" And the answer was: "Yes! for it is written; 'That you walk in the way of good men.' " The clothes were returned. The workers, however, were not yet satisfied. "We have worked all day and we are hungry," they said, claiming their wages. Ruled Rab: "Go and pay them their wages." Once again Rabba asked: "Is this the law?" and the answer was given: "Yes! For the verse in Proverbs concludes: 'And keep the paths of the righteous.' "[7] Legalistically speaking, Rabba, of course, was right. Such was not the law. But the case before Rab presented one of those characteristically halakhic problems. There was the law of damages. But there was also the obligation to care for the disadvantaged. Once again, the decision was made on the basis of a rabbi's appreciation of the more comprehensive concern of the Torah. Rab's decision was not in accordance with the specific law of damages, but with the total purpose of the Law of the Torah. It was *halakhah*.

We shall conclude with the discussion of two more cases. In recent times, due to a *cause celebre* in Israel, the problem of the *mamzer*, of the bastard according to biblical law, became for a while the preoccupation of many of us. Without commenting on the case itself, let us see how certain aspects of the problem were dealt with in the Talmud. There is, for instance, a statement by Rabbi Yo h anan, the leading teacher of his time in Eretz Yisrael, who swore that he could prove that *mamzerim* were present in a family. According to the law, that would disqualify its members from intermarriage with the "pure families." Yet he refrained from revealing the facts. As he said: "What can I do? Some of the *gedolei hador*, the great men of this generation, are mingled among them."[8] The question might well be asked: Who gave Rabbi Yo h anan the authority to disregard a biblical commandment and allow marriage with members of a family who were, by the law of the Torah, to be excluded from the community? But once again we have before us the typical halakhic problem. There is the law on *mamzerut* in conflict with another law and concern of Judaism, the respect due to the *gedolei hador*, the great men of Israel, who are bearers and teachers of the Torah, whose function is vital for the preservation of Judaism and the Jewish people. There was no code extant to tell Rabbi Yo h anan how to act. On the basis of his total understanding of what Judaism demands of the Jew, he decided not to reveal the facts. In the Talmud itself, his decision is related to a principle formulated by Rabbi Yitz h ak: "Once a *mamzer* has 'sunk' into a family, leave him there," meaning that even though one could determine which part of the family is "pure" and which is not, do not investigate, do not ferret out the *mamzer*. This principle is further broadened into the rule that if one knows with certainty of a *mamzer* who could be simply singled out, but the case is not generally known, one is not permitted to reveal the truth. One might wonder how such leniency could be justified in the face of a clear biblical ruling on the exclusion of the *mamzer* and his descendants all generations from intermingling with the community. Undoubtedly, here, too, biblical teachings in conflict with each other in a given situation had to be considered. On the one hand, the law concerning the *mamzer*; on the other, considerations of justice and pity for the innocent person and his offspring. (The rabbis in various places had the courage to question the justness of the law regarding the *mamzer*.) Thus, with true halakhic boldness, out of their comprehensive interpretation of Judaism's meaning, they limited the application of the law.

One of the most striking examples of halakhic boldness and independence found in the Talmud is the great debate about the *tanur shel Akhnai*, the oven of Akhnai. The subject matter of the debate itself is irrelevant to our discussion. The dispute over the law in this case raged between Rabbi Eliezer, the son of Horkenos, and the other masters. Since his colleagues did not accept his arguments, the mighty Rabbi Eliezer wrought a number of miracles to prove that he was right. The miracles were disregarded. Finally, a voice from heaven came to the support of Rabbi Eliezer declaring: "What do you want from Rabbi Eliezer? The *halakhah* is always as he teaches it!" What was there for the rabbis to do? The Talmud continues the story: Rabbi Joshua then stood up and said (quoting from the Bible, somewhat out of context): "It is not in heaven!" And this explanation is given: Said Rabbi Jeremiah: "What does it mean, 'It is not in heaven?' The Torah has already been given to us on the mountain. We pay no attention, not even to a heavenly voice. Because You (God) have already written in the Torah at the mountain: 'Decide according to the majority.' "[9]

How did the rabbis resolve the confrontation between the divine voice, which they clearly received, and their own consciences as to what was the right decision in the case of the oven? They beat the divine voice with God's own words, as they understood those words. However, their own personal share in the decision is obvious. For one could have easily argued with Rabbi Joshua: it is true that one should rule in accordance with the majority opinion, but only when the discussion is among men. However, in a debate with God Himself, how dare you rule against God? Indeed, how dare you enter into a debate with Him? Yet, the rabbis did rule against the voice from heaven. Once again, there was a conflict between two demands of the Torah: whether to obey the heavenly voice or to administer the law in a given case as they were able to understand it. Once again, the conflict was resolved on the basis of a more comprehensive principle which, in the rabbis' own estimation, deserved priority. The story itself finds its charming conclusion as follows: Rabbi Natan met the prophet Elijah (who, in Jewish lore, occasionally walks among the people and reveals himself to them) and asked him, "What did the Holy One, blessed be He, do in that hour (of the great debate)?" Said Elijah: "He laughed and exclaimed, 'My children have defeated me, my children have defeated me.' "[10] The postscript to the story is decisive. To His own joy, God is overruled. A specific word of God is controlled by a more comprehensive divine command. Therein lies the secret of the creative vitality of the *halakhah*. We might now formulate it more generally. When, in a given situation, a specific law is in conflict with another law, principle or concern of the Torah, the specific law may be limited in its application, reinterpreted, adapted, suspended or changed in this one situation, but not abolished, by the overruling concern of the total Torah.

We may now be in a better position to understand why the *Torah SheBikhetav*, the Written Torah, is not enough, why it needed to be completed by a *Torah SheBe'al Peh*, the Oral Torah and why the *halakhah* could not be anything else but oral teaching. Every written law is somewhat "inhuman." As a code laid down for generations it must express a general idea and an abstract principle of what is right, of what is desired by the lawgiver. But every human situation is specific and not general or abstract; in a sense, every human situation is unique. No general law speaks to the specific situation. The uniqueness of the situation will often call for additional attention by some other principle, which has its validity within the system. Two witnesses are necessary to establish a fact. That rule has general validity. But the woman whose husband has disappeared is in a specific situation. The law of the Torah itself calls for responsible care for her specific right. Resolution can be found only in the totality of the ethos of the law. But no written code can provide the resolution. Once you write it down as a code you have generalized it. Only the Oral Torah, alive in the conscience of the contemporary teachers and masters who can fully evaluate the significance of the confrontation between one word of God and another in a given situation, can resolve the conflict with the creative boldness of application of the comprehensive ethos of the Torah to the case. Thus, *Torah SheBe'al Peh*, as *halakhah*, redeems the *Torah SheBikhetav* from the prison of its generality and "humanizes" it. The written law longs for this, its redemption, by the Oral Torah. That is why God rejoices when He is defeated by His children. Such defeat is His victory.

According to an opinion in the Talmud, God concluded His covenant with Israel only on account of the Oral Tradition.[11] A covenant is a relationship of mutuality. The covenantal relationship could find no expression in the revelation and acceptance of the Torah at Sinai. It was a case, as the Talmud puts it, of *kafah aleihem har kegigit*, a law given, imposed. Only in *halakhah* is the covenant, as mutuality of relationship, fully present. *Halakhah* is not subjective adjustment at all (though a specific law may be adjusted, but not for the sake of adjusting to the situation). The very essence of covenantal mutuality cannot be subjectivity; but neither can it be without subjective involvement on both sides. *Halakhah* is not subjective, but it has a subjectively creative element to it. The halakhist recognizes the will of God as expressed in the Torah; he is wholly committed to the law and the teaching of the Torah. But in the mutuality of the covenant the responsibility has fallen to him to take upon himself the risk of determining, in the light of the totality of Torah teaching and Torah living, the manner in which the will of the other party to the covenant is to be realized in a specific situation. Ultimately, he has to do that in the independence of his own Torah-imbued conscience. This is our share in the covenant, the existential component of our participation in it. Loyalty to the Torah, to the divine partner to the covenant, demands that we accept the responsibility, notwithstanding the risk involved in the subjective aspect of our participation. Only thus may the generality and abstractness of the written Torah be transformed into *Torat Hayyim*, its realization in whatever situation Jews may find themselves in the course of history.

As we confront unanticipated situations, can we in this generation proceed with the same surety of method and authenticity of purpose as did the teachers in the time of the Talmud and, in some measure, for a while even beyond it? Unfortunately, for the time being, the answer has to be in the negative. In the course of the ages a calamity has overtaken the *Torah SheBe'al Peh*, the Oral Torah. In the course of time, what was to be oral teaching became more and more committed to writing. The first "text" of the Oral Torah was the *Mishnah*. In the Gemara, which is usually understood to be the explanation of the mishnaic text, one notices the struggle of the Oral Torah, still very much alive, with the mishnaic phase of its solidification. There is a continuous tension between the oral teaching and the written word of what, too, was, in its origin, *Torah SheBe'al Peh*. The text is "corrected"; often a law formulated in the *Mishnah* as a general principle is interpreted to mean only a single rule in a specific case. The plain meaning of the text is often changed into its very opposite by an insertion. Interpretation is often "creative," in that it may disregard syntax and literal meaning. The whole of the *Gemara* testifies to the unavoidable struggle of the spoken word of the *halakhah* with its solidification in a text. But then, the *Gemara*, too, was "concluded." And now the Oral Torah had been committed to two texts. However, the second text has a much less solidified form of the oral teaching than the first. There is an essential difference between the spoken and the written word. Whereas the *Mishnah* was, indeed, a transformation of the spoken word into the written one, the *Gemara* was the writing down of the spoken word in a manner that preserved its essential spoken quality. The *Mishnah* is a text; the *Gemara* is more like notes for a text.

Then came the third phase, that of the codifiers, Maimonides, for instance, in his *Mishneh Torah*, imitating the mishnaic style, transformed the "notes" of the *Gemara* into a text, and thus transformed the entire extent of the Oral Torah into a new kind of *Torah SheBikhetav*. The ultimate outcome of this process was, of course, the *Shul h an Arukh*.

Thus, what was not meant to be did come about: the Oral Torah became a written one. In fact, this whole development took place in actual violation of a principle of the Torah, according to which it was forbidden to commit the Oral Torah to writing.[12] Why, then, was it done? One might apply to this entire development what was said in the Talmud of Rabbi Yo h anan and Rabbi Shimon be Lakish, who allowed themselves to study the written version of certain parts of the oral tradition. It is said that they did it following a verse in Psalms[13] which, in a famous Talmudic interpretation reads: When it is time to act for God, one may violate His commandments.[14] They meant to say that, since it was impossible to preserve the entire body of the oral teaching in memory alone, some parts of it had to be put into writing, especially in the light of the vicissitudes, uncertainties, and destruction of communities and talmudic academies in the history of the Jewish people in many lands. This conclusion is supported by Maimonides' Introduction to his monumental halakhic work, the *Mishneh Torah*.

This means that the transformation of the Oral Torah into a text was brought about by the course of history. When the spoken word was forced into the straitjacket of a written mould it was an unavoidable violation of the essence of *halakhah*. It was no one's fault; nevertheless, it was a spiritual calamity of the first magnitude. Orthodoxy is, in a sense, *halakhah* in a straitjacket. Having had to transform the Oral Torah into a new written one, we have become Karaites of this new *Torah SheBikhetav*, forced upon us by external circumstances.

It was part of the spiritual tragedy of the *Galut* that exactly what *halakhah*, in its original vitality and wisdom, was intended to protect us from, has happened. God can no longer rejoice over His "defeat" by His children. It is a condition we have had to accept. It is the price we have paid for the preservation of our identity and Jewish survival.

Today however, we are faced with unprecedented new challenges and problems, problems of a true halakhic nature, which require solution in the true halakhic spirit. This is true in the free societies in which Jews live, but it is compellingly manifest in the State of Israel. When some leading rabbinical authorities there maintain that *halakhah* can solve all of the problems that may be raised for Judaism in a modern state they are right and they are wrong. They are right, for *halakhah*, in its present strait-jacketed state, cannot fulfill that function.

This is certainly no plea for reform. We believe that many of our inherited moulds are leaking and cannot meaningfully contain the life that has fallen to the lot of our generation. What is needed, first of all, is to retrace our steps. To return to the original *halakhah*, to rediscover it, and, having rediscovered it, to restore it to its original function. If only the problem were thoroughly understood, it would liberate us from the stultifying burden of this "Karaite *halakhah*." We would then see that in this generation, we have been called upon, as it were, by another *bat kol* to accept the responsibility to make use of whatever is still left of the Oral Torah in its textual solidification. It would be the beginning that would lead us back to the original source and strength of *halakhah*. It would be the beginning of its restoration to its original vitality and dignity, for the sake of which God concluded this covenant of mutuality with Israel. What is needed is not less study of Torah, but better study of Torah. What is needed is at least one talmudical research institute that would be dedicated to this task of rediscovery of *halakhah* and—at first—its intellectual restoration. What is needed is not less dedication to *halakhah*, but more faith in *halakhah*. Where there is greater faith, greater boldness is justified.

As in the past, because it was a time to act for God, and shackles had to be placed on the Oral Torah in violation of God's command, so now the hour has come when the need to act for God places upon us the responsibility to free the Oral Torah from its shackles in obedience to God's original command. There are risks involved in such an undertaking. Because of it we need, not less, but more *yirat shamayim* (fear of God).

The Status of Woman Within Judaism

In recent times, Jewish communities the world over have been perturbed by a number of problems of Jewish life which remain unresolved in accordance with the Torah. Is it really so that, because of the unfortunate transformation of the Oral Torah into a stubborn text, nothing can be done until we have succeeded in reversing the process from the text to the living word? There are vast possibilities still present in the *halakhah* to come to grips with problems arising from the contemporary situation. Although the *halakhah*, contrary to its original essence and function, has become solidified, it has not become petrified. Notwithstanding what has been imposed upon it, due to the vicissitudes of the external history of the Jewish people, it has still retained a high measure of its original vitality. To this day, one may sense how the original life of the *halakhah* tends to burst through the bonds of the written-down form of the Oral Torah. Whether one is able to deal meaningfully with contemporary problems halakhically is not just a matter of the extent of halakhic scholarship. It is to a large extent dependent on the understanding of what *halakhah* is about. One may be a great halakhic scholar and yet be lacking completely an appreciation of the purpose and the functioning of *halakhah*. Since *halakhah* deals with the concrete situation, it is essential that the halakhist himself be personally involved in the life of the community within which the problems arise. There is no *halakhah* of the ivory tower. The attitude to human needs is decisive. Without understanding, without sympathy and compassion, one cannot be an authentic halakhist.

1

Unfortunately, very little is being done to cope with some of the most serious problems that afflict the Jewish people internally, which bodes ill for the future of Judaism. This is most disturbing in the ethical and moral realm. Our first concern in this regard is the status of woman within Judaism.

In the context of a religious civilization, the thought that the union between a man and a woman may be deserving of the company of the Divine Presence suggests a dignity granted to the woman which may hardly be surpassed. Nevertheless, it is extremely difficult to gain a clear view of how the woman was seen in Jewish tradition, how she was evaluated. There seems to be no consistent philosophy about her nature, no uniform designation of her function and place in society. Her position appears to differ on the different levels of experience and thought.

There are numerous statements in which the teachers in the Midrash and the Talmud expressed their opinions on the nature of women. Some of these are outright offensive, to which—we assume—no Jew can subscribe any longer; others are only a little less objectionable. For example, basing itself on the relevant Hebrew word of the biblical text, one homily comments:

Before God made woman out of the rib, he considered whether he should not make her from some other part of the body. The head. No! Not from the head, he said, for she would carry her head too high. Not from the eye that she should not desire to see everything. From the ear? Not from the ear either; she would be listening in to everything. From the mouth? She would become a chatter-box. Making her from the heart would make her an envious creature. He would not make her from the leg that she might not become a run-about, or from the hand, for she should want to touch everything. He made the woman from the rib, which is hidden in the body, that she might become retiring and modest. It did not help. All these characteristics are in her.[15]

As if this were not enough, others add that women are gluttonous, lazy, quarrelsome, and thievish.[16] They were believed to be addicted to witchcraft. Even the most kind and humane of teachers, Hillel, observed: The more wives, the more witchcraft.[17] Women were said to be weak-willed.[18] The woman was considered considerably more sensuous than man. It was maintained that a woman preferred one measure (*kab*) of life with sexual license to nine measures of it with the obligation of chastity.[19] We find also some appreciative statements. Women are merciful, more hospitable than men, more considerate of the needs of a stranger, and have greater understanding for them.[20] Yet, when Rab took leave of Rabbi Ḥiyya to go from the land of Israel to Babylon, Rabbi Ḥiyya blessed him with the words: May God protect you from what is worse than death. At first Rab did not understand. Could there be anything worse than death? He thought about it and found the verse in Ecclesiastes: ". . . and I find more bitter than death the woman. . . ."[21] However, could indeed this be the final biblical word about women? Did not the author of *Proverbs*, who according to tradition is identical with that of *Ecclesiastes*, declare the very opposite when he said, "Whoso findeth a wife findeth a great good, and obtaineth favor of the Lord"?[22] How is the contradiction to be resolved? Simple. If she is good, there is no end to her goodness; if she is bad, there is no end to her wickedness.[23] Needless to say all these generalizations carry little convincing power. We shall yet discuss what we consider to be their significance.

It is surprising that such negative opinions could find their place beside more positive expressions of appreciation of the function of woman in the life of the people. The views of a number of rabbis in the Talmud may be condensed in the following comprehensive statement:

A man without a wife is not a complete human being; together they are Adam. A man without a wife dwells without joy, without blessing, without goodness, without atonement, without Torah, without peace; yes, without life.[24]

In the light of this, it is easily understandable that the rabbis should also have taught that a man should love his wife as himself and honor her more than himself.[25] Similarly, Rabbi Halbo taught that man should forever be caring about the respect with which he treats his wife, for blessing is found in the house only on account of her.[26] In the course of Jewish history, these appreciative views determined the quality of Jewish marriage and family life. In general, the wife was loved and respected to a greater degree than in any other culture and civilization. This was the source of the strength of the Jewish home in antiquity, through the Middle Ages, and right up to our own days, the source of its strength, joy and blessing. This view of the woman and her importance has guided Jewish family life as if the negative evaluation did not exist at all. It is rather mysterious how such contradictory outlooks could be part of the same tradition. Shall we perhaps say that there is no contradiction here? Different people thought about the same subject differently. After all, the same biblical phrase in the Hebrew original that, as we saw, was used in order to suggest that God was contemplating from which part of Adam's body to form Eve and thus became the basis of the rather objectionable description of the feminine characteristics, is in another place used to prove that God gave a greater measure of understanding and insight to the woman than to the man.[27]

It is difficult to accept such an explanation. The function of the woman has been established metaphysically in the Bible. Even if we should accept the biblical story at its face value, Eve was intended by God to be a helpmate to Adam. As such, it is hardly conceivable that those negative characteristics could be attached to her by nature. The biblical statement would then be the seed of any Jewish view of woman that in itself would bestow a certain dignity on her because of her place in the scheme of creation. One might say that her existential dignity received its metaphysical affirmation in the *Song of Songs*. Rabbi Akiba declared: All the songs (in the Bible) are holy; the *Song of Songs* is the holy of holies.[28] It is true that the love between Shulamit and the King was mystically interpreted as the love covenant between God and Israel, yet the very fact that the love relationship between a man and a woman could serve as a symbol for the purest and holiest of relationships within the reality of the Jewish experience elevates it to the rung of the holy of holies. The words "Love is strong as death,"[29] are illustrated in the Midrash as much by the love with which God loves Israel as with the love a husband loves his wife.[30] The comparison does not mean that a sensuous element is being introduced into the God-Israel covenant, an idea which, as a result of questionable influences, abounds in certain forms of Jewish mysticism. On the contrary, the comparison is only possible because love between a man and a woman is the highest form of personalized relationship. This, however, should exclude those negative appreciations of female characteristics that we have quoted earlier from talmudic and midrashic sources. How is such a personalized relationship possible with one who is a gluttonous runabout, quarrelsome, thievish, and addicted to witchcraft? It would seem that there is a tension between teaching and certain forms of male experience.

2

Before suggesting a solution as to how the tension between teaching and experience might have come about, we shall have to consider another level on which the status of the woman finds its expression. From what has been shown thus far it should be obvious that it is always men who express views about women. While there are statements about how good a good wife is and how bad a bad one is, there is not a single saying recorded about how good a good husband is or how bad a bad husband may be. And even when statements are most appreciative of the women, they speak of her importance *for* man, as if the meaning of her existence were fully comprehended by what she represents as an adjunct to complete the life of a man. An opinion transmitted in the name of Rab, of whom we know that his marriage was not a very happy one, is characteristic. Regarding the importance of the man in the life of the woman he maintained: "A woman is a *golem* (an unfinished product). She will make a covenant only with one who makes her into a (completed) vessel."[31] At the root of it all is the idea that the manner in which the male and female principle complete each other in the world is determined by the aggressive or active nature of the male and the passive and receiving nature of the female.

This is mainly reflected in the legal status of the woman. Because of the legal form of the marriage contract she was originally greatly disadvantaged. While the husband could divorce her at will and against her will, she could not, and cannot to this day divorce her husband. The husband would inherit her property, but a widow does not inherit her husband and has to be maintained by her children from the estate they inherit. The heirs of a man are his sons, not his daughters. The daughters have to be supported and must be provided with an appropriate dowry, but they do not inherit as equals with their brothers. Women are not admitted as witnesses or as judges. Similarly, their religious status is also severely limited. They are under no obligation to fulfill the highest commandment of Judaism, to study Torah. Since they are not obligated to study, they can have no obligation to teach. Therefore, while it is incumbent upon a father to teach his son Torah, the same duty does not apply to the mother. But not only was there no obligation for a woman to study Torah, the teaching of the written law to her was actually frowned upon, while the teaching of the oral tradition was forbidden.[32] Her place as a member of the religious community is strictly limited. While she is obligated to adhere to all the negative commandments, she is exempted from the duties to practice most of the positive commandments whose observance depends on a specific time of the day or the year. She does not have to put on *Tefilin* (phylacteries) or to wear *Z i z it* on the corners of her clothes, she does not have to dwell in booths during the *Sukkot* festival, etc. She cannot be part of *Minyan*, a quorum of ten Jews required for a congregational religious service.

We may now be in a better position to understand how those negative opinions about female characteristics might have come about and might, notwithstanding their exaggerated generalization, often have been derived from experience. There is little doubt that notwithstanding these rather limiting rules and regulations, Judaism produced numberless *Z adkaniyot*, women who were pious, chaste, virtuous, and charitable often in a self-sacrificial sense and to an ideal degree. Yet we have to consider what must have been the effect of the position granted to the woman on the great majority of their sex. Since education was essentially Torah education, many women had no education at all. They were of course taught the duties appertaining to their responsibilities as wives and mothers, and also learned from the example of the living tradition that surrounded them. As compared to the education of the sons, many of the daughters of Israel must have been intellectually as well as emotionally stunted. They were largely excluded from and were often mere spectators of the drama of the creative forms of religious life. Their legal status, too, was often that of a passively receiving, protected member of society. It should not, then, be surprising if many of them were thievish, because they might have felt that they did not have the share in the family fortune that was due to them. That they were quarrelsome is quite believable; dissatisfied people often react to their surroundings in such a manner. With our better psychological insight, we may well understand that a deeply frustrated person may seek comfort in over-eating and become gluttonous. Some of the other negative characteristics, too, which were ascribed to women in talmudic times, are better understood as psychological reactions to their condition. We need not at all be convinced that the good woman, whose goodness was said to be limitless, was indeed potentially a better human being than the bad one, whose wickedness, it was maintained, was without end. Could it not have been that the good woman was meeker by nature and because of that readily accepted her status, whereas the bad woman was more vital, more energetic, with a stronger will of her own and because of that, much more frustrated. Her "wickedness" might have been her unconscious rebellion against her inability to make meaningful use of her natural gifts. Rabbi Eleazar, a talmudic teacher of the early part of the third century, has an interesting comment on the creation of woman, which has a bearing on this aspect of our discussion. We read in the Bible that God said, "It is not good that man should be alone; I will make him a help meet for him."[33] This rather awkward English phrase stems from the fact that an attempt is made to give as accurate a rendering of the idiosyncrasy of the Hebrew text as possible. A more literal translation of the second part of the sentence would read: I will make him a help meet *opposite* him.

The phrase, "opposite him," is explained by Rabbi Eleazar to mean: if not, she will be *"opposite* him," i.e. against him.[34] It may well have been the case that the numerous shrews about whom the talmudic records know were the kind of women that the society of some men deserved. All those sweeping generalizations about women may say very little about what women are, but rather about what they become in the circumstances in which they had to live.

3

In fact, talmudic tradition shows a great deal of compassionate awareness of the disadvantaged position of the woman. Rab, with whose opinions relating to women we are now somewhat familiar, urged husbands to be extremely careful not to hurt their wives by unkind words. For since a woman's tears run easily, the punishment is fast.[35] While a man had the right to divorce his wife, and legally it could be done for the least of reasons, yet, maintained Rabbi Eleazar, he who does it, causes the altar in the sanctuary to weep. He applies to the case the words of the prophet Malachi:

> And this further ye do:
> Ye cover the altar of the Lord with weeping, and with sighing,
> Insomuch that He regardeth not the offering anymore
> Neither receiveth it with good will at your hand.
> Yet ye say, 'Wherefore?'
> Because the Lord hath been witness
> Between thee and the wife of thy youth,
> Against whom thou hast dealt treacherously,
> Though she is thy companion,
> And the wife of thy covenant.[36]

Whereas Rabbi Eleazar states that the very alter of God weeps over the wrong done to a woman betrayed by an arbitrary divorce, the plain meaning seems rather to suggest that it is the women, in their misfortune, who surround the alter with weeping and sighing. Indeed, that is how Rabbi Haggee understood it and therefore applied the prophet's castigation to an event in the history of the Jewish people. According to him, the prophet, who lived during the period of the second Temple, was referring to the behavior of some Jews after they had returned from the Babylonian exile. During the long and arduous journey from Babylon to the land of Israel, the faces of their wives were blackened and parched by the sun, and they lost their attractiveness. At that, their husbands left them. The women came to the alter of God weeping. Said God: How could I receive your temple offerings, when the misery of these women calls to Me from the same alter where you want to serve Me! You have robbed, you have violated, you have taken her beauty from her, and now you send her away. I am astounded."[37] This is a remarkable statement. God rejects their divine service, because of the injustice they have done to their wives. Yet what they did was perfectly legal. According to the marriage contract one may send one's wife away even because one has found a more attractive woman.[38] It is then the conscience of Judaism that finds fault with the moral quality of an action that is completely legal. Implied in the statement of Rabbi Haggee is a criticism of the form of that legality. Malachi's phrasing, that these men acted treacherously against their "companions" and "the wives of their covenants," is significant. Companionship is a fully personalized relationship, and it is because the union between a man and a woman is meant to be a covenant that it could have served as a symbol of God's covenant with Israel. It is then in the light of the covenant idea, identified as the fully realized personalization of the relationship, that the nature of the legality of the divorce becomes morally objectionable. One cannot live in an adequately realized covenanted relationship with God if one lives with one's wife in impersonality. Impersonality is injustice towards another human being, a crime; in the sight of God, sin.

The following moving story is told in the Talmud, illustrating the critical awareness with which Judaism viewed some of the practices which prevailed in the Jewish community in the talmudic period. It was customary for married students to leave their wives for long periods in order to go to distant school to study Torah. In the Talmud, the question is discussed, if such a husband leaves his wife without her permission, how long would he be permitted to stay away from home: thirty days, or even two to three years? The codes disagree as to which opinion to follow. Nevertheless, it was said that even those who leave home for only thirty days without the consent of their wives were taking their lives into their hands. In support of the story it is told that one, Rabbi Rehumee, was wont to study Torah with Raba in Me h oza. Normally, he would return home on the day before *Yom Kippur* (the Day of Atonement). Once, being deeply involved in his studies, he delayed returning. His wife was waiting anxiously, saying to herself: he is coming now, now he is coming! As he did not come a tear fell from her eyes. At that very moment her husband was on a roof; the roof collapsed under him and he died.[39] Needless to say, the death of her husband was not much help to the poor woman, yet the story shows an insight into the sacrificial service of these women. The severity of the punishment indicates that Rabbi Rehumee had no adequate appreciation of the loneliness of his wife. Though what he did was the accepted practice, there was something very wrong about it in the view of the Talmud itself, if an inadvertent delay could have brought death down on the man. Once again, we have an example of the moral conscience implying a rather severe criticism of a legally established form of married life.

It would seem that the conscience of Judaism was ill at ease with certain forms of the institutionalized order of the husband and wife relationship. This had its consequences for the legal status of the woman as well. Already in talmudic times certain aspects of the original marriage and divorce laws were modified in favor of the woman. In certain cases, for instance, when a condition developed after the marriage of a kind that the woman could not be expected to live with her husband, the authorities would compel the man to divorce his wife.[40] According to some authorities this meant that one could even use corporal punishment if he refused to do as he was ordered.[41] With what right one could do that presented a problem. According to the law, a divorce could only be effected by the husband himself and never against his will. Yet, these were situations when from the point of view of the conscience of the teachers of the Torah, one had to free the wife from the obligation of continuing the marriage. A solution was found by bringing pressure on the husband until he says, I am willing to divorce her. The legal validity of this formula has been well explained. It is important, however, to understand that the ethical conscience required and found a way to modify the application of the original law within the framework of the law. There are other similar cases where an even more drastic modification of law application was established within the confines of the law itself. In certain situations when problems arose, the rabbis hit upon much more elegant solutions. They formulated the phrasing of the declaration that is needed for the legal conclusion of the marriage in such a manner that they reserved to the recognized rabbinical authorities the right even to invalidate a marriage retroactively.[42]

Even more striking is the case of the *Moredet*, the "rebellious" wife, who refuses to continue to live with her husband. Basing himself on the Talmud, Maimonides formulates the law in this case as follows: "One (i.e., the court) asks her why she "rebels." If she says: "I dislike him and cannot willingly be intimate with him," one compels him (i.e. the husband) to divorce her immediately. For she is not like a prisoner that she should (be forced to) have intercourse with one whom she hates."[43] Maimonides' formulation reveals his psychological insight into what might be expected from the continuation of such a relationship. It starts out as incompatibility. The wife dislikes her husband. However, should she be compelled to continue the marital relationship with him, her dislike is bound to turn into hatred. Once again we have an example of how ethical considerations drastically limited the power of the husband to divorce his wife or to refuse to divorce her.

Similar considerations for the well-being of the woman brought about modifications in other areas of the law. We have discussed earlier the fact that in order to establish the death of a husband and thus free his widow to remarry, the legal requirement to establish a fact by two witnesses was dispensed with, and the testimony of a single witness was admitted as sufficient testimony. And whereas normally women could not qualify as witnesses, in this case the testimony of a woman was also accepted. Of course, very sound reasons were adduced in the Talmud for allowing this—and other changes—in the law. What matters is that in cases of conflicts between a moral principle that demanded the protection of the personal dignity and well-being of a woman, and the impersonal objectivity of the law, a specific law had to yield to the transcending ethos of the comprehensive concern of the Law. We might say that in all these cases the ultimate comprehensive concern of the Law in general was allowed to modify the form of the application of a specific law. Finally, toward the end of the tenth century, Rabbenu Gershom of Mayence imposed the *Herem* (a form of excommunication) against divorcing a woman against her will.

4

There exists, then, a tension between the moral conscience of the tradition or, as we may also put it, between the ultimate ethos of the Law, and its institutionalization in specific laws. There can be little doubt that the tension is normally due to the fact that, inevitably, the actual institutionalization of the ethos is always time-conditioned; it cannot be achieved independently of the people whose adherence to it is demanded. This need not contradict the faith of a religious Jew who believes that the Torah as God's revelation has validity.

No less a halakhic authority than Maimonides expressed the same idea in his well-known interpretation of the biblical divine service by means of animal sacrifices. According to Maimonides, prayer, while not the highest form of divine service, is yet superior to that by animal sacrifices. Yet the sacrificial service was allowed, for, says Maimonides, human nature does not change suddenly. Since in biblical times animal sacrifices were the generally understood mode of serving a god, the Torah—in order, as it were, to wean the Jews from idolatry—tolerated sacrifices, but ordered the children of Israel to offer them to God and not to idols. At a certain juncture in the spiritual and social development of the Jewish people, this was the only way of teaching them how to serve the One God. To quote Maimonides' own words: ". . . God refrained from prescribing what the people by their natural disposition would be incapable of obeying, and gave the above mentioned commandments (i.e. regarding animal sacrifices) as a means of securing His chief objects, viz., to spread a knowledge of Him . . . and to cause them to reject idolatry." This educational method is ascribed to the "wisdom" of God. There was no other way of dealing with the problem, for while God may work miracles in the world, "the nature of man is never changed by God by way of miracles."[44]

Now theologians and religious thinkers may disagree with Maimonides' interpretation of the meaning of the sacrificial service in the Temple, but the principle of interpretation that he uses will still have his authority. For one who believes in the eternal validity of the Torah, the divinely revealed teaching, Maimonides' principle is vital to safeguard his faith. Is it not possible for a believing Jew to make peace with certain biblical laws without applying to them Maimonides' principle of interpretation? This is not the place to discuss the subject comprehensively, but let us consider one or two examples. Let us take the case of the Jewish slave. That a Jew should buy another Jew as a slave is an intolerable thought which is rejected by everything that the teaching of the Torah in its religious and ethical significance stands for, yet it was a fact accepted and incorporated in a law.[45] Obviously slavery was an institution that in biblical times, given human nature, social and economic conditions, could not have been abolished by any law. So the law limited the duration of the slavery. The slave had to be set free after six years of service. The Bible insists on calling the slave "thy brother," and prescribes how he is to be treated: "Thou shalt not rule over him with rigour; but shalt fear thy God."[46] The rabbis in the Talmud then went on to explain that the slave's standard of living had to be equal to that of the master. "Do not yourself eat fine bread and give him the coarse one. Do not you drink old wine and let him have only new wine. Sleep not on a soft bed, while he has to sleep on straw. So much so that people would say: 'He who buys himself a Jewish slave buys a master for himself.' "[47] The biblical law regarding a father selling his minor daughter (less than twelve years and a day old) to be a maid-servant is similar in essence.[48] It is inconceivable that today the most orthodox of orthodox Jews would allow such a practice. Even if the State of Israel were established in full conformity with Torah and Jewish law, it is inconceivable that both these laws should not be completely abolished and with the full approval of the orthodox rabbinate. Both cases are examples of time-conditioned practices, which could not be abolished by the law abruptly, but which were, however, legally limited, modified, humanized. They were absorbed by a net of laws and regulations that incorporated the thrust of the transcending ethos of the Torah, thus educating the people and guiding their moral development along lines which would lead to the complete abolition of the objectionable practices. What we learn from Maimonides' principle of Torah interpretation[49] is that no matter what the meaning and the truth of the teaching may be *sub specie aeternitatis*, when the ethos of the teaching is incorporated in the legalized and institutionalized forms of social organizations, one cannot disregard the capacities of human nature to understand and to implement the imperative of the teaching. This is the root cause of the tension that often prevails between the law and the transcending spirit that formulates the law, which has been responsible for the process within the *halakhah*.

Can there be any doubt that the status of the woman reflected in the Talmud was, to a large extent, influenced by the climate and the mores of a passing day? For instance, according to the Midrash, it is the "way" of the woman to stay in her house, whereas the "way" of a man is to go out into the market place and learn wisdom from other people.[50] This understanding of the "way" of the woman found its formulation in the code of Maimonides in the following manner:

> Every woman has the right to leave her house in order to visit her parents, pay condolence calls, to attend festive meals (on the occasion of weddings, etc.), rendering loving-kindness to her female friends or relatives so that they in turn would

visit her, for she in not in a prison that she should not be able to go and to come. However, it is shameful for a woman to go out regularly, outside the house or into the streets. A husband should prevent his wife from doing this. He should not allow her to go out more than once or twice a month, according to need. For it is becoming for a woman to sit in the corner of her house, as it is written: All glorious is a king's daughter within the palace.[51]

The biblical quotation may, of course, easily be interpreted differently and brought much nearer to its intended meaning. Yet this is how the verse was used in the Talmud and, in view of the mores of the times, with full justification. This has nothing to do with the intentional oppression of the woman. Considering the moral climate of the times, the daily life of the people in the streets and the market places, it might indeed have been in the best interest of the woman to stay indoors as much as possible. The reference to "a king's daughter" has to be taken seriously. In the consciousness of those days, the restriction on her movements did not contradict her dignity as a woman. On the contrary, it was understood as society's concern for the protection of her dignity as a princess. The duties of a wife toward her husband were formulated as follows:

"Every woman has to wash the face, hands, and feet of her husband, mix for him his cup of wine, prepare his bed, and stand and serve him, for instance, by handing him water, a dish, and clearing away from before him."[52]

Needless to say, the law as such is incompatible with the status that the woman had in the ethos of Judaism. In the actual practice of married life it could hardly have been reconciled with the injunction that one should honor one's wife more than oneself and love her as oneself. Surely, these "duties" were at cross purposes with the terms which the prophet Malachi uses for married woman: a "companion," a "wife of the covenant." Once again, we have here an example of the tension between the more fundamental conscience of the Law and its formulation in a specific case in view of circumstance whose practical strength could not be ignored. From the point of view of the transcending conscience of the Law, the real significance of its formulation in this specific case found its expression not in what it imposed on the wife, but in that from which it liberated her. For this is how Maimonides, on the basis of the talmudic determination, concludes the paragraph we have quoted: "However she does not have to stand and serve his father and his son." In the language of the time, the fact that she owed certain services only to her husband and not to any other member of his family meant that she was a wife and not a servant. In the circumstances of the times this was a great step forward. A law of this kind, joined to the moral admonition to honor her more than oneself and to love her like oneself, was in fact moving Jewish society towards the goal of the covenantal relationship between husband and wife.

What we have to see is the success of this method in bringing about the rich penetration of the Jewish marriage by the ethos of the covenantal personalization of the relationship between a man and a woman in the course of history. Indeed, through the ages the marital union in the Jewish home was sufficiently pure and consecrated to serve as the symbol of the covenant between God and Israel. There was no question at all of the woman not being granted the full dignity due to her as a person. The functions of husband and wife were different, the heavier burden did fall on the woman in the house, yet as to their equality in human dignity—in general—there could be no doubt. Normally, the ethical climate in the Jewish marriage was determined by the comprehensive ethos of Judaism, as if the legal disabilities of the wife did not exist.

5

What follows from all this for the contemporary situation? There can be little doubt in the mind of any thinking Jew that those time-conditioned elements that, in talmudic times and later still, influenced the formulation of the laws regarding the status of the woman, have been overcome to a very large extent by the Jewish people of today. And we are not thinking here of the majority of Jews who today may be considered secularists, but of the majority of religious Jews, who accept the Torah as divine revelation, who adhere to the laws of Judaism and strive toward the fullest realization of *halakhah* in their own lives as well as in that of the community. Who among religious Jews still adheres to the old law that, since "her house is not a prison," a wife should be permitted to leave it once or twice a month, according to need? Which Jewish husband still expects his wife to look upon him as if he were "a prince and a king,"[53] simply because he is her husband? In our understanding, a man who, independently of being a husband, indeed deserves to be respected like a "prince and a king," would neither demand of his wife such respect nor would he accept it from her. On the other hand, should he demand or even accept it, it would itself be proof that he was not worthy of it. Do religious Jews today allow their wives to serve them by washing their faces, hands, and legs, and fulfilling those other duties which are prescribed by the law? Apart from the respect due to our wives as human beings, our self-respect would not allow us to accept this kind of service from our wives, or even from any other human being. This is so not because we are modern Jews, not because this is the second half of the twentieth century. This is so because we are Jews. This has been so for many generations, on account of what Judaism has made of us. In my home in Rumania, we had a village girl working for us as a servant. In the morning, she would clean the shoes of the family, she would set the table and, of course, put a jug full of water on it. Occasionally, as would be the case with children, we would dirty our shoes during the day, but we were not permitted to ask the maid to clean them again for us. During the day, if we wanted clean shoes, we had to clean them ourselves. When during a meal the water bottle would be emptied, the maid might have been asked by the lady of the house to bring another jug of water to the table, but we children were not allowed to ask her to bring a glass of water especially for us. Our father explained: the maid has certain duties in this house, she works, and she is paid for her work. But she is not the personal servant of anyone in the house. Our father was not a modern Jew. His education was chiefly Bible, Talmud, and the codes of Jewish law. He was teaching his children what Judaism had taught him. Could it have been conceivable to him to pay any regard to those "duties" of a wife to her husband, with whose talmudic sources and codification he was well familiar?

The truth is, that in the Torah-education Jewish conscience, the ethos of Judaism has overcome many of the time-conditioned elements that unavoidably found their way into the legal formulation of the Law in a distant past. Notwithstanding the biblical law of inheritance, today in orthodox Jewish families, wives do inherit their husband's property and daughters inherit together with sons. Of course, there are ways of justifying this within the *halakhah*. What is decisive is that these ways were found and a new practice has developed within the framework of the Law. We have heard that a woman cannot be admitted as a witness in court. Yet we also heard that in certain cases her testimony was accepted. Is this the ultimate limit of what is possible within the system of the *halakhah*? Of course, there was a reason for the exception; but have all the possible reasons been exhausted? A woman cannot be a judge, yet Deborah of biblical fame was a judge, indeed the supreme judge of her time. Again, there is an explanation for this exception,[54] but again one might ask, have all the explanations of what is possible within the Law already been given? One does not ask these questions because the Torah has become a burden and one wishes to break away from it; one asks because one believes in the eternal vitality of the divine revelation, because one is committed with one's whole existence to the proposition that the teaching is *Torah Ḥayim*, the way of life for the Jew.

We saw how within the *halakhah* itself there have been significant developments that would limit the power of the husband by compelling him, in certain cases, to divorce his wife by annulling the marriage retroactively, and recognizing the freedom of the wife to demand a dissolution of the marriage in certain circumstances. Yet we have to acknowledge that more has still to be done. The case of the *Agunah*, of the deserted wife or the wife whose husband has been missing for a long period of time, is still challenging the conscience of the Law for a solution. In our own days, with civil divorce, there are many cases when, after a marriage has been dissolved by the civil authorities, the husband, often out of spite, refuses to divorce his wife by the giving of a *Get* (a divorce document) as required by Jewish law. Many human tragedies result from the present situation.

In a halakhic work, published several years ago in Jerusalem, I have shown how these and other related problems may be solved and, thus, a great deal of human suffering avoided, within the rules of *halakhah*.[55] It is halakhically possible to introduce conditions into the *ketubah* (the marriage contract) that if certain eventualities should arise in the future, the marriage is to be annulled retroactively. Thus, for instance, in the case of soldiers missing in action, or in cases where civil divorce had taken place but the husband refuses to give a *get*, under appropriate safeguards the marriage would be annulled and the wife would be free to remarry. According to *halakhah*, annulment would have no detrimental effect on either the legal or moral status of the children.

Another problem that could easily be resolved is that of *Halitzah*. According to biblical law, when a man dies without leaving any offspring behind, his brother must marry the widow and if he refuses, the ceremony of *Halitzah* is to be performed. The widow is not free to remarry without first having been released by that ceremony. However, already in talmudic times, the levirate marriage was largely discontinued and replaced by *Halitzah*. Needless to say, in the present social and moral climate, the institution of levirate marriage has lost its original meaning and purpose. On the other hand, that it has been in the main abandoned renders some aspects of the *Halitzah* ceremony objectionable for the widow as well as for her brother-in-law. Understandably, in many cases, both parties are greatly embarrassed by it. In addition, all kinds of problems may arise as, for instance, when the whereabouts of the surviving brother cannot be ascertained. At times, the brother-in-law refuses to go through with the *Halitzah* ceremony because he considers it demeaning. In other cases, worse still, he uses the need for his consent in order to blackmail the family of the widow. Every practicing rabbi is familiar with the human agony arising from such situations, which befall especially Torah-observant women. I have proven conclusively that in the case of the husband's death, a childless marriage can be annulled retroactively by means of a *tenai* (condition) appropriately incorporated in the *ketubah*.

Unfortunately, the rabbinical establishment moves very slowly, if at all. At the time of this writing, two men are imprisoned in Israel. One, convicted as a rapist, has been condemned to a long prison term. He is married and the rabbinate, with the authority of the state, imposed an additional jail sentence on him until he divorces his wife. The other is a case of a Jew who, all through his married life, neglected his wife and family, never worked, and never accepted any king of responsibility. He too was imprisoned and will have to stay there till he agrees to divorce his wife of his own free will. Both men are adamant in refusing to obey the demand of the rabbinate. It is difficult to understand how the Israeli rabbinate can remain insensitive to the indignity imposed upon the Torah itself by such degrading wrestlings with the inadequacies of human nature. In the meantime, of course, the misery of the wives deepens with every passing day. When these cases will be resolved, if they ever should be, other cases of a similar kind will follow and the indignity and the suffering will be repeated. Yet all this could be prevented by the introduction of an appropriate formula into the marriage contract, for which there is sufficient validation within the *halakhah*.

We are confronted with a challenge to the conscience of Judaism, with a very test of its humane quality. Apart from the happiness of numerous human beings, which alone should be a matter deserving the highest compassionate priority among the concerns of the rabbinate, the moral dignity of the Law itself is at stake. The situation is ethically intolerable.

The day will come when the problem of the *Agunah* and other similar problems will be solved, as they well may be, within the framework of the *halakhah*. More and more young couples who abide by the *halakhah* are now demanding that appropriate conditions be included in their *ketubah*. They do this as a requirement of their Jewish conscience, out of loving concern for each other, in order to avoid possible human misery in the future, and in order to protect the ethical dignity of their marriage. There is little doubt that as more and more Torah-observant young couples will realize that there are halakhically valid possibilities to eliminate those problems that have plagued us in the past, the pressure on the rabbinate will become strong enough to turn the halakhically possible into the humanly real.

In addition to the legal status of the woman, a new concern that agitates many of us today is the religious status of the woman in the daily life of the Jewish community. This is truly a contemporary problem, resulting from radically changed intellectual, social, and economic conditions. The concern deals with what should be the place of the contemporary Torah-observant woman, who adheres to the rules of the *halakhah*, in the religious life of the community. Many of these women are well educated at colleges and universities, and have a broad, and often highly specialized, secular education. Is it conceivable that they should continue to be excluded from any serious study of Torah and Talmud, and of the other disciplines in the study of Judaism, as they were in the past? What is bound to be the quality of Jewish life, in the homes and the communities, if intelligent, mentally alert women, otherwise fully involved in the moral, political, social and economic issues of the day should be—as a matter of religious principle—relegated to the status of the ignoramus within the realm where they ought to have their spiritual and religious roots, the realm of Judaism? Is the Jewish woman of today, who intellectually, socially, and, often professionally too, is indeed the equal of her husband, to remain only a passive participant in the daily religious life of the community, often only the spectator to Judaism which, apparently, is essentially a male concern and responsibility?

Once again, we have reached a juncture at which the comprehensive ethos of the Torah itself strains against its formulation in specific laws. It is, however, the very essence of the *halakhah* to be responsive to such a strain, and by its resolution to bring about an even richer realization of the Torah itself. Not only is the status of the woman at stake, but the status of Judaism itself. For if in its application it could not do full justice to the Jewish woman in her present state as she is longing for participation in the drama of Jewish realization in accordance with her capacity and spiritual need, its form of such application becomes itself highly questionable. Those who understand the true nature and function of *halakhah*, and are committed to halakhic Judaism, cannot accept such a suggestion. With unreserved openness and sensitivity to the genuineness of the problem, with faith in the vitality of the *halakhah*, with humility and yet with intellectual courage, the necessary halakhic work will be accomplished that will define the status of the woman anew, justly and meaningfully.

Endnotes

[1]*b. So ṭ a* 44b.
[2]See above, 27.
[3]*Sefer Ha-Ikkarim* III, ch. 23.
[4]*b. Git.* 36b, 37a.
[5]See *b. Yebam.* 88a, and the relevant commentaries *ad locum.*
[6]Ibid.
[7]*b. B. Me ṣ .* 83a.
[8]*b. Qidd.* 71a.
[9]*b. B. Me ṣ .* 59b.
[10]Ibid., ibid.
[11]*b. Git.* 60a.
[12]Ibid. 60b.
[13]Psalms 119:126
[14]*b. Git.* 60a.
[15]*Ber. Rab.* 18.
[16]Ibid. 45.
[17]*m. 'Abot* 2,8.
[18]*b. Šabb.* 33b; *Qidd.* 30b.
[19]*b. So ṭ a* 20a.
[20]Ibid. *Meg.* 14b; *Ber.* 6b.
[21]Eccl 7:26. For the talmudic reference see *b. Yebam.* 63b.
[22]Prov 18:22.
[23]*Midr. So ḥ er Tov* 59.
[24]Cf. *b. Yebam.* 63a; 62b; *Midr. Rab. Kohelet* 9,7.
[25]*b. Yebam.* 62b.
[26]*b. B. Me ṣ .* 59a.
[27]*b. Nid.* 45b.
[28]*m. Yad.* 3,5.
[29]Song of Songs 8:6.
[30]*Midr. Rab. Shir HaShirim.*
[31]*b. Sanh.* 22b.
[32]See *b. So ṭ a* 20a; Maimonides, *Yad Ha Ḥ azakah, Talmud Torah* 1,13; *Shul ḥ an Arukh, Yoeh De'ah* 246,6.
[33]Gen 2:18.
[34]*b. Yebam.* 63a.

[35]*b. B. Meṣ.* 59a.

[36]Malachi 2:13-14. For Rabbi Eleazar, see *b. Git.* 90b. It is true that because of the biblical reference to "the wife of thy youth" he speaks only of a first divorce. Our concern is with the spirit of the statement, rather than its homiletical technicality.

[37]*Midr. Rab., Ber.* 18,8.

[38]Cf. the last *Mishnah* in *Git.*

[39]*b. Ketub.* 62b.

[40]Cf. e.g., *b. Ketub.* 77a.

[41]See *Tosafot*, ibid. 70a. *Yotzee Veyitten Ketubah.*

[42]Cf., for instance, ibid. 3a.

[43]*Yad HaHazakah, Hilkhot Ishut* 14,8.

[44]Maimonides, *The Guide for the Perplexed*, III, 32, trans. M. Friedlander.

[45]Exod 21:1-6.

[46]Lev 25:39-43.

[47]*b. Qidd.* 22a.

[48]Exod 21:7-11.

[49]That it does have general validity and was not used by Maimonides exceptionally in the case of *Korbanot* (animal sacrifices) one can see by the fact that it is in essence the principle that guides his interpretation of the reasons for the biblical commandments (*Ta'amei HaMitzvot*) practically in its entirety.

[50]*Midr. Rab., Ber.* 18.

[51]*Yad HaHazakah, Hilkhot Ishut* 13,11; the biblical quotation is from Psalms 45:14.

[52]Ibid. ch. 21,3.

[53]Cf. Maimonides, *Yad HaHazakah, Hilkhot Ishut* 15,20.

[54]See *b. B. Qam.* 14a, *Tosafot, Asher Tasim Lifnehem.*

[55]Cf. my work *T'nai Bᵉ Nisu'in uveGet,* Mosad Harav Kook (Jerusalem, 1966).

Chapter 10

Sabbath as Temple: Some Thoughts on Space and Time in Judaism

Arthur Green

The law of the Torah comes to religious expression in the Sabbath, the day of rest that is observed every seventh day. It is the one point at which faithful Judaists hope all of humanity will meet the Torah, as Green says, "[we] ask ourselves what sort of inspiration we hope humanity might derive from the collective experience of the Jew," and, he argues, find the answer with the Sabbath. It is what is absolutely unique to Judaism, and it also forms what Judaism can contribute to the sanctification of all humanity. He finds this lesson: "any place where the glory of God appears, in however transient a manner, is to be treated as God's holy Temple . . . a sacred day . . . may be carried anywhere . . . any place where that Sabbath is proclaimed holy comes to have just a touch of Jerusalem residing within it." The importance of this reflection on the Sabbath is to show us how the laws serve to create a realm rich in theological meaning, and yet a realm that overspreads the home and hearth. The concreteness of Judaism, its capacity to consecrate the ordinary and sanctify the profane, comes to full expression in this discussion of the meaning of the laws that create of the Sabbath a day that is wholly other.

***

In 1945, just as the European Holocaust (and with it the second great age in Jewish history) was drawing to a close, Abraham Joshua Heschel gave voice to a hope that later Jewish history would one day be recognized and sanctified by the world, as has the history of biblical Israel:

> When Nebuchadnezzar destroyed Jerusalem and set fire to the Temple, our forefathers did not forget the Revelation at Mount Sinai and the words of the Prophets. Today the world knows that what transpired on the soil of Palestine was sacred history, from which mankind draws its inspiration. A day may come when the hidden light of the East European period will be revealed.[1]

We look at Jewish history throughout the Diaspora period—going here beyond Heschel and extending back from Eastern Europe to the Roman destruction —and ask ourselves what sort of inspiration we hope humanity might derive from the collective experience of the Jew. Surely the basic insights of our religion, moral as well as spiritual, are by now accessible outside of Judaism, whether through her younger sister faiths or altogether independently. The particularizing nuances of Jewish faith and expression, vital as they may seem from within, will not constitute a major new source of understanding. It is rather from the experience of Jewish history, and within this overwhelmingly from the experience of *galut*, that the world has to learn. Homelessness, alienation, permanent insecurity, the feeling of living as unwelcome guests in a society not of our making: these long-known characteristics of life as a Jew are now increasingly the lot of millions of others in a world where the uprooting of populations, the migration of labor forces, and, above all, the ongoing urbanization and detraditionalization of people are taking place far faster than anyone can record.

Surely the great miracle of Jewish existence is our survival of *galut*. But if we ask ourselves what exactly *galut* is, and what means the Jewish people used to combat its corrosive power, our answer will necessarily be manifold. Our interest here is in the specifically religious quality of *galut*, in distinction (a historical artificiality, to be sure) from its political, economic, linguistic, and other aspects. It was in religious terms, after all, that premodern Jews generally and most successfully expressed themselves, and it is around religious symbols, not surprisingly, that a great deal of the discussion of *galut* is focused.

Umi-penei h a t a'enu galinu me-'ar z enu- "because of our sins we were exiled from our land." Such phrases abound in Jewish liturgy, alternating always with the prayers for restoration. If we take such liturgical expression as a standard for the Jews' images of their history, it becomes clear that *h urban* and *galut*, the destruction of the Temple and the exile from the land, are invariably treated as one. This is the case despite the fact that they did not come at the same time in the all important second destruction. Ere z Yisrael remained a major center of Jewish life and creativity for four or five hundred years after the Temple was destroyed. The paradigmatic event for classical Jewish self-understanding was the *first* destruction, even though it was in the crucible of the second that rabbinic Judaism had its birth. Sin and prophetic warring, followed by destruction and exile as one event—this is the way the Jewish people chose to remember it.

In order to see the meaning of this exile in religious terms, some patterns perceived elsewhere in the study of the history of religions should be recalled. Israel is a people living in what its God has designated as a holy land, proclaimed as such through the various deeds of revered ancestors in times long gone. In that holy land God has chosen one place "to cause His name to dwell there" (Deut 12:11) and at that spot has commanded His faithful servant to build a Temple. True, many among Israel had learned, especially by the second Temple period, that their God was not purely a local tribal deity, that the Creator could be worshipped from anywhere and by others as well as Israel. And yet the religion of Israel had never fully abandoned its tribal roots. The Land of Israel, Jerusalem, and the Temple were still the *right* places—if not the only places—for Israel to stand before its God. The clearest expression of this viewpoint in the Bible is probably the prayer of Solomon, with which he reportedly dedicated the House of God. It is worth calling to mind some excerpts:

> But will God really dwell on earth? Even the heavens and their uttermost reaches cannot contain You, how much less this house that I have built! Yet turn, O Lord my God, to the prayer and supplication of Your servant, and hear the cry and prayer which Your servant offers before You this day. May Your eyes be open day and night toward this House, toward the place of which You have said: "My name shall abide there"; may You heed the prayers which Your servants will offer toward this place. And when You hear the supplications which Your servant and Your people offer toward this place, give heed in Your heavenly abode—give heed and pardon.
>
> In any plague or in any disease, in any prayer or supplication offered by any person among all Your people Israel—each of whom knows his own affliction—when he spreads his palms toward this House, O hear in Your heavenly abode, and pardon and take action! . . .
>
> When Your people take the field against their enemy by whatever way You send them and they pray to the Lord in the direction of the city which You have chosen, and of the House which I have built to Your name, O hear in heaven their prayer and supplication and uphold their cause.   (1 Kings 8:27-30; 38-39; 44-45)

Although this prayer was probably composed long after Solomon, and possibly after the first exile, it shows how central the chosen city and Temple remained in Israelite eyes. Historians of religion have shown that early societies are generally constructed around a geographical "sacred center." Such a center serves to embody the values and aspirations of each society. It is also in one way or another the very real dwelling place of the deity, the locus out of which divine power radiates, or at least the place on earth where humans are most apt to be touched by the Presence. The Bible is somewhat reserved about the expression of this concept, at least in some of its more mythological aspects. The notion that the Temple is the opening to heaven and hell, or stands on the spot with which Creation began, or is located just below a great heavenly Temple, does not find direct narrative expression in Scripture. They are of course indicated by biblical language and terminology. *Beth El* and *Sha'ar ha Shamayim* are two of the more obvious examples. The fact that these terms grow forth into full and explicit narratives in the post-biblical sources, where less care was taken with regard to such anti-mythic "orthodoxy," and sometimes in forms quite strikingly parallel to expressions in Mesopotamian literature of more than a millennium earlier makes it rather likely that these concepts were indeed a part of the unrecorded folk legacy of ancient Israel.[2] This notion of center ties together visions of ideal past or origins and restoration in the harmonious future which is to say that it stands at the very core of what the Bible understands as both cosmology and history. It has also been suggestively argued that the biblical narrative itself, taken as a literary whole, may be said to have underlying it an ongoing sense of sacred center, extended from the tree of Eden down through Abraham's discovery of the Holy Land, Jacob's Bethel vision, and the tabernacle in the wilderness, until it received its final articulation in the city of David and the Temple of his son.[3]

Bearing in mind this view of Temple as the center of cosmic orientation, we can now pose more clearly our question about the religious meaning of *galut* to the Jewish people and how post-biblical Judaism has been a reaction to it. First, we should reiterate that the destruction of the Temple made *galut* a fact; a visit or even settlement in the Holy Land could not change that. The Land of Israel *sans* Temple and altar was still sacred, to be sure, but it had lost much of its luster in Jewish eyes. Medieval Jewish visitors to the Land, rather than glorying in their return home, joined the land in its mourning. It was as though the burning of Jerusalem had caused the land itself to go into exile. Our primary focus, however, should not be upon Judaism's mourning but upon its growth and renewal. Given the role that the Jerusalem center played in the cosmology of ancient Israel, and given the later biblical insistence that only there could the cult of Israel be practiced, how was the transition made in the religious life of the Jewish people from Temple to synagogue, from a sacrificial cult at the Center to a liturgical faith that could thrive anywhere?[4] To answer this we should look at the attitudes of the early synagogue and its religion, especially as reflected in the liturgy, toward the old cult and Temple. Fortunately, this very question has been addressed in an illuminating study by Robert Goldenberg entitled "The Broken Axis."[5] In examining early rabbinic liturgy the author notes that the rabbis never resolved the dilemma of whether or not their religion of prayer, *halakhah*, and study successfully superseded the Jerusalem cult. They proclaimed with Hosea (14:3) that "We shall render for bullocks the offering of our lips" and they structured their daily *'amidah* prayers as though they were filling the role of sacrifices. But they also made sure, in the midst of those prayers, to express a longing that "the Temple be rebuilt soon, in our own days," that "You restore the priests to their service and the Levites to their song and music," and, quite explicitly, that "there we shall eat of the sacrifices and the Paschal offerings as their blood reaches the side of Your alter, in fulfillment of Your will."[6] Goldenberg reaches the following conclusion:

> The self-conception of rabbinic Judaism is built on the contradictory assumptions that the earlier worship in the Temple has been successfully left behind, but that things will never be quite right until it has been restored. If considered theologically, that amounts to a stark contradiction or at best an ambivalent paradox; seen as an effort to preserve the old religious orientation after its basis has been swept away, it makes sense. We can then see here the outlines of a system which took advantage of the disorientation caused by the fall of Jerusalem, but did not fall victim to it. The continuity of religious life was thus protected, even as all the forms of religious life had to be changed.

This ambivalence toward the sacred center is placed into clearest relief when the position of rabbinic Judaism is contrasted with that of its rival and fellow heir to ancient Hebrew cosmology, the early Church. Classical Christianity took the clear and unambiguous step that the rabbis declined to take: the old Temple has been replaced. Christ has become the center; sacred space has been recast into Christ the Temple. Sacred person completely dominates the cosmological stage; as Jesus the Christ is Torah enfleshed, so is he God's house re-established. His cross and his body are the meeting-place of heaven and hell. His body, through its presence in the eucharist, is able thus to consecrate real sacred space over and over again. It is the clear negation of the old *axis mundi* that allows Christianity the power to symbolically create new sacred space in a way that Judaism was never able (nor did it seek) to do. The cathedral and its architecture seek to recreate and embody the primal world; through the death of sacred space and its rebirth, creation can happen anew. The synagogue, though sometimes called *miqdash me'at*, is viewed so much as a temporary replacement for the only *real* sanctuary that its structure, however loved and sometimes embellished, could not be granted such significance.

Lacking an unambiguous resolution of this question, the Judaism of the rabbis moved on several fronts at once. The Day of Atonement, liturgy, and good deeds all serve in one or another rabbinic pronouncement to replace the altar. Sacred person has a very limited role in early post-exilic Judaism, and assumes major proportions only—to the distress of many—in the Hasidism of the eighteenth century.[7] An area that is less obvious, largely because it is not articulated directly by the rabbis, is our concern here: the transfer of attention from sacred space to sacred *time*. Diaspora Israel are deprived of space, the land they are in is profane in their sight, not capable or worthy of sanctuary. The only truly holy place, far off from most, in any case lies in presently irreparable ruin. What has remained untouched by the conqueror, however, and, moreover, what remains consistently portable for a wandering community, is the realm of time. It is to time, and of course particularly to the Sabbath, that the rabbis sought to turn Israel's attention. The development of the already ancient Sabbath as the central ritual/halakhic institution of rabbinic Judaism was a specific reaction to the era of destruction, and represented an unconscious shifting of primary Jewish allegiance from the spacial to the temporal realm.

It was Heschel, whose words introduced this study, who first called the attention of modern Jews to the Temple-like quality of the Jewish Sabbath. His book *The Sabbath* made frequent reference to *shabbat* as a "palace in time" and went on to describe Judaism as a time-oriented rather than space-oriented way of viewing the world. Heschel did not, however, set the centrality of *shabbat* in historical context, a move that might have been inappropriate to an essentially poetic work.[8] In asserting the superiority of time over space as an eternal Jewish value, however, and in consigning the love of space to the realms of the ancient pagan and the modern materialist, the work inevitably wound up in deprecation of space, despite Heschel's claims to the contrary.

The remainder of this study may be viewed as an extended postscript to *The Sabbath*, a claim that *shabbat*-centered piety belongs specifically to the second era of Jewish history, the result of particular spiritual/historical circumstances.

Anyone familiar with the life of a traditional Jewish community needs no proof of the centrality of *shabbat* in Jewish religious life. The ongoing love affair between Jew and *shabbat* is so well attested in Jewish folk literature, and has been so beautifully described by Heschel and others, that it would be worse than superfluous to try to capsulize it here. It might be worth noting that there are ways in which the Jewish community actually *defined* itself religiously as a community of Sabbath-observers: one who keeps the Sabbath is part of the group, but one who profanes it (for the Sabbath was proclaimed holy at Creation) is not. A Sabbath-observer may be trusted as a witness before a rabbinic court; a Sabbath-profaner may not. Food served in the home of a known Sabbath-observer may be assumed ritually fit; among others one could take no chances. Probably the closest one could come to speaking of an "Orthodox" Jew in premodern Jewish parlance, as used within the community, was *shomer shabbos*. Such evidences are, of course, popular and informal; they reflect general opinion rather than *halakhah*,[9] and are not necessarily early. One might wonder, however, whether the Talmudic tale of the final encounter between Elisha ben Abuya and Rabbi Meir does not represent something similar. It is as Elisha rides off on his horse beyond the Sabbath-barrier, leaving Meir behind, that the final break is made by the heretic who has left the rabbinic fold.[10]

The observance of the Sabbath has always been one of the major concerns of Jewish law: definitions and categorizations of forbidden labors, punishments for Sabbath-violations, and the application of old categories of forbidden labor to ever-new situations of advancing human technology have occupied Jewish legalists since very early times. While we do not know as much as we would like about the observance of the Sabbath in prerabbinic times, there is much evidence from the later period of the Second Temple, both internal and external, to indicate that Sabbath rest was a central part, if not actually the defining characteristic, of the religion of the Jews.[11] Evidence from the Dead Sea sectarians shows that their Sabbath was rather like that of the later rabbis in terms of its halakhic nature;[12] some indications are now found that lead scholars to trace later forms of Sabbath observance back to biblical times, despite the lack of written evidence for them.[13]

Our claim is *not*, then, that Sabbath became *important* only after the destruction of the Temple. This would be foolish; the ten commandments are ample testimony to the contrary. It is rather this: *the Sabbath gradually supplanted the Temple as the central unifying religious symbol of the Jewish people.* This shift took place originally in the context of the sectarian strife of the Second Temple period, and was ultimately confirmed by the destruction of the Temple.

The best symbol for this movement from space-oriented to time-oriented piety is in the formula that the rabbis use to encapsulate the Sabbath regulations; the thirty-nine categories of forbidden labor. According to Talmudic report (originally disputed but later widely accepted by the tradition)[14] the biblical basis for almost the entirety of the Sabbath prohibitions lies in Exodus 31:13: "Moreover you shall keep My Sabbaths. . . ." This Sabbath command is inserted, seemingly without reason, in the midst of the ongoing discussion of the building of the tabernacle, the Torah's prototype of an ideal Temple. Since the word *'akh*, with which this Sabbath verse opens, is a term of exception in the technical vocabulary of rabbinic exegesis (i.e. it comes to teach that what follows is an exception to the previously stated rule), the rabbis concluded that all forms of labor involved in any way in the construction of the tabernacle were meant to be forbidden on the Sabbath. These include such general categories, e.g., as planting, shearing, dyeing, sewing, and striking a hammer. The point seems to be obscure and arbitrary, that so much of Sabbath law should be unmentioned in Scripture and derived from a seemingly innocuous two-letter Hebrew word. The rabbis themselves called it "mountains hanging by a hair."[15] But perhaps it is neither arbitrary nor obscure. The commandments for the tabernacle tell how to construct sacred space, elaborating in full and rich detail the place that was to be Israel's center and opening to heaven. Now, because of changed circumstances, a new such center was needed, temporal rather than spatial in character. The ancient and revered institution of *shabbat* is the vehicle, of course, but the detail of *shabbat* observance is lacking in Biblical basis and especially lacking in a coherent structure to lend it meaning. By the deft interpretation of an *'akh*, the rabbis have succeeded in transferring all that Biblical detail from the realm of space, where it had been rendered useless, to that of time. The phenomenon is one of reversal: by *doing* all these labors in the particular prescribed configuration, one creates sacred space. By *refraining* from these same acts, in the context of the Sabbath, one creates sacred time. Here the legalistic device, far from being arbitrary, is used in a highly sophisticated way to effect a basic change in religious modality.

The Talmudic rabbis had not read Mircea Eliade. For them such notions as "sacred time" and "sacred space" hardly existed as categories of thought. There was, of course, no conscious decision taken one fine day at Yavneh to fashion the Sabbath after the fallen Temple.[16] How then, according to our reading, could such a transference have come about? How could Temple and *Shabbat*, two seemingly unrelated institutions of ancient Judaism, be so linked? The question requires a brief examination of the theological rationale provided for these institutions in the Biblical and rabbinical sources, one that will uncover a deep though mostly unspoken link between the two, a link that makes this shift of focus after the destruction considerably more understandable.

Rav Judah in the name of Rav (Babylonia, 3rd cent.) teaches that Bezalel, architect of the tabernacle, "knew how to perform those permutation of letters through which heaven and earth were created."[17] Why should Bezalel, of all people (and not Moses or Aaron), be privy to this secret? The tradition makes sense only if his single task is somehow especially related to the original Creation. We do not have to go far to see that this is the case:

"These are the accounts of the tabernacle: (Exod 38:21) . . . Said Rabbi Jacob ben Assi: Why does Scripture say "Lord, I love the habitation of Your House and the place where Your Glory dwells" (Ps 26:8)? Because it [God's house] is parallel to the Creation of the world. How is this?

Of the first day it is written: "In the beginning God created the heaven and the earth." It is also written "He stretched forth the heavens like a curtain." (Ps 104:2). And what is written regarding the tabernacle? "You shall make curtains of goatskins." (Exod 26:7)

On the second day: "Let there be a firmament," and separation is mentioned, as it says: "Let it separate waters from waters." And of the tabernacle: "And the veil shall separate for you between the holy and the holy of holies." (Exod 26:33)

On the third day water is mentioned: "Let the waters be gathered." And in the tabernacle: "You shall make a brass basin with a brass base . . . and place water there." (Exod 30:18)

On the fourth day He created the lights, as it says: "Let there be luminaries in the heavenly firmament." And in the tabernacle: "You shall make a gold candelabrum." (Exod 25:31)

> On the fifth day He created the birds: "Let the waters swarm with every living thing and let birds fly." Parallel to them in the tabernacles are sacrifices of lambs and birds. [Alternative reading: "And in the tabernacle: 'The cherubim spread their wings upward.' " (Exod 25:20)]

> On the sixth day man was created, as it says: "He created man in His image. He created him through the glory.[18] Man (Adam) in the tabernacle is high priest, anointed to serve and minister before the Lord. . . .[19]

The continuation of this midrash will be quoted below, but there is enough here for our present purposes. The parallel raises to an ultimate height the cosmic significance of the drama that takes place within the tabernacle or Temple. The priest is now Adam or the embodiment of all mankind, the candelabrum gives off the radiance of the sun, and so forth. While the language is that of metaphor, the intent seems clearly symbolic: thus is the cult to be understood. The rabbis speak of sacred space as microcosm, the tabernacle reproducing in a sacralized context the entirely of Creation. In other passages the relationship between Creation and the tabernacle is adumbrated somewhat differently: Creation is not quite complete or secure until it has been "sealed" by the erection of the sacred shrine:

> "Who has established all the ends of the earth" (Prov 30:4). The tent of meeting, as it says: "it was on the day that Moses completed setting up the tabernacle" (Num 7:1). The world was set up with it. Rabbi Joshua ben Levi in the name of R. Simeon ben Yohai: It does not say *LeHa-QYM Ha-MiSHKaN*, but rather *LeHa-QYM 'et [with] Ha-MiSHKaN*. What was set up "with" it? The world, for until the tabernacle was erected the world trembled; when the tabernacle was set up the world was firmly established. . . .[20]

Here too we see a theme that is familiar from other cultural contexts. The shrine finally validates (and hence guarantees) the existence of the world itself; only at this point is Creation complete.

Viewing the tabernacle/Temple from this perspective, we understand that the rabbis took it as no coincidence that the Sabbath command of Exodus 31:12 followed immediately upon the details of its construction. Only then is Moses told (31:1ff.) that God has called upon Bezalel and his associates to execute the work. The Sabbath warning comes before work can actually begin. Theologically as well as halakhically, there is no arbitrariness; as God rests on the seventh day after *His* work of Creation, so do you rest on the seventh of yours. The repetition of the Sabbath command in Exodus 35:1-3, just as the actual work is to get underway, makes it clear that in this case what the rabbis saw was probably *peshat*, at least the intent of a Scriptural editor.

The Sabbath, according to Genesis, is the apex of Creation. There is no holiness in God's world until He finds rest. Only after Creation has been completed and He ceases from work does He bless and hallow. And it is not the fruit of His labors that is sanctified, but the day of His rest.

The building of a Temple is, for religious societies, the most meaningful of human labors; in it man makes an earthly dwelling-place for the presence of his God or, in Israel's case, a symbol of His presence in their midst. But this labor too remains unhallowed until completion. The laborers who constructed the Temple, we are told, were able to come and go throughout, even walking through what was to become the holy of holies, until their work was done.

No wonder then that the closing chapter of Exodus repeats the step-by-step structure of the opening chapter of Genesis, concluding with the unmistakable refrain *Va-yekhal Mosheh et ha-mel'akhah.*[21] A biblical redactor, having before him an account that reached from Creation to the tabernacle, sought to "seal" that account with a conclusion that has an appropriate parallel to its beginning. Creation is completed by its repetition as a human act; God's work finds fulfillment only as something of His power to create to imitated by humans. In this linking of sacred-space construction to the original Creation, the Torah also implies a link spoken only with the subtlety of juxtaposition and linguistic parallel, between Temple and Sabbath.

Now we may proceed with the passage from *Midrash Tanhuma* that we cited above. The six days of Creation, we recall, have already found their match in the tabernacle. And now:

> On the seventh day: "Heaven and earth were completed." And in the tabernacle: "All the work was completed" (Exod 39:32). Of Creation: "And God blessed [the seventh day]," and of the tabernacle: "And Moses blessed them" (Exod 39:43). Of Creation: "God completed," and of the tabernacle: "On the day when Moses completed" (Num 7:1). Of Creation: "And He made it holy," and of the tabernacle: "He annointed it and made it holy" (ibid.).

It was the rabbis' sensitivity to this nuance of biblical meaning, barely hinted at in text but deeply implanted in the structure of the two institutions, that allowed them, in the face of the need of their age, to perform the delicate manipulation of an *'akh*[22] that had so great a meaning for all of the Judaism that was to come.

Jewish thinkers writing under the influence of Kabbalah, beginning in the thirteenth century, were able to articulate most fully this link between Temple and Sabbath. In the works of the Spanish Kabbalists, well known for their deft use of symbols and their ability to rapidly translate from one symbol-system into another, it is frequently made clear either that Temple (or tabernacle) and Sabbath are one or else that they are the classic pair which need to be drawn together. Here we are dealing with a literature of mysticism, one in which both time and space will perforce be relativized. The chief focus of the Kabbalists' interest is the realm of the *sefirot*, seen at once as the stages of divine unfolding or emanation and as the rungs in the ladder of the mystic's ascent to the One. As the adept moves by successive degrees ever "upward" or "inward" toward realization, points along the journey must perforce somehow be designated. These designations, drawn especially by the *Zohar* in a full array of colorful symbols, may be characterized by terms that have their origins either in the temporal or the spatial realm. Either is acceptable for this purpose because neither is quite adequate. The divine effulgence does not first flow through either spatially locatable points or temporarily determined moments; neither does the mystic in his ascent to God. In order to speak of his universe in human language, however, he must designate the states in symbols taken from one realm or the other. It is not surprising, then, to find in his writings moments in "time" and objects in "space" that turn out to be identical with one another. As symbols of light may turn into water as one proceeds from line to line on the same page of *Zohar*, so may figures in space "reveal themselves" to be figures in time. What we have here is no merely external literary device, but a representation in symbolic language of an essential characteristic of mystical experience.

The central figures in most discussions of the sefirotic universe are the sixth and the last of these ten manifestations. The sixth *sefirah* represents the deity as generally depicted in the earlier biblical and rabbinic sources. This is the God-figure, Father and King, who is the source of the written Torah, the object of nonmystical prayer, and whose being represents a constant balance of the potentially warring forces of justice and love, the "Holy One, blessed be He," as He is most frequently called by the rabbis. The tenth *sefirah* is the *shekhinah*, the presence of God indwelling, the hypostatized Community of Israel, and most importantly, the object of divine affection, the bride of the mystical Song of Solomon. The most essential and daring theological innovation of the Kabbalah was the claim that the Canticle, long read by the rabbis as a lovesong between God and His people Israel, was now to be seen as documenting a love that takes place *within* God, between two poles of the divine self symbolically designated as male and female, a relationship in which Israel were no longer seen as the direct object of divine *eros*, but rather as its offspring and devotees.

The association of the Sabbath with the feminine aspect of the divine world is widespread in the Kabbalah and is quite well known, if only through its presentation in the Sabbath hymn *Lekha Dodi*. Many Kabbalistic writings speak of two Sabbaths, or of male and female aspects within the *shabbat* itself (these resting on earlier speculations around *zakhor*—"remember" the Sabbath (Exod 20:8) and *shamor*—"keep" the Sabbath [Deut 5:12]. But it is with the *shekhinah* as bride and queen that the mystics' Sabbath is finally identified:

> The secret of Sabbath: *she* is Sabbath as she cleaves to the mysterious One, causing that One to shine upon her. . . . When Sabbath comes, she is unified and separated from the "other side." All evil forces of judgement are removed from her, and she dwells in union with the holy light. She is crowned with many crowns as she faces the holy king—her face shines with a sublime radiance as she is crowned from below by the holy people. . . .[23]

The tabernacle/Temple too is identified with the *shekhinah* throughout the literature of the Kabbalah. House, Tent, Temple are all classic symbols of the feminine archetype: that which is entered, gathering place, womb, etc. It is in this symbolic garb that the last *sefirah* serves as the meeting-place for God and Israel: the flow of divine energy from the *sefirot* "above" and the devotion of Israel's prayers "below" are joined together in this *bet mo'ed le-khol ḥai*. It was in some of their most daring moments that the Kabbalistic authors allowed Moses (or the adept in the guise of Moses?) to share with God the role of bridegroom of the *shekhinah*. Hence this rather startling passage is made possible:

> "They brought the tabernacle unto Moses" (Exod 39:33). Why did they *bring* the tabernacle? Because that was the hour of Moses' marriage—for this reason "they brought the tabernacle unto Moses"—just as the bride is brought to the bridegroom. First the bride must be brought to her groom, as Scripture says: "I have given my daughter to this man as a wife" (Deut 22:16). Only afterwards may he [the bridegroom] come to her, and it says "and he came unto her," as is written "Moses came unto the tent of testimony" (Num 17:23). Here, however, what is written? "Moses could not come in to the tent of meeting for the cloud abode upon it" (Exod 40:35). For what reason? She was preparing herself for him, as a woman prepares and adorns herself for her husband. At the time when she is adorning herself it is not proper for her husband to come in to her. That was why "Moses could not come in to the tent of meeting" and it was for that reason that "They brought the tabernacle unto Moses."[24]

This rather courtly vignette of Moses and the *shekhinah* as bridegroom and bride is paralleled by a number of passages, particularly in the *Zohar*, where the lovely damsel or chaste and faithful wife appears as symbolic representation of the *shekhinah*. It is generally understood that these refer in the first place to *shekhinah* as the bride of God, but not exclusively so. With regard to the Sabbath too, it should be recalled, there is reason in old Midrashic sources to think of her as *Israel's* bride: "Israel will be your mate," God says to the lonely seventh day.[25] The poetic genius of Alkabeẓ' *Lekha Dodi* lies in his steadfast refusal to name the *dod* to whom the hymn is addressed, thus maintaining a certain enriching ambiguity in the identity of the Sabbath's bridegroom.[26] This *shabbat*, for whom one must prepare "as one prepares a canopy for a bride," is also the one who is "shut and sealed on the six weekdays," in a passage that quotes from Ezekiel's vision of the restored Temple

(46:1): ". . . but on the seventh day she is open to receive her husband."[27] The identification of Temple and Sabbath is sometimes associated with the exegesis of Lev. 19:30: "You shall keep My Sabbaths and fear My Temple." So, for example, Rabbi Bahya ben Asher of Barcelona, a contemporary of the *Zohar*:

> " 'You shall keep My Sabbaths.'. . . One is the Great Sabbath, that of 'remember,' and the other is the Temple, the Community of Israel, mate of [the upper] Sabbath. This one is 'keep,' and for that reason it was not proper that the work of [building] the Temple supersede this Sabbath/Temple."[28]

Here the lower Sabbath, that of 'keep' and thus particularly identified with the prohibitions among the Sabbath commands, is identified at once with *shekhinah* and Temple. For the Kabbalist it is perfectly a matter of course that the command of Sabbath was so placed in the Bible as to infer that the work of construction had to cease on the seventh day: anything else would have been self-contradictory, for the Sabbath, and particularly the cessation from labor, *is* the Temple.[29]

If the medieval Kabbalists were able by means of their mystical symbolization of space and time to bring Temple and Sabbath to a state of identification, the free-wheeling associative patterns of the later Hasidic homilies were able to do the same. Popular impressions to the contrary, their method was not at all that of the Kabbalists, but rather an extension, sometimes seemingly *ad absurdum*, of the classical methods of Midrashic exegesis. Although the rubric of the *sefirot* is formally preserved in Hasidic discourse, its content has been largely vitiated. The Kabbalistic system is generally used (*HaBaD* is the great exception here) as only one more device in the hands of the homilist. Thus "Sabbath" and "Temple" in the following passages are no longer ciphers for the *shekhinah*, but once again the real Sabbath and Temple of time and space, with perhaps just a slight added nuance of Kabbalistic meaning.

The first Hasidic passage comes from the *Degel Ma h aneh Ephraim*, the collected homilies of Rabbi Moses Hayyim Ephraim of Sudilkov, first published in 1810/11. Ephraim was the grandson of the Ba'al Shem Tov,[30] and his teachings often reflect the thoughts of the movement's first central figure:

> "The children of Israel shall keep the Sabbath, observing the Sabbath throughout their generations as an everlasting covenant; it is a sign forever between Me and the children of Israel" (Exod 31:13). The *Ba'al ha-Turim* notes that the words *'et ha-shabbat le-dorotam* may be abbreviated as *'HL* (consonantally) *'ohel*, "tent."

> In commenting on this we must first recall the verse "They shall make Me a tabernacle and I will dwell in their midst." (Exod 25:8). We might then think that without such a tabernacle it would not be possible for the *shekhinah* to dwell amidst us! But the matter must be understood thus: "A foretaste of the world to come is the

Sabbath day of rest." The best counsel [since there is no tabernacle] is to keep the Sabbath properly. In this way may we merit, as it were, the indwelling of the Presence, for the Sabbath is a sort of sanctuary. In that way too is it a foretaste of the future world [i.e. of the rebuilt Temple].

It was for this reason that the Torah hinted at the word "tent" in the phrasing of this verse, showing that the Sabbath too is a form of tent or tabernacle. The word *le-dorotam* also hints at the notion of "dwelling" (*DoRoTaM = DiRaTaM*), as in the dwelling of a Temple. In this way God dwells in our midst, and that is why Scripture continues: "As an *everlasting* covenant": by means of the Sabbath, the Lord, blessed be He, dwells in our midst . . . and the words *'ot hi'le-'olam* again form the word *'ohel*, showing that this sign goes on without interruption. Even in times when there is no Temple, the Sabbath has not been negated, *and it is the Temple*.[31]

Operating here outside that symbol-structure that had so utterly relativized space and time, the Hasidic master produces his own spiritualized rereading of the Scriptural command. His spirituality remains halakhic, to be sure, for it is only by "keeping the Sabbath properly (*kehilkhato*)" that this new Temple is maintained. His essential point, however, is far-reaching, one that goes to the very core of the religious radicalism of the Hasidic movement. The destruction of the Temple does not represent an *essential* change in the relationship of God to His world and to Israel. The Presence remains in our midst as previously; only the medium of primary access to it has been shifted. The immanentism that the Ba'al Shem Tov's religion represented had to find a way to overcome the sense of divine distance that permeates so much of rabbinic and later Judaism.

A second Hasidic example, as likely to have been well-known to Heschel as was the first, is found in the *Mey ha-Shiloaḥ* , by Rabbi Mordecai Joseph Leiner of Izbica (1800/01–1854). Izbica was an important school of Hasidic thought in central Poland; its founder, Mordecai Joseph, had at one point been quite close to Rabbi Mendel of Kotzk, whose latter-day disciples Heschel knew so well in Warsaw. R. Mordecai Joseph writes:

"You shall keep My Sabbaths and fear My Temple" (Lev 19:30). 'My Sabbaths' [in the plural], for every dwelling of the *shekhinah* at any time, no matter how temporary, is called a Sabbath. The blessed Lord commanded us to honor all the places where His *shekhinah* has dwelt, however temporarily. "And fear My Temple"—the Targum renders this as "be in fear *for* My Temple": you still should long for the deepest [eschatological] good to be found in each of the commandments. The Sabbath as we have it now is much diminished; only in the future will God grant us "the day that is wholly Sabbath," when we shall have no need for any labors. We must long for this, while still giving honor, meanwhile, to that which God has commanded us.

> This may be compared to a king who moves from place to place: you show honor
> to each of his lodgings, while still looking forward to his own resting-place. . . .

> This was the mistake of Hophni and Phinehas: they saw that God's dwelling in
> Shiloh was only a temporary one, and therefore they treated it lightly. Of such
> conduct Scripture says: "You have despised My Temple." . . .[32]

Here we have the lesson drawn out for us in a strikingly modern-sounding formulation: the juxtaposition of Sabbath and Temple teaches us that any place where the glory of God appears, in however transient a manner (and indeed what place is not capable of such description?) is to be treated as God's holy Temple. Yes, Judaism has become a religion of sacred time, learning through the bitter experience of exile that geographical locus alone could not suffice to describe the manner in which God dwells on earth. This time-centeredness, however, also served to expand and "liberate" the notion of sacred space, a process we see reaching its culmination here in the *Mey ha-Shiloah*. The history of exile teaches Israel that a sacred day, unlike a sacred mountain or a sacred shrine, may be carried anywhere and remain safe from outward attack. The hidden lesson here learned also inevitably points to the idea that any place where that Sabbath is proclaimed holy comes to have just a touch of Jerusalem residing within it. The legacy of wandering Israel to the world may lie precisely in this: home does not have to be abandoned as you are forced to leave it. The transformation of space into time may allow us to be bearers of our homes and origins, however far away from them modernity may lead us, so that the values they represented in our lives need not fade into mere pleasant memories of things past.

Endnotes

[1]*Der Mizrekh-Eropeisher Yid* (New York: Schocken Books, 1946) 44f. Expanded translation as *The Earth Is the Lord's* (New York: Schuman, 1950) 99.

[2]These sources have been collected and discussed by Raphael Patai in *Man and Temple*, London, 1947. See also the dated but still important treatment by Victor Aptowitzer in *Bet ha-Miqdash shel Ma'alah" Tarbiz* 2 (1931). For the older Mesopotamian parallels see particularly the works of Geo. Widengren, including *Sakrales Königtum im Alten Testament und im Judentum*, Stuttgard, 1955, and the various ancillary studies.

[3]Michael Fishbane, "The Sacred Center in the Bible," in *Texts and Responses: Studies Presented to Nahum N. Glatzer* (Leiden: Brill, 1975) 6ff. See also his *Text and Texture: Close Readings of selected Biblical Texts* (New York: Schocken, 1979). I am grateful to Professor Fishbane for several suggestions he has made in connection with this article.

[4]I do not mean to oversimplify a long and complex process. Of course I am aware that the synagogue began to come into being before the Temple was destroyed, etc. The question is asked from a long-range historical vantage-point.

[5]Robert Goldenberg, "The Broken Axis," *Journal of the American Academy of Religion* 45 (1977): 353ff.

[6]The phrases are all from the liturgy: daily *'amidah*, festival *mussaf 'amidah* and Passover *haggadah*.

[7]See the author's "The *Zaddiq* as *Axis Mundi* in Later Judaism," *Journal of the American Academy of Religion* 45 (1977): 327ff.

[8]It is perhaps noteworthy, however, that the tale of Rabbi Simeon ben Yohai and his son plays so prominent a role in that volume, certainly serving to focus the reader's attention on the generation immediately after the destruction.

[9]As to witnessing, for example, Maimonides' *Mishneh Torah*, Laws of Testimony 10:2 makes it clear that a violator of *any* Torah law of a certain magnitude may not testify; no special point is made of the Sabbath.

[10]*y. Ḥag.* 2:1 (77b).

[11]The Sabbath attracted a good deal of attention among Latin writers, and not only those who had a particular interest in the Jews. For the sources see Radin, *The Jews among the Greeks and Romans*, 245ff. and J. Hugh Michael, "The Jewish Sabbath in the Latin Classical Writers," AJSLL 40 (1923/24): 117ff.

[12]See the thorough treatment by Lawrence Schiffman, *The Halakhah at Qumran* (Leiden: Brill, 1975) 77ff.

[13]See the treatment by Y. D. Gilat, *"Le-Qadmutam shel 'Issurey Shabbat 'Aḥadim"* in *Bar-'Ilan* 1 (1963): 106ff. A summary of Sabbath ritual in the Second Temple is found in *EJ* 15, col. 977. See further M. Fishbane's "Revelation and Tradition as Religious Categories in the Bible" in a forthcoming *Journal of Biblical Literature*.

[14]The "derivation" of the 39 labors from the construction of the tabernacle is given in Shabbat 49b; see also 96b. It is clear that this is a rubric added later to an accumulation of forbidden labors of diverse origins. *Tosafot* ad loc. seems nearly to admit as much. On the 39 labors see further Y. D. Gilat, "39 *'Avot Mel'akhot Shabbat"* in *Tarbiz* 28 (1959/60): 226ff.

[15]*Ḥagigah* 1:8, *Tosefta Ḥagigah* 9:9 and *'Eruvin* 11:23. The actual derivation from *'akh* is not found in the extant rabbinic sources, but only in the Middle Ages: RaSHI to Exod 31:13. We do have a source in the *Mekilta* (ed. Horwitz/Rabin, 345) that derives the relationship from the similar juxtaposition in Exod 35:1ff. On the question of *'akh*, see the extended discussion by M. M. Kasher in *Torah Shelemah*, 21:58, n. 34.

[16]But consider the parallel between our matter and the decision recorded in *Rosh Hashanah* 4:1: "When the holiday of Rosh Hashanah occurs on the Sabbath, the *shofar* is blown in the Temple but not in the town. When the Temple was destroyed, Rabbi Yoḥanan ben Zakkai decreed that it should be blown wherever there is a *bet din*." Here is a rather clear symbolic statement that the seat of rabbinic authority takes on something of a Temple-like quality. On this see Neusner, *A Life of Yoḥanan ben Zakkai*. Second edition (Leiden: Brill, 1970) 205f. and *Development of a Legend* (Leiden: Brill, 1970), Index s.v. Sabbath.

[17]*Berakhot* 55a. The biblical text itself already seeks to link Hiram, architect of Solomon's Temple, with Bezalel. Note the linguistic parallel of 1 Kings 7:14 with Exod 31:3. Further material on Bezalel of a similar sort is found scattered in rabbinic sources. See Ginzberg, *Legends*, s.v. Bezalel.

[18]I am emending *bi-khevod yoṣero* to *b-kavod yeṣaro*, which seems to make more sense, particularly if the phrase is a medieval gloss. I find no way of understanding the text as it stands.

[19]Tan ḥ uma, *Pequdey* 2. A parallel version is found in *Leqa ḥ Tov*, ad loc., and a somewhat better text of the Tan ḥ uma is preserved in *R. Bahya* to Exod 38:21. A rather different version is found in *Midrash Tadshe'* 2 (*Bet ha-Midrash* 3, 164f.) See also the sources discussed in Ginzberg's *Legends*, 6:67, n. 346, and by Chavel *ad loc.* in his edition of the Bahya commentary. See Bahya also on Exod 40:16.

[20]*Pesikta de-Rav Kahana*, ed. Buber 5b–6a, as emended by the editor. Perhaps an even stronger statement is found regarding Solomon's Temple in *Pesikta Rabbati* 6, ed. Friedmann 25a. There it is suggested that Solomon's very name SHeLoMoH) indicates that it was he who completed (hiSHeLyM) the making of heaven and earth.

[21]This has been noticed by Cassutto, *Commentary on the Book of Exodus* (Jerusalem, 1967) 176 and 483. Cassutto does not mention that he had been preceded by the Midrash and especially by *R. Bahya* in this insight. M. Fishbane informs me that "there is an ancient Near Eastern pattern, embedded in Enumaelish, that the end of Creation is construction of a temple for the victor god." Fragments of this, he notes, appear in the Bible (Exod 15; Ps 29) and this concluding pattern of Exodus is to be seen as a transformation of that pattern.

[22]Taken symbolically; see note 15 above.

[23]*Zohar* 2:135a–b. On the two Sabbaths in early Kabbalah see Nahmanides on Exod 20:8 and 31:13. His comments are based on those in *Bahir* 181–82 (ed. Scholem 124). See further Tishby's *Mishnat ha-Zohar*, 2:487ff. Sabbath as bride in the Kabbalah is of course also based on earlier motifs; the figure of Sabbath as queen is mentioned occasionally in rabbinic literature. Much is made of this theme in the Falasha treatise *Ta'azaza Sanbat*, but that development seems entirely unrelated to the Kabbalistic expansion of this idea.

[24]*Zohar* 2:235a. "And he came unto her" is not part of the verse in Deut 22:16, but has slipped into the author's mind from elsewhere.

[25]*Bereshit Rabbah* 11:8. Elsewhere, however (*Shemot Rabbah* 25:11, for example), shabbat is taken as a token of the intimacy that exists between God as King and His lady Israel.

[26]See the extended discussion of the bride and queen motifs in Heschel's *Sabbath*, 126ff., n. 4. The rabbinic sources to which I refer in n. 23 above are there listed in full.

[27]*Zohar* 3:272b; *Tiqquney Zohar* 36, ed. Margaliot 78a.

[28]*Bahya* to Lev 19:30; ed. Chavel, 2:532.

[29]One cannot help but wonder also whether the Safed Kabbalists did not have this association somehow in mind when they chose Psalm 95 as the opening to Kabbalat Shabbat. The closing line of that Psalm stands before the Sabbath as a liturgy of entry: "So I vowed in My anger that they would not come in to my *menu ḥ ah*." Of course in the context of the Psalm *menu ḥ ah* clearly refers to the Land of Israel. Here, however, it cannot but refer to the Sabbath, and the Psalm then challenges the worshiper, much as does Psalm 24, to examine whether he is ready to "enter" the Sabbath as *Sanctum*. This same verse, by the way, was used earlier, exactly as one might expect, with regard to the Temple. See *Yalqut Shime'oni*, 2:189. I am indebted to Rabbi Jack Riemer for this insight.

[30]On R. Ephraim, see the references in my *Tormented Master*, a study of his nephew, R. Nahman of Bratslav. The sources on him have been collected by M. Y. Guttman, *Geza' Qodesh* (Tel Aviv, 1950/51) and in Horodezky, *Ha-Ḥasidut weha-Ḥasidim* 3:7ff.

[31]*Degel Ma ḥ aneh Ephraim, Ki tissa'*, ed. (Jerusalem, 1962/63) 131f.

[32]*Mey ha-Shiloa ḥ*, part one, *Qedoshim* 38b. The verse with which he concludes is not to be found in Scripture. He seems to be misquoting from 1 Samuel 2:29ff.

Chapter 11

The Distinctive Expression
of the Category of Worship in Judaism

Manfred H. Vogel

From the specifics of prayer, we come at the end to an account of how prayer in Judaism exhibits quite special characteristics. Before us is a complex argument, which places prayer into the context of a complete theological system. Here is how the concrete points made in the preceding chapter are recast as elements of a whole and comprehensive statement of theological truth. For prayer pertains not only to us but to the structure of our faith; it is not personal, therefore, it is a chapter in a larger book of belief that many read and understand, and that is why Vogel has chosen to formulate prayer in the terms of a governing theological structure. Worship in Judaism has taken place in sacrifice of worldly produce, the gifts of nature, to God; prayer; and study of the Torah. But there is no doubt that of the three, prayer—human address to God—best formulates the divine-human interchange. In sacrifice, humanity gives to God, and in study of the Torah, God speaks to humanity; prayer is an interchange of an I to a You. Prayer is a form of address to God, the moment at which, for the faithful, God is most real, most personal, most present. But it is always an act of a "we," not an "I," and it is always governed by halakhah. Since it is God who revealed the Torah, the fact that the Torah governs, also, how we pray, closes the circle. As Vogel says, ". . . now the act of prayer is no longer grounded in man but in the divine. It is no longer a communication to God originating in man but rather a communication to man originating in God. It is an act of divine revelation to man rather than an act of man's address to God. Rather than being an act of human spontaneity, it is an act of divine command. For it is not God who wishes man to pray and commands him to do so." Here is how the concept of revelation in the Torah links up with the piety and quest for God's presence of the private person and makes of prayer the ultimate act of revelation and self-revelation, all at once, in the here and now. Vogel's chapter is certainly the most difficult in this book, but because of the question that he answers, it also is the most important.

***

*From *A Quest for a Theology of Judaism: The Divine, The Human nad the Ethical Dimensions in the Structure-of-Faith of Judaism. Essays in Constructive Theology,* by Manfred H. Vogel. Copyright © 1987 Univeristy Press of America. Reprinted by permission of the editorial board of *Bijdragen Tijdschrift voor Filosophie en Theologie,* in which the essay originally appeared, volume 43 (1982): 350-382.

Worship is a central category in the structure of faith of all religions. The purpose of this essay is to attempt to explicate the basic signification of this category; moreover, it is to show that in the case of Judaism, specifically in its mainstream expression, the category expresses itself in a special and distinct way.

I

We take the category of worship to signify the relating of man to that which is taken to constitute the ultimate being. Thus, worship in its basic and most inclusive signification signifies an act of relating—not, however, just any act of relating but that act of relating which is specifically directed to the ultimate being, and then only when it signifies the relating as it emanates from the side of man and not vice-versa as it emanates from the side of the ultimate being. It is this relating of man to that which he takes to be ultimate, irrespective of the shape, form, manner or content of the relating, which constitutes the very essence of the category of worship, all other characterizations being in the last analysis implicated by it.[1]

But as such the category of worship necessarily implicates the further category of transcendence inasmuch as we take the category of transcendence to signify the act of surpassing, the act of going beyond oneself (or commensurately, that entity which surpasses, which exists beyond oneself). For clearly, in signifying the relating of man to an ultimate the category of worship necessarily implicates the act of surpassing, of going beyond oneself on the part of man, i.e., it necessarily implicates an act of transcendence on the part of man. Indeed, any act of relating necessarily implicates an act of transcendence; the category of worship being constituted as an act of relating is thus constrained by its very constitution to implicate the category of transcendence.[2]

This assertion, however, requires further clarification. For, in the light of our delineation of the category of transcendence the category may implicate two different kinds of acts. On the one hand, it may implicate an act whose surpassing remains within the confines of the space-time continuum, within the totality of the world of our experience. On the other hand, it may also implicate an act whose surpassing goes beyond the very confines of the space-time continuum.[3] Using graphic imagery as a convenient short-hand, we may denote the latter act as a "vertical" act of transcendence and the former act as a "horizontal" act of transcendence. Thus, an act of transcendence can be either a vertical act or a horizontal act, seeing that by definition any act of surpassing is an act of transcendence and that the act of surpassing need not be exclusively a vertical act but can also be a horizontal act.

But surely, we would not want to say that in the context of biblical faith, specifically in the context of Judaism, the act of worship implicates an act of transcendence that is merely horizontal. Surely we would have to say that the act of transcendence which the act of worship implicates here must be specifically vertical.

This is so because in the context of biblical faith the ultimate to which one relates in the act of worship is clearly vertical, i.e., it exists outside the space-time continuum. Thus, with respect to biblical faith, i.e., to Judaism, the act of worship must indeed implicate an act of transcendence that is exclusively vertical. It is not sufficient, therefore, to say here that the act of worship necessarily implicates the act of transcendence and let it go at that—one must specify that the act of transcendence implicated here is exclusively vertical.

We should note, however, that the specific, exclusive implication of the vertical act of transcendence is not universally valid with respect to all acts of worship. For although the act of worship signifies by definition a relating to an entity that is taken as ultimate, an entity need not be vertical in order to be taken as ultimate. One can relate to a horizontal entity as the ultimate thus characterizing the relating as an act of worship and in this case one would have, of course, an act of worship that implicates an act of transcendence that is horizontal and not vertical. Thus, for example, one can relate to a nation, to a party, to a cause, to art, to money or to power as one's ultimate and we do, indeed, often characterize the relating in such circumstances as an act of worship, i.e., we say "he worships money" or "he worships power," etc. But these entities are clearly horizontal, i.e., they exist within the space-time continuum, and the relating to them is, therefore, clearly an act of transcendence that is horizontal. Thus, generally speaking, the act of worship can implicate an act of transcendence that is not only vertical but also horizontal. Still, one may argue that in allowing the notion of worship to implicate an act of transcendence that is horizontal one is really vitiating the authentic signification of the notion. For one would want to say that, strictly speaking, the notion of worship belongs to the religious domain and that in the religious domain the ultimate can be constituted only by an entity that is vertical. Thus, although in principle one can take as ultimate an entity that is horizontal, and as such make the implication of a horizontal act of transcendence by the act of worship come within the purview of the definition of worship, still, it would not be valid to suppose that the act of worship can implicate an act of transcendence that is horizontal since, strictly speaking, the category of worship belongs to the religious domain and in the religious domain an entity that is horizontal would not be taken as ultimate. The notion of worship can be taken to implicate an act of transcendence that is horizontal only when the notion is used in a derived and imprecise signification, when it is a pseudo notion of worship—when the notion signifies a relating to what is taken to be ultimate (hence its linkage with the authentic signification of the notion) but which from the religious viewpoint—which after all is the authentic, primary context where the signification of the notion is formulated—is not really an ultimate (hence its being pseudo).

But is this argument really valid? For although we may readily grant that the authentic signification of the notion of worship must be formulated in the context of the religious domain, is it further really valid to maintain that in the religious domain the only acceptable ultimate is the ultimate constituted by a pantheistic orientation as a legitimate orientation within the domain of religion (as many religionists would no doubt insist on doing). For pantheism in identifying God, i.e., the ultimate, with the world of the space-time continuum, must inescapably implicate an ultimate that is horizontal. Indeed, pantheism by definition, i.e., by its very essence, cannot implicate an ultimate that is vertical. Thus, to the extent that pantheism is a legitimate orientation within the domain of religion, one cannot make the sweeping claim that for the domain of religion as such an authentic ultimate can only be an ultimate that is vertical. But while one cannot validly make this claim with respect to the domain of religion *as a whole* one can certainly make this claim with full validity with respect to the *theistic* orientation within the domain of religion. For evidently, the theistic orientation in placing God, i.e., the ultimate, over-against the world of the space-time continuum necessarily implicates that the ultimate here must be an entity that is vertical and that consequently the relating to it can only be an act of transcendence that is specifically and exclusively vertical. Thus, it is only when the religious domain is identified exclusively with the theistic orientation that one can argue that inasmuch as the category of worship belongs authentically to the domain of religion it implicates exclusively and specifically an act of transcendence that is vertical and not horizontal.

Now, such identification with the theistic orientation, while by no means characterizing the religious domain universally, does characterize biblical faiths. Indeed, in biblical faiths this identification is not peripheral or accidental but constitutes the very essence of the structure of faith—biblical faiths are by their very essence theistic in orientation. As such, it is specifically in biblical faiths (and consequently, as regards our case, specifically in Judaism) that the act of worship necessarily implicates not only an act of transcendence but also verticality, i.e., that it necessarily implicates an act of transcendence that is specifically and exclusively vertical and not horizontal. Indeed, since the theistic orientation constitutes an essential and inextricable aspect of biblical faiths it follows that the implication of verticality by the act of worship is likewise an essential and inextricable aspect of biblical faiths.[4]

Indeed, as such, the implication of verticality can serve as the criterion by which, from the perspective of biblical faiths, the distinction between the authentic religious orientation and the merely pseudo-religious orientation can be established. For one cannot really establish the distinction on the basis that only the authentic religious orientation can provide an all-encompassing *Weltanschauung*, an all-encompassing structure of meaning, a "home" for man to dwell in. Nor can one establish the distinction on the basis that only the authentic religious orientation can implicate ultimacy and the self-transcendence of man. Pseudo-religious ideologies can do the same. Indeed, as has been pointed out, pseudo-religious ideologies (see, for example, Communism) exhibit remarkable similarity to authentic religious formulations on practically every point in the structure (hence the reference to them as "religious"). The only point where a fundamental distinction can nonetheless be validly established is with respect to the implication of verticality—pseudo-religious ideologies do not implicate verticality while the authentic religious orientation ("authentic," of course, in the sense of reflecting the theistic-biblical vantage point) must by its very essence implicate verticality (hence their qualification as *pseudo*-religious).

But even more fundamentally, the implication of verticality can serve as the criterion by which the essential distinction between the authentic religious orientation (again, when viewed from the theistic-biblical vantage point) and the orientation of secularism can be established. For as in the case of the pseudo-religious ideologies, so also here, the aspect of an all-encompassing *Weltanschauung*, of self-transcendence or of ultimacy cannot apply as the criterion of distinction. Secularism can provide these aspects just as well as the authentic religious orientation. But what secularism, in contradistinction to the authentic religious orientation, cannot provide is verticality—the ultimate which exists vertically over-against the world or the act of transcendence which is vertical rather than horizontal. Indeed, we would suggest that the very essence of the notion of secularism lies in its signifying the abrogation of any and all verticality. In the last analysis, this is what the notion really signifies. Namely, it does not signify the absence of ultimacy or the abrogation of transcendence as such (clearly, these are feasible when they are horizontal) but rather the absence of ultimacy which is specifically vertical and the abrogation of transcendence when it is, again, specifically vertical rather than horizontal.

Finally, it should be clear that this implication of verticality by the authentic religious orientation (when taken in the theistic-biblical context) must quality the argument that inasmuch as man is by his very essence constituted as a self-transcending being he is by his very essence also constituted as a *homo religiosus*. For although there is no denying that man is by his very essence constituted as a self-transcending being (seeing that by his very essence he is constituted as a conscious being and that consciousness necessarily implicates self-transcendence, inasmuch as every act of consciousness is an act of going beyond, of surpassing oneself, towards something else), this does not in any way require that the transcendence must be vertical. Indeed, the consciousness of man can express itself fully in the horizontal act of transcendence—man's inherent aspect of self-transcendence can be fully met by horizontal transcendence and does not require recourse to vertical transcendence. On the other hand, however, what constitutes (in the theistic-biblical context) *homo religiosus* is not just any act of transcendence but the act of transcendence that is specifically vertical. Horizontal transcendence would not constitute here a *homo religiosus*. Thus, it does not follow from the fact that man is by his very essence constituted as a self-transcending being that he is also by his very essence constituted (in the theistic-biblical context) as a *homo religiosus*. All that one can say (seeing that man is constituted as a self-transcending being) is that the vertical transcendence constituting *homo religiosus* here is an authentic and viable option for man, thus allowing other considerations to make the case that man ought to express his self-transcending in vertical transcendence.

We must repeat and emphasize the point, however, that delineating worship as implicating not just any act of transcendence but specifically only that act of transcendence that is vertical and the considerations that follow from this (i.e., the distinction between the authentic religious orientation, on the one hand, and the pseudo-religious and secularist orientations on the other, and the implications for the question of *homo religiosus*) are applicable only when religion is viewed from a theistic-biblical vantage point. They are not applicable when religion is viewed from a pantheistic vantage point and thus from the vantage point of most, if not all, non-biblical religions. Indeed, from the theistic-biblical vantage point the very formulation of pantheism itself (and thus of all non-biblical religions manifesting this vantage point) must be rejected as a viable expression of the authentic religious orientation; rather it must be viewed as an expression of the pseudo-religious orientation, an expression that, if not actually belonging in the last analysis to the secularist orientation, is nonetheless close and congenial to it.[5]

Of course, if what constitutes the authentic religious orientation is to be defined not from the exclusive theistic-biblical vantage point but rather from some other broader vantage point, then not only pantheism but also the various pseudo-religious orientations and, indeed, even secularism itself may become valid expressions of the authentic religious orientation (namely, the distinction between the authentically religious, the pseudo-religious and the secularist orientation in the fundamental sense proposed here falls away). We should be clear, however, that any such alternative broader vantage point would have the marked disadvantage that in its terms the delineation of the authentic religious orientation would become vague and that, indeed, it would become questionable if one can really use such a delineation in any meaningful and useful way. To paraphrase a rabbinic saying, "If you catch a lot you don't really catch anything." In any event, since our task here is to explicate the signification of the category of worship in the religious context of Judaism, a religion which is certainly a theistic-biblical religion, the theistic-biblical vantage point would clearly apply here and consequently the distinction delineated above between the authentic religious orientation on the one hand, and the pseudo-religious and secularist orientation on the other, should also apply here. But even more to our point, the signification of the category of worship, as a category operating in the authentic religious domain, should implicate here not just the act of transcendence as such but the act of transcendence that is specifically and exclusively vertical.

Saying, however, that worship necessarily signifies a relating that is vertically transcendent does not necessarily implicate the further saying that the *mode* of the relating must be exclusively *direct*, i.e., a relating initiated at a specific point in the horizontal flux of space and time moving away from such a point *perpendicularly* towards the vertically transcendent being. In other words, the mode of the relating must not be exclusively away from this concrete world—the concrete world merely serving at a certain point in its space-time continuum as a jumping-board from which one launches towards the vertically transcendent being. Of course, such a direct mode of relating is possible, and indeed manifests itself quite extensively within the religious phenomenon.[6] But it is also possible that the mode of the relating be *indirect*. Namely, while the relating is horizontal, i.e., between two points in the horizontal flux, this horizontal relating will at the same time implicate a relating to the vertically transcendent being. One relates here to the vertically transcendent being through a relating to the world, i.e., to that which is horizontally transcendent.[7] The relating here would thus proceed through the world; it would be mediated by the world. It would be, so to speak, refracted through the horizontal dimension. Still, such an indirect mode of relating would constitute authentic worship just as much as the direct mode of relating, for *ultimately* the relating here is also directed towards the vertically transcendent being and this after all is what counts. The way by which this relating is carried out, namely, whether it is direct or refracted, exclusive or involving a relating to other intermediary entities, is a secondary consideration which, inasmuch as it does not change the fact that the relating here is *ultimately* directed towards the vertically transcendent being, does not in any way undermine the relating being an authentic act of worship. Thus, the act of worship as delineated here allows either the direct or the indirect mode of relating.

We would suggest, however, that this alternative between the direct and indirect mode of relating is actually linked to the alternative between the ontological and ethical perspective in terms of which an essential structure of faith may formulate itself. (By an "essential structure of faith" we mean the formulation which impinges on (1) the perception of what is taken to constitute the ultimate predicament of man and (2) the salvation that is anticipated commensurately with the perceived predicament—these two considerations determining, in turn, all the other considerations constituting the overall structure of faith as, for example, the kind of divinity implicated, its role, the vocation of man, the cosmological setting, etc.) Namely, a case can be made that the direct mode of relating is linked to the ontological perspective while the indirect mode of relating is linked to the ethical perspective. The rationale for this is as follows: given the content and orientation of the ontological perspective (for example, that the ultimate predicament lies in the finitude of being), there is really nothing in its inner-logic that would require that the mode of relating be refracted through the horizontal dimension. The horizontal dimension, i.e., the world, has no role to play if what is at stake is the transformation of man's ontological constitution. Indeed, if anything, it would seem that such an ontological transformation can be effected only by a source transcending the horizontal dimension and consequently the inner-logic of the situation here should implicate a relating that is exclusively in the direct mode. As against this, the inner-logic of the ethical perspective clearly implicates the requirement that the relating be refracted through the horizontal dimension. For the ethical consideration can really arise only in the context of the horizontal dimension, i.e., in the context of the concrete world, seeing that it impinges upon conduct and relations which are embedded specifically within the horizontal dimension; ethics, strictly speaking, does not impinge upon conduct and relations which transcend the world. Thus, if a structure of faith is to formulate itself from the ethical perspective, namely, if the religious relation, i.e, the relation to the vertically transcendent being, is to be infused with ethical meaning, then the religious relation must be refracted through the horizontal dimension, in other words, the structure of faith must resort to the indirect mode of relating.

Indeed, the alternative between the ethical and ontological perspectives is a fundamental alternative which, in turn, implicates any number of rather significant alternatives impinging upon the category of worship. Thus, in addition to showing that it implicates the alternative between the direct and indirect relating, it can also be shown to implicate the further alternative between the individual and the collectivity when these impinge on the human role in the context of worship. Namely, it can be shown to implicate whether the human bearer of the relating expressing worship, i.e., the human pole in the man-god relation, is to be constituted by the individual person or by a collectivity of persons, whether worship is primarily an affair of the individual or of the collectivity. For clearly the ontological perspective would implicate the individual and not the collectivity, seeing that the relating here is ultimately for the sake of an ontological transformation and that such a transformation can be effected only in terms of the individual and not of the collectivity (the notion of collectivity can enter the picture here only secondarily as that which signifies the sum total of individuals seeking or being granted such an ontological transformation).[8]

As against this, the ethical perspective implicates the collectivity rather than the individual. For the ethical impinges not on the aspect of man's constitution but rather on the aspect of his conduct and action. It thus implicates man in relation to an other rather than man in his monadic individuality and the context of man in relation to an other constitutes already a collectivity, albeit not necessarily an exclusively human collectivity (for the "other" need not be here exclusively man—it can be any entity of nature). Still, we would argue that in the case before us the collectivity that is implicated must indeed be a human collectivity, i.e., that the "other" in the relating must be specifically one's fellow-man. For we are not dealing here with the ethical perspective as an independent philosophical perspective grounded in its own terms but rather we are dealing with the ethical perspective as it is grounded in the biblical religious domain. This means, however, that we cannot be dealing here with an ethical perspective that bases itself on egocentric criteria, thus expressing itself, for example, in such formulations as the utilitarian or eudemonistic formulation; we must be dealing with an ethical perspective that bases itself on the criteria of accountability and responsibility to an other. But as such this, in turn, means that it must be an ethical perspective in which the 'other' in the relating is specifically also man, i.e., an ethical perspective in which the ethical concern impinges specifically on the relating of man to his fellow-man. For only a conscious, personal being can exact accountability and responsibility for the action directed towards it and among all the beings of nature only man is a conscious, personal being. Thus, the ethical perspective that is before us here implicates a relating that is specifically a relating between man and his fellow-man, thus implicating a human collectivity (the individual enters the picture here only secondarily and then only by virtue of his membership in the collectivity). Needless to say, this collectivity being a collectivity of men (of men who are not only conscious spirits but also flesh and blood), it is inescapably a this-worldly collectivity. Furthermore, if the ethical perspective is to express itself fully, i.e., if it is to impinge upon the whole gamut of relations that can arise between man and his fellow-man—impinge upon relations belonging to the social, the economic and the political domains of life—the collectivity which it implicates must be the ethnic-national collectivity. For only in the ethnic-national collectivity can all these relationships between man and his fellow-man be encompassed. In any other collectivity, be it sub-national or extra-national (as, for example, the family, the clan, or any professional, ideological, spiritual or political association), only some of these relations, but never all of them, can be encompassed. The ethnic-national collectivity thus becomes a central and primary category in the structure of faith that formulates itself from the ethical perspective. It is transformed by the ethical perspective from being essentially a category of history into being a fundamental religious category—the category which provides the matrix through which the indirect relating to the divine can express itself.

Even more significantly, perhaps, the alternative between the ethical and the ontological perspectives implicates the further alternative impinging on whether the vertically transcendent being, i.e., the category of the divine, involved in the structure of faith is to be constituted as a Thou or as an It. Namely, we would suggest that the ethical perspective (being here specifically an ethical perspective that bases itself on the criteria of accountability and responsibility) would necessarily implicate that the vertically transcendent being involved in the structure of faith be constituted as a Thou (i.e., a conscious, personal being) and not as an It (i.e., an impersonal being of Power devoid of consciousness). For inasmuch as the relating here is subject to accountability, and seeing that although it be refracted through the horizontal dimension it is nonetheless directed ultimately towards the vertically transcendent being, the relating must implicate that the vertically transcendent being be constituted as a Thou. For as we have argued above, only a being constituted as a Thou can exact accountability and responsibility for the action, i.e., the relating, directed towards it. A being constituted as an It cannot do it and consequently a relating subject to accountability cannot arise with respect to it. But that the relating be subject to accountability is the very mainstay of the ethical perspective. Thus, an ethical perspective and a vertically transcendent being that is constituted as an It are mutually exclusive; an ethical perspective must implicate that the vertically transcendent being be constituted as a Thou.

As against this, the otological perspective need by no means implicate the exclusion of a vertically transcendent being that is constituted as an It. Indeed, a case can be made that while, strictly speaking, the inner logic of the ontological formulation can encompass a vertically transcendent being that is constituted either as a Thou or as an It, its tendency would be to implicate, in the last analysis, a vertically transcendent being that is constituted as an It. For the tendency here would be to place the category of being, the category in terms of which the predicament is perceived, in the sphere of Power (i.e., perceiving being as the manifestation or expression of Power). Thus, for example, if the predicament in the ontological formulation is ultimately perceived in terms of the *finitude* of being (as we would want to argue is generally the case), then the category of being is indeed taken here in terms of the sphere of Power as can readily be seen by the mere fact of its quantification. But if the predicament is perceived in the context of the sphere of power, then commensurate to it the envisioned salvation will be formulated likewise in the context of the sphere of Power and consequently the vertically transcendent being will be constituted as an It.[9] Thus, in the context of the ontological perspective (and in clear contradistinction to that of the ethical perspective) not only can the implicated vertically transcendent being be constituted as an It but it is very likely to be so constituted.

Now, this alternative between the Thouness and Itness of the vertically transcendent being impinges, in turn, on a most significant aspect in the delineation of the category of worship. Namely, it impinges upon the *kind* of worship, i.e., the *kind* of relating, that is made feasible. For clearly, the only authentic relation that is feasible with respect to a Thou is the relation of address—the affirmation of the other in its otherness. As against this, with respect to an It the only feasible relation is the relation of utilization—either a theoretical utilization which is then tantamount to orientation (i.e., to the "capturing" or the "fixing" of the other in description), or a practical utilization which is then tantamount to manipulation (i.e., to the handling of the other for one's interests). But this, in turn, would clearly implicate the following: (1) that with respect to a vertically transcendent being constituted as a Thou the relating, if it is to be authentic, must be circumscribed to expressing itself either as prayer (when the relating is directly vertical) or as ethical conduct (when the relating is indirect, i.e., refracted through the horizontal dimension), seeing that the only viable authentic expressions for a relating that is constituted as an address are prayer and ethical conduct; (2) that conversely, neither prayer nor ethical conduct could be feasible expressions for a relating directed towards a vertically transcendent being that is constituted as an It, seeing that both prayer and ethical conduct are inextricably expressions of address and that it would simply not make sense to address an It; (3) that, on the other hand, with respect to a vertically transcendent being constituted as an It, the relating, if it is to be feasible, will have to be circumscribed to expressing itself either as divination (when the relating is theoretical) or as magic (when the relating is practical) inasmuch as it is these expressions which constitute respectively orientation (albeit with respect to the future) and manipulation; (4) that these expressions of divination and magic are, in turn, not feasible with respect to a vertically transcendent being constituted as a Thou. Thus, whether the vertically transcendent being is constituted as an It or as a Thou would clearly determine the *kind* of worship that is feasible—magic and divination in the case of the former, prayer and ethical conduct in the case of the latter.

Finally, there are two further sets of alternative characterizations involved in this context and they require some clarification. First, we have the alternative between the relating constituting worship being carried out verbally and it being alternative, i.e., in terms of the literal signification of its notions (when "verbal" is to signify the mere emitting of sounds and "action" is to signify soundless bodily movements), the alternative is clearly peripheral and not very significant. For, as such, it is an alternative that impinges merely on the outward means of expressing the relating rather than on its very content and signification. Furthermore, it is not really relevant to the further elucidation of the options impinging upon the category of worship in connection with the basic alternative characterizing it, i.e., the alternative between the Itness and Thouness of the vertically transcendent being. For one cannot establish here any exclusive correspondence between the action or verbal expression of the relating, on the one hand, and the Itness or Thouness of the vertically transcendent being, on the other hand. Thus, a verbal relating can clearly be linked with a vertically transcendent being that is a Thou; but it can also be linked with a vertically transcendent being that is an It as, for example, in the case of verbal magic. Conversely, a relating expressing itself in action can certainly be linked with a vertically transcendent being that is an It; but it can also be linked with a vertically transcendent being that is a Thou as, for example, in the case of ethical conduct.

This alternative can become, however, much more significant if we expand its signification, namely, if we take "verbal" to signify not merely the emitting of sound but actual speech and "action" to signify not just bodily movements but the impingement of brute force devoid of intention on an other. For clearly, in terms of these expanded significations the alternative would not impinge on the very content of the relating. Furthermore, one would not be able to establish an exclusive correspondence between a relating that is verbal and the vertically transcendent being that is a Thou, on the one hand, and between a relating that is action and the vertically transcendent being that is an It, on the other hand, seeing that actual, authentic speech can be directed only to a being that is a Thou and that brute force devoid of intention can impinge only upon a being that is an It. As such, it would appear that with this expanded signification we do have here, after all, a *bona fide* additional alternative impinging on the category of worship in conjunction with the basic alternative between the Itness and Thouness of the vertically transcendent being. A moment's reflection will show, however, that in terms of this expanded signification the alternative here is really reduced, for all intents and purposes, to an alternative which was already delineated above, i.e., to the alternative between address and manipulation. For in saying that "verbal" signifies speech we are really saying that in essence it signifies address, and likewise in saying that "action" signifies the impingement of force we are really saying that in essence it signifies manipulation (by the way, in terms of these significations verbal magic would, of course, have to be taken as a relating that is action while ethical conduct would have to be taken as a relating that is verbal). Thus, there is nothing new here except for the terminology. We must conclude, therefore, that the alternative between verbal and action is not too significant—it is either peripheral or it is a restatement, in a different terminology, of another more essential alternative, the alternative between address and manipulation.

Secondly, and lastly, we have the alternative between intention and precision. This alternative is actually implicated by the foregoing alternative, i.e., the alternative between verbal and action, in its expanded signification, thus, when it actually signifies the alternative between address and manipulation. For clearly, a relating that is an address would implicate that the efficacy of the relating be determined exclusively by its intention while a relating that is manipulative would implicate that the efficacy of the relating be determined exclusively by its precision. The very constitution of an address, it being an act of affirmation (the affirmation of an other), lies in its intention. There can be no affirmation without the intention to affirm—the act of affirmation is an act of intention. On the other hand, in manipulation intention counts for naught. The results here depend exclusively on how the action is executed—to secure the desired results the commensurate action must be executed with perfect precision. This, and this alone, provides its success. This rationale is further buttressed by the consideration that an address is a relating that is linked exclusively to a Thou while manipulation is a relating that is linked exclusively to an It and clearly with respect to a Thou it is intention which exclusively determines the efficacy of the relating while with respect to an It it is exclusively precision. Thus, this alternative fits very neatly into the array of alternatives delineated above. Indeed, whether a relating is "verbal" or "action" (in the expanded signification of the terms) and consequently whether it is a relating to a Thou or to an It can be established by whether its efficacy is determined by intention or by precision. Thus again, for example, verbal magic can now be determined as a relating that is action, i.e., manipulation, by the additional consideration that the efficacy of its relating lies in its precision, and conversely ethical conduct can now be determined as a relating that is verbal, i.e., address, by the additional consideration that the efficacy of its relating lies in its intention.[10] Furthermore, this alternative, unlike the former alternative between verbal and action, is a legitimately new alternative which cannot be reduced to any of the alternatives delineated above. For it impinges on the category of worship from a new angle—it does not impinge on the content, the mode or the object of the relating but rather on the criterion that determines the efficacy of the relating. Still, as we have seen, it is very consistent with these other alternatives even though they impinge on quite different aspects of the relating.

In view of the analysis presented here, therefore, one would have to conclude that the signification of the category of worship (once its basic signification as a relating to a vertically transcendent being is established) is clearly bifurcated—the array of alternatives delineated above could arise only on the basis of such a bifurcation. Thus, we actually have two distinct and quite different expressions of the category of worship depending on whether the category constitutes itself in the context of a structure of faith that formulates itself from the ethical perspective or in the context of a structure of faith that formulates itself from the ontological perspective or, to put the matter more conclusively, depending on whether the category constitutes itself in the Thou-sphere or in the It-sphere.

II

With the help of the above analysis we can now proceed to examine how the category of worship functions in the context of Judaism. The first thing to note is that in the context of Judaism, when it is taken in its all-inclusive entirety, one may encounter both alternative expressions of the category of worship. This should not really be surprising. For Judaism in its concrete, historical manifestation (as, indeed, the other biblical faiths when taken in their concrete, historical manifestations) is by no means monolithic with respect to its structure of faith. Actually, in its concrete, historical manifestation one can encounter a mixture of structures of faith; specifically, one can encounter both the structure of faith which is grounded in the Thou-sphere and the structure of faith which is grounded in the It-sphere. In view of this and in view of the fact, as we have seen above, that the category of worship is determined by the structure of faith, it should not be surprising to find that corresponding to the manifestation of the two basic structures of faith (the one grounded in the Thou-sphere and the other in the It-sphere) the two alternative expressions of the category of worship are also manifested.

Thus, for example, the expression of the category of worship which formulates itself in the It-sphere can clearly be encountered in the sacrificial cult as presented in Hebrew Scriptures. For in the sacrificial cult, irrespective of which of the various interpretations may be given to it (be it that it signifies the "feeding" of the divine on a *quid pro quo* basis or be it the reverse, that is signifies the "eating" of the divine which is present in the sacrificial animal), one inescapably encounters a relating that is directly vertical, a relating that is constituted as manipulation (specifically, the utilization of the divine) and whose efficacy lies in its precision rather than in its intention. In the last analysis, the relating here is by its very essence constituted as a transaction of power and as such it inevitably implicates a vertically transcendent being that is an It and a signification that is ontological rather than ethical—its intention is to increase the power, and thus to strengthen and fortify the being of the sacrificer. Similarly, this expression, i.e., the expression formulating itself in the It-sphere, can also be encountered in the act of prayer and the observance of the commandments when these are taken in terms of the signification accorded to them in the context of Jewish mysticism. For in this context these acts are constituted as means for the mystic's ascent towards union with the divine or, alternatively, they are constituted as means for the mystic's endeavor to unify anew the being of the divine. In either case these acts are constituted here as a "technique" and thus as signifying manipulation rather than address. Indeed, they clearly implicate for the structure of faith in which they operate an ontological rather than an ethical perspective—they clearly impinge ontological transformations in the constitution of the mystic or of the divine rather than on their ethical conduct—and as such they implicate a vertically transcendent being which is, in the last analysis, an It rather than a Thou. Thus, although the act of prayer and the observance of the commandments would generally be taken (and rightly so) as articulating the category of worship that formulates itself in the Thou-sphere, when these acts are taken now in the context of mysticism, i.e., when the signification of these acts is provided by the context of mysticism, the acts clearly articulate the category of worship that formulates itself in the It-domain.

But while we can encounter in Judaism the manifestation of the category of worship that formulates itself in the It-domain, it must be admitted that we can encounter this formulation of the category of worship only in these strands of the phenomenon which do not constitute the mainstream expression or, even more significantly, the distinctive expression of Judaism. For the category of worship that formulates itself in the It-domain can be encountered in the main only in the "priestly" strand of Hebrew Scriptures and in the mystical strand of Rabbinic Judaism and while these strands are certainly part and parcel of the all-encompassing phenomenon of Judaism they certainly do not constitute the distinctive or, for that matter, the mainstream expressions of the phenomenon.

Indeed the structure of faith that formulates itself in the It-domain, i.e., the structure of faith that formulates itself from the ontological perspective and which implicates a vertically transcendent being that is constituted as an It, is quite universal and consequently expressions similar to the "priestly" and mystical strands in the phenomenon of Judaism can be encountered in most other religions. To locate the distinctive expression of Judaism one must turn to the "Prophetic" strand in Hebrew Scriptures and to the non-mystical *halachic* strand in Rabbinic Judaism. For the underlying structure of faith in these strands is one that formulates itself in the Thou-domain, i.e., it is a structure of faith which formulates itself from the ethical perspective and which implicates a vertically transcendent being that is constituted as a Thou, and such a structure of faith is, indeed, distinctive to Judaism (or, more precisely, to biblical faiths) seeing that it is not generally encountered in other religions. But as such, we should, of course, expect to encounter here the category of worship that formulates itself in the Thou-domain, namely, the category of worship which implicates a relating to a vertically transcendent being that is constituted as a Thou rather than as an It, which delineates the relating as address rather than as manipulation, and where the signification of the relating is ethical rather than onto-logical. This, indeed, is the case. To fully appreciate this, however, we must keep in mind what our analysis above has established, namely, that while the direct mode of relating will, of course, be present here (and given the nature of the relating it will have to be delineated *qua* address), the burden of the relating, in view of its signification being ethical, will tend towards the indirect mode. Only as such, can we come to understand how the category of worship really functions in these distinctive strands of Judaism. Failing to keep this in mind and, therefore, looking only for the direct mode of relating is bound to leave us with an unsatisfactory and, indeed, warped picture of the way the category functions in these strands. For while the direct mode in the form of prayer *qua* address is certainly present in these strands, its presence is not as central and important as one should expect nor is its structure (specifically in the *halachic* strand) quite commensurate with its signification as address. Indeed, if the category of worship in these strands were to consists only of prayer *qua* address, one would be left with a rather perplexing situation—the category which constitutes the very heart and essence of the religious phenomenon functioning in a rather peripheral way and in a manner which does not quite correspond to its signification.

Let us attempt to briefly explicate this contention. To start with the "prophetic" strand, there is no denying that prayer *qua* address can be encountered in this strand —the prophets, though not all of them, certainly pray and some of the most striking and powerful instances of prayer are to be found in this literature.[11] Still, the fact remains that the amount of prayer found in the prophets is quite meager. Moreover, it is quite clear that, strictly speaking, prayer is not part of the prophetic vocation; if anything, it is a clear interruption of it. Indeed, most pertinently, if prayer were to be completely extirpated from prophetic literature, that literature would hardly be affected. Thus, prayer can hardly be taken as the central expression of prophecy. While prayer when it occurs in prophesy is indeed authentic prayer, i.e., it is prayer *qua* address, it actually occurs only to a small extent and rather peripherally.

Moving to the non-mystical *halachic* strand, one must likewise readily admit that prayer can be encountered also here. Indeed, prayer manifests itself here to a con-siderably larger extent and in a way that is much more central and significant than is the case in prophecy. Even more telling, it is accorded an established status as an expression for the human-divine relating. Still, even so, the status and role of prayer here are by no means what we should expect if prayer *qua* authentic address were indeed *the* central expression of the category of worship, i.e., *the* central expression of the relating of man to the divine. For first, it must be noted that this established status is, strictly speaking, accorded to prayer only on a provisional basis. Namely, prayer is accorded this established status only because it comes to take the place of the sacrificial cult when the sacrificial cult becomes inoperative upon the destruction of the Temple and it is to retain this established status only for the duration, i.e., only as long as the sacrificial cult cannot be reinstituted. Thus, "officially" speaking, prayer is not the permanent, let alone the inherent expression for the relating—the sacrificial cult is. Prayer is merely a substitute and, in principle, a provisional substitute at that. This is hardly an impressive status. Now, to accord prayer this status, i.e., the status of being merely a provisional substitute, must clearly indicate that it is not viewed as a fundamental expression—it is hardly the status one would expect for the central expression of the category of worship.

Of course, one can argue that this unsatisfactory state of affairs as regards the status accorded to prayer is brought about only because of the legalistic mode of thought characterizing the *halachic* strand, but that from the phenomenological vantage point, i.e., from the vantage point of the structure of faith characterizing the strand, the expression of prayer is really permanent and inherent to the *halachic* strand and that, therefore, its status is in reality also much more substantial and significant to the strand. Namely, legalistically speaking the *halachic* strand cannot indeed accord prayer any other status than that of provisional substitute, seeing that in the legalistic context of the *halacha* the Pentateuchal Law is taken as the sole all-encompassing record of revelation, thus as the only authoritative and binding source of its prescriptions, and that the Pentateuchal Law nowhere prescribes prayer. Specifically, its prescription for the direct mode of relating to the divine (the relating which prayer could appropriately express) is that it be expressed exclusively through the sacrificial cult. The expression of prayer is in no way grounded in revelation and consequently, given the legalistic orientation of the *halacha*, it can in principle have no status in its own right. Indeed, its very institution was made feasible only through a rabbinic decree and then only when, upon the destruction of the Temple, the sacrificial cult became inoperative, thus creating a lacuna in the expression of the direct mode of relating which required that it be filled in. This being the case, it is clear that from the legalistic vantage point the status of prayer could not be otherwise than that of provisional substitute, i.e., a substitute only for the duration in which the sacrificial cult remains inoperative.

However, when one proceeds to view the matter not from the legalistic vantage point but from the phenomenological vantage point, i.e., from the vantage point of the requirements of the structure of faith characterizing the strand, a quite different assessment of the status of prayer and of the sacrificial cult emerges. For from this vantage point it becomes quite clear that the only authentic mode of expression in the *halachic* strand for the direct mode of relating is prayer and that the sacrificial cult, its prescription in the Pentateuchal Law notwithstanding, is quite untenable as a mode of expression. After all, as we have seen, the *halachic* strand formulates itself from the perspective of the Thou-dimension and as such it requires that all its expressions be similarly articulated in terms of the Thou-dimension, seeing that it is simply not tenable for an expression articulating itself in terms of the It-dimension to operate authentically and validly in the context of a structure of faith that formulates itself from the perspective of the Thou-dimension (and vice-versa). This being the case, it is clear that prayer, inasmuch as it articulates itself in terms of the Thou-dimension, constitutes an authentic expression for the *halachic* strand; the sacrificial cult, on the other hand, being clearly an expression that articulates itself in terms of the It-dimension, is fundamentally an incommensurate expression for the *halachic* strand. Indeed, the legalistic orientation in attributing the expression of the sacrificial cult to the *halachic* strand was in effect placing an untenable strain upon the *halachic* that could not have been maintained for any appreciable duration. By the way, one may well surmise that with respect to this issue (though not, of course, with respect to other issues), the destruction of the Temple causing the sacrificial cult to become inoperative was rather fortuitous as it provided a ready and convenient way out of the dilemma and that had the Temple not been destroyed the *halachic* strand would have found or devised another rationale to make the sacrificial cult inoperative; by the same token one may well conjure that the *halachic* strand would see to it that the conditions prerequisite for the reinstitution of the sacrificial cult would never be satisfied. Thus, when viewed from a phenomenological rather than from a legalistic vantage point prayer in the *halachi* tradition is far from being a substitute and it is hardly provisional. Its status as a provisional substitute is merely a formal matter necessitated by legalistic considerations; in reality it is inherent within the strand as one of its authentic expressions and is indeed instituted, for all intents and purposes, as a permanent expression.

Still, even so, granting the validity of these observations, the fact remains that the *halachic* strand could acquiesce in the fact that it attributed to prayer, albeit merely in a formal way, the status of being a mere provisional substitute, indeed, that it accommodated itself to such an evaluation and did not feel compelled to change it. This certainly indicates that the *role* which prayer plays within the *halachic* strand is not essential or central. For if prayer were not only an authentic expression for the *halachic* strand but actually constituted its essential and central expression, one would have had every right to expect that the strand would not have acquiesced in attributing to it the status of being a mere provisional substitute and a way would have been found to change it, the legalistic considerations notwithstanding. Surely, an essential and central expression cannot be characterized by the status of being a mere provisional substitute. Furthermore, it is significant to note that the Pentateuchal

Law does not prescribe any other expression for the direct mode of relating aside from the sacrificial cult. For this means, of course, that it is only the "priestly" strand in the Law, i.e., the strand formulating itself from the perspective of the Thou-dimension, is unconcerned with the question of the direct mode of relating. Now, this observation is most telling, for it clearly suggests that the direct mode of relating is not an essential and central mode of relating for the "prophetic" strand. Indeed, had it been an essential and central mode, the "prophetic" strand would have surely been constrained to address itself to it. Thus, it would seem to us that the fact that the "prophetic" strand in the Pentateuchal Law can ignore prescribing an expression for the direct mode of relating and that the *halachic* strand can acquiesce, albeit merely on the formal-legal level, in the status of prayer being merely that of a provisional substitute, clearly indicates that in these strands prayer does not constitute the essential and central expression of the relating to the divine.

But even more problematic than the fact that the *halachic* strand accords prayer the status of a mere provisional substitute are some of the features which the *halachic* strand imposes on prayer. Thus, the *halachic* strand fixes set times for the recitation of prayer. Furthermore, it fixes the content of prayer, i.e., it predetermines from the outside what is to be recited on what occasion. Lastly, it formulates the content of prayer in terms of the collectivity rather than of the individual, i.e., it is in terms of the "we," the people Israel, rather than in terms of the "I," the individual person, that the content of prayer is formulated. Clearly, these features are very problematic for authentic prayer, i.e., if prayer is to be taken as an act of address. For prayer *qua* address must be spontaneous, an affair of the heart, seeing that it is constituted by its intention and not by the form of its outward expression. It must be the articulation, in whatever outward form, of the intention of a specific, particular moment. As such, it cannot be the act of a collectivity but only of the individual person (the very notion of collectivity can enter the picture here only secondarily and in the abstract as a designation for a summation of praying individuals). Nor can appointed times or content be determined for it in advance or from the outside, i.e., by others. Indeed, the very notion of its prescription or recitation is already a corruption of its authenticity *qua* address. Thus, the fact that in the *halachic* strand prayer is delineated in terms of these features must raise serious questions as to its authenticity, namely, whether prayer is really constituted here as an address.

No doubt the imposition by the *halachic* strand of these features upon prayer is in part due to the fact that, as we have seen, prayer is introduced here as a substitute for the sacrificial cult. For after all it would be quite understandable if one were to transfer to the substitute features which characterized the entity that it has supplanted. This means, of course, that in our case it should be quite understandable if prayer, having been instituted as a substitute for the sacrificial cult, were also to be characterized, as a result of this substitution, by features which really belong legitimately to the sacrificial cult. Indeed, we can readily see that with respect to the sacrificial cult such features as collectivity, pre-determined content, appointed times (and, indeed, also appointed places) are quite feasible and legitimate, seeing that the sacrificial cult expresses itself in terms of the It-dimension and that in this context the relating is constituted as a transaction in Power and not as an address. Certainly, with respect to the imposition of appointed times upon prayer, we know that the rabbis consciously and explicitly imposed them to parallel the schedule of appointed times set for the sacrificial cult in the Temple (e.g., the morning and afternoon sacrifice on weekdays and the twofold morning sacrifice on the Sabbath and holidays). But even more fundamentally, perhaps, the imposition of these features is also due to the fact that prayer is institutionalized in the *halachic* strand (as, indeed, it would be in any other concrete expression of religion). For institutionalization certainly implicates uniformity and consequently specification as regards the contents and time of prayer. Namely, in an institutionalized context one would clearly need to have determined when one ought to pray and what one ought to pray.[12] But be this as it may, there is no escaping the fact that the imposition of these features does compromise the authenticity of prayer, i.e., it does compromise prayer *qua* address.

Indeed, it would seem that the rabbis who fashioned the *halachic* strand were aware of this contradiction which arises between the imposition of these features and the requirements of prayer *qua* address and that they tried as best they could to mitigate it. For while arrogating prayer to the collectivity, i.e., formulating it in terms of the "we" rather than the "I," they nonetheless provide an occasion within the set structure of the prayer for the individual, if he is so moved, to express himself spontaneously (they provide a place for a "prayer of the heart"); similarly, while determining in advance and from the outside the contents of prayer they nonetheless keep emphasizing the importance of injecting *Kavanah*, i.e., proper intention, into the set words of prayer.

This clearly shows that the rabbis were aware of the requirements of authentic prayer and that, indeed, they tried to satisfy them. Still, these attempts do not really change, in the last analysis, the situation. For the provision of an opportunity for spontaneous prayer by the individual does not change the fact that the overwhelming bulk of prayer is determined in advance from the outside and is arrogated to the collectivity (and, indeed, this provision is rarely availed of in the ethos of the *halachic* strand). And even more significantly, the emphasis on *Kavanah* does not change the fact that *Kavanah* does not really influence the criterion which determines the efficacy and validity of prayer. Indeed, the signification of the emphasis on *Kavanah* is to be located only in the context of idealism and perfection. Namely, it expresses an ideal desideratum—ideally speaking, prayer should be infused with *Kavanah*. Thus, it is not that *Kavanah* must be an inextricable factor in the very constitution of prayer as such; only that, ideally speaking, prayer, being as such already constituted, be in addition infused with *Kavanah*. It is precisely in this qualification of "ideally speaking" that the rub lies. Indeed, the fact is that even if

Kavanah is not forthcoming it is still incumbent upon the Jew to recite the set prayers at their appointed times; it is incumbent upon him, so to speak, to go through the motions and perform that which has been prescribed. Moreover, in the last analysis it is precisely this performance which counts. What counts is the execution of the prescription as it is prescribed. Namely, what counts is conformity in action rather than *Kavanah*. Here lies the real crux of the problem. For as such, from the viewpoint of authentic prayer, i.e., from the viewpoint of prayer as address, the act of prayer is inevitably compromised.[13]

It would appear, therefore, that although authentic prayer, i.e., prayer *qua* address, certainly manifests itself both in the "prophetic" and in the *halachic* strands (the strands which constitute the distinctive and main expression of the phenomenon of Judaism), its manifestation is far from adequate if it is to be the main expression by which the relating to the divine in these strands is delineated. For the category of the relating to the divine is the essential and crucial category in the constitution of any structure of faith and consequently its authentic expression must be prominent, central and unambiguous. But while prayer *qua* address is, indeed, an authentic expression for delineating the relating to the divine in the "prophetic" and *halachic* strands (seeing that these strands formulate themselves in the Thou-domain) it is far from occupying in these strands the central, unambiguous and prominent position that is called for. For as we have seen, it is decidedly peripheral in the "prophetic" strand while in the *halachic* strand its constitution *qua* address is rather ambiguous and its position is far from being central or prominent. Thus, if the relating to the divine in these strands were to be delineated exclusively or even primarily by prayer, a most unsatisfactory situation would exist. For it would mean that in the distinctive strands of Judaism the most essential category in the structure of faith, i.e., the category of relating to the divine, would be inadequately expressed. If this were really so, it would be a most puzzling and, indeed, a most untenable state of affairs.

It is at this point, however, that our analysis of the category of worship presented above can come to the rescue and prove most helpful. For this analysis has shown that in structures of faith which formulate themselves from the ethical (rather than the ontological) perspective the relating to the divine need not be exclusively a *direct* vertical mode of relating; it can also be an *indirect* vertical mode of relating, i.e., a relating that passes through the horizontal. Indeed, as we have seen, this latter mode of relating is not only possible here but it actually constitutes the main and essential mode of the relating. It follows from this, therefore, that in structures of faith which formulate themselves from the ethical perspective prayer as a delineation of the direct vertical mode of relating need not be the only expression of the relating to the divine—the relating to the divine can find its expression (indeed, it can find its main expression) in a delineation of the indirect vertical mode of relating. Thus, in the "prophetic" and *halachic* strands, seeing that these strands manifest structures of faith which formulate themselves from the ethical perspective, the relating to the divine needs by no means be exclusively expressed by the direct vertical mode of relating. It can be expressed (and, indeed, it is most likely to be expressed) by the indirect vertical mode of relating. Consequently, the fact that prayer *qua* address (it being the direct vertical mode of relating) is peripheral or compromised in these strands is not so serious in its implications as suggested above. For it does not necessarily mean that the relating to the divine, i.e., that the category of worship as such, is devoid of proper expression here (this would have been indeed untenable). It only means that we have to look for it here in the indirect vertical mode of relating which expresses itself, as we have seen above, in the ethical act and concern. In short, our analysis of the category of worship presented above allows us to realize that in the "prophetic" and *halachic* strands we must not look at prayer as the exclusive delineation for the relating to the divine; rather we must see that ethical concern and the ethical act can just as well delineate the relating to the divine and, therefore, constitute the expression for the category of worship in these strands.

But if this be the case, namely, if in the "prophetic" and *halachic* strands (they being strands that formulate themselves from the ethical perspective) the relating to the divine can express itself in the indirect vertical mode of relating, i.e., in ethical concern and the ethical act, then it can be shown that the relating to the divine, i.e., the category of worship, is after all properly and adequately expressed in these strands. For there is no denying that the burden of biblical prophecy lies in its critique of the social, economic and political policies pursued by the community, thus manifesting a deep and all-evasive ethical concern. Indeed, this ethical concern constitutes the very essence of biblical prophecy—take it away and biblical prophecy remains an empty shell. Similarly, there is no denying that the burden of the *halachic* strands lies in its legal formulation, i.e., in the *halacha*. The *halacha* is its central and all-encompassing expression and the *halacha* in its essential and distinctive trust clearly manifests ethical concern. Of course, the *halacha* covers every aspect of life including the ritualistic aspect and one would certainly not want to claim ethical concern for the ritual legislation. But then a good case can be made that the ritual legislation does not constitute the essential and distinctive thrust of the *halacha*; rather it is the civil, political and criminal legislation which constitutes it.[14] Thus, inasmuch as we are talking here of the essential and distinctive thrust of the *halacha*, we are perforce dealing with its civil, political and criminal legislation (and not with its ritual legislation) and this legislation clearly constitutes itself as an organon which impinges upon the relations between man and fellow-man, which means that it clearly carries ethical signification. Indeed, in the last analysis, it is but the formal, concrete expression of the ethical concern. It is but the crystallization of the ethical concern, i.e., the concern to establish righteous relations between man and man, in universal and objective legal maxims. It is but the concretization of the ethical concern in ethical acts that are delineated *a priori* and universally in prescriptive laws.[15] Thus in both the biblical "prophetic" strand and in the rabbinic *halachic* strand the category of worship is in fact fully and centrally operative (as, indeed, it should be with respect to such an essential category) if we only look for its expression not in the direct vertical mode but in the indirect vertical mode of the relating.[16] In the biblical "prophetic" strand it expresses itself essentially in the social, economic and political critique raised by prophecy while in the rabbinic *halachic* strand it expresses itself essentially in the civil, political and criminal legislation of the *halacha*.

Indeed, so pervasive and all-encompassing is the thrust of the indirect vertical mode of relating in the *halachic* strand that it actually encompasses even the act of prayer. Namely, we would suggest that prayer is not to be viewed here primarily as an expression of the *direct* vertical mode of relating, an independent expression paralleling and supplementing the expression of the *indirect* vertical mode of relating represented by the *halacha*. Rather, it is to be viewed as part and parcel of the *halacha* and thus as an expression of the *indirect* vertical mode of relating. For the *halachic* strand reduces prayer into the structure of the *halacha*—it constitutes prayer as one of the prescriptions of the *halacha*. As such, prayer becomes one of the ways in which the *halacha* expresses itself and since the *halacha* constitutes itself essentially as an institutionalized expression of the indirect vertical mode of relating, this means that prayer becomes here one of the ways in which the indirect vertical mode of relating expresses itself when operating in an institutionalized context. Of course, if this be the case, then clearly the validity and efficacy of the act of prayer are not to be judged by the criterion of the direct vertical mode of relating, namely, by whether or not the act of prayer actually constitutes an inward act of direct vertical address. Rather they must be judged now by the criterion of the *halacha*, namely, by the criterion of the indirect vertical mode of relating that is institutionalized. Thus, the determining criterion becomes now (as it does indeed, with respect to all other *mitzvot*, i.e., to all other commandments prescribed by the *halacha*) whether or not the act is executed precisely in conformity with the prescription of the *halacha*. Its validity and efficacy lie in the fact that one is fulfilling a *mitzvah*, a commandment, rather than in the fact that one is directly addressing the divine.[17]

Indeed, in view of this consideration there should be now no problems with the way the act of prayer is delineated in the *halachic* strand, namely, the problems encountered above in connection with the *a priori* and universal determination of the content and timing of prayer, with its collective characterization, with the fact that it lacks a distinctively fundamental status within the ethos of the community, with the fact that its outward performance rather than inward intention constitutes the determining criterion for its efficacy and validity—all these problems can now be set aside. For these problems arose only because we have applied to prayer the criterion of the *direct* vertical mode of relating. But if prayer is constituted as a precept of the *halacha* and if, therefore, the criterion that must be applied is not the criterion of the direct vertical mode but the criterion of the *indirect* vertical mode of relating, then the delineation of the act of prayer in the *halachic* strand would no longer be problematic. Indeed, far from being problematic such delineation is actually called for if prayer is constituted as a precept of the *halacha.*

Thus clearly, an *a priori* and universal determination of the content and timing of prayer is made feasible by the fact that now as a *halachic* precept prayer is constituted as an expression of the indirect vertical mode of relating. For while such an *a priori* and universal determination in the context of a direct vertical mode of relating certainly throws into question the authenticity of an expression that formulates itself in terms of the Thou-dimension (as we have seen with respect to prayer when constituted as a direct vertical address), in the context of an indirect vertical mode of relating the authenticity of the expression can be preserved, albeit not in its most ideal form (as was also the case with respect to ethical action). Furthermore we can see that such an *a priori* and universal delineation is actually called for by the fact that the *halacha* implicates institutionalization and that institutionalization must delineate its expressions in an *a priori* and universal way. Prayer, therefore, when constituted as a precept of the *halacha*, would indeed require that it be delineated in an *a priori* and universal way. Only as such can it be fulfilled as a precept, i.e., executed in accordance with the *halacha.* For clearly, in order for the community to act in conformity with the *halacha* its dictates must be spelled out in advance in the greatest detail and made equally incumbent upon any and every member of the community. Indeed, the very thrust of the *halacha* is precisely to provide in advance such detailed determination that is universally applicable for all its precepts, and prayer as one of these precepts cannot be an exception. Certainly, at the very least, it would have to be determined in advance as to what and when one is to pray, making such determination applicable to any and every person, in other words, at the very least its content and timing would have to be determined in an *a priori* and universal way.

By the same token, it should be clear that the constitution of prayer as an act of the collectivity rather than of the individual i.e., that it is the collective "we" rather than the individual "I" that is the entity that prays, is similarly made feasible by the fact that as a *halachic* precept prayer is constituted as an expression of the indirect vertical mode of relating.[18] Indeed, while in the context of the direct vertical mode of relating such a constitution would simply not make sense (the praying entity, i.e., the primary category, in this context must be the individual, the collectivity being here only a secondary, abstracted category signifying the sum total of all individuals sharing the common denominator of being praying individuals), in the context of the indirect vertical mode of relating such a constitution is not only feasible but is actually called for. This is so by virtue of the fact that the indirect mode of relating expresses itself, as we have seen in ethical action and concern and that this implicates the collectivity and not the individual as the primary category. For ethical action and concern can be constituted only in terms of the collectivity and not in terms of the individual in himself. In relating to the divine, therefore, through ethical action and concern the human pole in the divine-human axis must be a collectivity of men rather than an individual person. Thus, inasmuch as prayer is constituted as a precept of the halacha, i.e., as a precept of a structure whose very essence lies in expressing ethical action and concern, its subject should indeed be the collectivity and not the individual.

And as for the lack of a distinctively fundamental status for the act of prayer in the ethos of the community, this can be accounted for by the mere fact that prayer here is constituted as a precept of the *halacha* (and without even having to resort to the further implication that as such it is constituted as an expression of the indirect vertical mode of relating). For the act of praying in being constituted as a *halachic* precept is after all but one of 613 precepts constituting the *halacha*, its binding-force and status being equal to that of any other precept—no less but also no more. Thus, while as an expression of the direct vertical mode of relating the status of prayer may have well been distinctively central, and, indeed, *sui generis* (seeing that the *halachic* strand formulates itself essentially from the Thou-perspective and that in this perspective prayer *qua* address is the *only* authentic expression of the direct vertical mode of relating), when prayer is incorporated into the structure of the *halacha* as one of its precepts its status is per force equalized to that of all the other precepts.

Lastly, the same consideration involved in the preceding characterization, i.e., the mere fact that prayer is constituted here as a precept of the *halacha*, should also account for the observation that in the *halachic* strand the approach to prayer centers by and large on its proper outward execution, i.e., on its execution in precise conformity with the prescription of the *halacha*, rather than on its inward intentional quality, i.e., on whether or not it constitutes authentic address. For a case can be made that inasmuch as the *halacha* is an expression of ethical concern, its attention must indeed be centered on the outward execution of the precepts. After all, ethical concern, one would want to argue, cannot fully express itself merely in inward intentions; in the last analysis it must impinge on overt, outward acts. But even if this is not granted, certainly the fact that the *halacha* is an objectified and legislated expression of the ethical concern must dictate that it centers its attention on the outward execution of the act. For clearly, objectification and legislation cannot be applied to inward intentions—they are applicable only to outward acts. Hence, it is understandable that for the *halacha* the validity and efficacy of its precepts (and this would, of course, include the act of prayer when it is constituted as a *halachic* precept) must ultimately lie in their outward performance. The proper inward intention accompanying the outward deed may well be an ideal desideratum; still, what really counts, in the last analysis, is the doing, the outward deed.

Thus, the fact that in the *halachic* strand prayer is constituted as a *halachic* precept can satisfactorily account for the various characterizations which, with respect to prayer as an act of direct vertical address, proved to be so problematic. But we must realize that in constituting prayer as a *halachic* precept the *halachic* strand radically transforms the nature and intent of the act of prayer. For now the act of prayer is no longer grounded in man but in the divine. It is no longer a communication to God originating in man but rather a communication to man originating in God. It is an act of divine revelation to man rather than an act of man's address to God. Rather than being an act of human spontaneity it is an act of divine command. For it is not God who wishes man to pray and commands him to do so. Clearly, in this context, man's role in prayer is not so much to address God as to conform to His will. As such, of course, the criterion for the validity and efficacy of the act of prayer must change radically. For now it clearly can no longer be the authenticity of address; rather, it must be the precision of execution in conformity with the dictates of revelation. What counts now is that the divine will be fulfilled. And this, in turn, would of course mean that the inward orientation accompanying the act can no longer be spontaneity, openness and immediacy but must rather be obedience. For in the face of divine revelation the only feasible inward orientation on the part of man is to obey. In this context, therefore, the act of prayer, i.e., the religious act, is no longer an act of address but an act of obedience.[19]

Clearly, the implications of transforming the act of prayer to a *halachic* precept and thus to an expression of divine revelation are far reaching. Indeed, not only the delineation but the very signification of the act undergo a fundamental change. One has certainly come a long way away from the signification and delineation of prayer not only when it is constituted as a direct mode of address but even when it is constituted as an indirect mode of address. How this has come about in the *halachic* strand is, however, a different story into which we need not enter here.

Thus, we may sum up the main thrust of this essay in the thesis that in the context of the mainstream and distinctive strands of Judaism, i.e., in the context of the "prophetic" and *halachic* strands, the category of worship is to be understood on the model worked out in our analysis above of the way the category is constituted in a structure of faith that formulates itself in terms of the ethical rather than the ontological perspective. This means that in the "prophetic" and *halachic* strands the expression of the category of worship is by no means to be confined exclusively to the direct vertical mode of relating; its expression, indeed, the main thrust of its expression, can just as well take place in the indirect vertical mode of relating. Indeed, in the *halachic* strand the tendency for the category to express itself in the indirect vertical mode of relating is so strong that even the act of prayer (which by its essence is an expression *par excellence* of the direct vertical mode of relating) can be constituted as an expression of the indirect vertical mode of relating. If such an exposition appears nonetheless somewhat forced and strange it is because the structures of faith of most religions tend to formulate themselves in terms of the ontological rather than the ethical perspective and consequently we have come to assume that the category of worship must express itself exclusively in the direct vertical mode of relating. It was precisely the purpose of this essay to disabuse us of this assumption and show that there is an alternative expression, namely, that in a structure of faith which formulates itself in terms of the ethical perspective—as is the case in the "prophetic" and *halachic* strands of Judaism—the category of worship can and does express itself in the indirect vertical mode of relating.

Endnotes

[1]Thus, for example, the various characterizations commonly assigned to worship, such as its inspiration of awe and reverence or its manifestation of the dimension of the wholly other, of the mysterious, originate and receive their rationale from the fact that the relating here is to the ultimate.

[2]The signification of transcendence as distance in contradistinction to proximity, i.e., its signification in the polarity of transcendence versus immanence, or its signification in the context of the polarity of the *deus absconditus* versus the revealing God, or, still further, in the polarity of the sovereign God versus the God of grace, is evidently a derived signification. Although these various significations are of great importance in the hermeneutics of theology and in the history of religions they are not of immediate concern to us here. For further background discussion of this subject see, for example, the contribution of K. Lehmann in *Encyclopedia of Theology*, ed. K. Rahner (New York: Seabury Press, 1975) 1734-42, and the contribution of J. A. Hutchinson of *Handbook of Christian Theology* (New York: Meridian Books, 1958) 363-66.

[3]Although we very often may tend to associate the notion of transcendence with the latter act, it is clear that the former act is just as legitimate an expression of transcendence. Indeed, we continuously surpass, i.e., transcend ourselves in acts that remain within the space-time continuum as, for example, in relating to a fellow-man, to an object, to an idea or to the future. Actually, every act of our consciousness is an act of transcendence and most of these acts remain within the space-time continuum. That we often tend to connect transcendence with the act that specifically surpasses the space-time continuum is due to our association of the category with its use in the context of biblical faith. For in this context, as we shall presently see, the distinctive connotation of the category is indeed linked to the act that surpasses the space-time continuum.

[4]Thus, from the vantage point of biblical faiths it is untenable to take a horizontal entity as the ultimate and commensurately to have the act of worship implicate an act of transcendence that is merely horizontal. Such an act is guilty of substituting that which is not truly ultimate for the ultimate and thus of misdirecting the act of worship. It is precisely what constitutes for biblical faiths the phenomenon of idolatry.

[5]This assertion may appear strange as pantheism is commonly associated with the religious domain. But if we examine the issue carefully we will see that its association with the religious domain is, indeed, centered mainly in non-biblical religions. And although pantheism has certainly penetrated to a considerable extent also the historical manifestation of biblical religions, there can be no denying that all biblical religions deemed it a pernicious and an heretical formulation which they, true to their essence, felt compelled to reject. Thus, the association of pantheism with the religious domain is established only by virtue of its

association with non-biblical religions. We, however, are judging it from the view-point of biblical religion and from this viewpoint such an association is, indeed, untenable. Indeed, this diametrically opposed view of pantheism reflects the fundamental and qualitative cleavage between biblical and nonbiblical religions (a cleavage which, by the way, dialectical theology rightly reflects in its distinction between "faith" and "religion"). And as to the further claim that pantheism is actually congenial to the secularist orientation, this can be seen in the fact that cultural awareness whenever secularized (as for example in the case of modernity) finds the pantheistic formulation much less of an anathema than the theistic formulation. This should not really be all that puzzling seeing that pantheism by its very essence abrogates any and all verticality and that, as we have suggested, the abrogation of the vertical dimension is precisely what constitutes the secularist orientation.

[6]See the many religious structures where one's relating to the divine, i.e., to the vertically transcendent being, is confined to specific places or to specific appointed times to the exclusion of all other places and times, thus constituting such places and times as sacred in contradistinction to all other places and times that are constituted as profane. Clearly, such points in space or time serve as jumping-boards from which man launches perpendicularly towards the vertically transcendent being, this status being precisely the factor that constitutes them as sacred in contradistinction to all other points which as such remain profane.

[7]Of course, the feasibility of such a mode of indirect relating would depend on the vertically transcendent being in some way implicated within the horizontal dimension. Such an implication would be clearly available in the pantheistic structure, for here the divine is identified ontologically with the world and consequently relating to the world is tantamount to relating to the divine. But as we have seen above the pantheistic structure is not viable with respect to the category of worship as delineated here. It is only within a theistic structure that the category as delineated here can find full and unambiguous expression. But the implication of the divine, i.e., of the vertically transcendent being, within the horizontal dimension, i.e., within the world, is certainly not self-evident in this structure. In its own terms the theistic structure provides no such implication—on the contrary, its very thrust is to separate the divine from the world. As such, any implication here of the divine within the world certainly cannot be ontological and will have to be provided extraneously. Such implication is provided in biblical religions by the tenet of creation which establishes the world as the possession of the divine and as such makes any act towards the world necessarily impinge upon the divine. In this context, relating to the world, i.e., to the horizontal dimension, is relating to something which belongs to the divine and consequently relating to the divine self, i.e., to the vertically transcendent being.

[8]True, such an ontological transformation can be effected in terms of the relating only when the relating proceeds from God to man and not when it proceeds from man to God. Namely, it can be effected only when the relating constitutes providence and not when it constitutes worship. Still it is clear that the relating when it proceeds from man to God (i.e., when it constitutes worship and when it cannot effect an ontological transformation) will have to be commensurate in its implications with the relating when it proceeds from God to man (i.e., when it constitutes providence and when it can effect an ontological transformation).

[9]True, the ontological formulation does not have necessarily to place the category of being in the sphere of Power; namely, it does not have to implicate the predicament exclusively in terms of the *finitude* of being, thus quantifying being and placing it within the sphere of

Power. It can deal with the predicament of being in qualitative terms and consequently implicate a vertically transcendent being that is a Thou. Thus, for example, one may encounter within the ontological formulation a formulation which perceives the predicament to be in the very presence of the It dimension in the It-Thou constitution of man (or even more generally in the It constitution of nature), and commensurate to this, envisioning salvation in terms of a qualitative ontological transformation of man from an It-Thou constitution (or of nature from an exclusively It constitution) to a pure Thou constitution—salvation thus being the constituting of man as a "new being" (or of nature as a "new creation"). In such a context the vertically transcendent being, by virtue of its representing the ultimate goal of salvation, will essentially be constituted as a pure Thou. Still, even here the vertically transcendent being is inescapably implicated in the sphere of the It and is thus constituted, if only provisionally, also as an It. For the effecting, as distinct from the representation, of such a salvation, i.e., of such a qualitative ontological transformation, must implicate the vertically transcendent being within the domain of Power, i.e., within the sphere of the It—incarnation, i.e., entering the sphere of the It, must precede and is a necessary step for effecting apotheosis, i.e., entering the sphere of the pure Thou. Thus, the ontological formulation even in the most optimal circumstances for constituting the vertically transcendent being as a pure Thou cannot really escape completely the constituting of the vertically transcendent being also as an It.

[10]It would also follow from this consideration that cult and ritual, inasmuch as their efficacy lies in precision, constitute a relating that is manipulation and consequently a relating that can be validly directed only to a vertically transcendent being that is an It; on the other hand, prayer, inasmuch as its efficacy lies in intention, constitutes a relating that is address and consequently a relating that can be validly directed only to a vertically transcendent being that is a Thou.

[11]Thus, see, for example, Jeremiah 15:15-18, 20:7-10; Amos 7:2. Indeed it would have been strange not to have prayer in this strand as a means of relating, seeing that the underlying structure of faith formulates itself here in the Thou-sphere. By the same token it is not surprising that in this context (i.e., the context of classical prophecy) we do not find the prophet relating to the vertically transcendent being through the cult; we may encounter the prophet praying but not performing cult (of course, this does not encompass the instances of cultic-prophets that may be encountered in Hebrew Scriptures, but then cultic-prophets, the name not withstanding, really express the "priestly" strand and not the "prophetic" strand). Indeed, no matter how much one may mitigate the prophetic critique of the sacrificial cult (for example, Isaiah 1:11-42, Jeremiah 6:20, 7:22-23 or Amos 5:5, 21-25) the fact remains that the prophet's own expression of the direct relating is not through the cult and that he accepts the cult only as a necessary *modus vivendi* and then only after devoiding it of its own signification and infusing it with a signification derived from his own perspective. Namely, the prophet appears willing to acquiesce in the sacrificial cult only if the cult were to be linked to moral conduct (one wonders, however, what justification and rationale the cult can have in such a context). No, the sacrificial cult can operate and have its rationale only in the "priestly" strand, but then in this strand there can be no authentic prayer. We may recall in this connection the interesting observation made by Yehezkel Kaufmann that in Hebrew Scriptures the sacrificial cult was conducted in utter silence—we do not find priests praying.

[12]This, of course, raises the question in a more general way whether authentic prayer, i.e., prayer *qua* address, can find expression in any religious context that is institutionalized. Our

considerations above would seem to indicate that the answer is no; it would seem that the contradiction between the dictates of institutionalized religion and the requirements of authentic prayer are too sharp to be overcome. The closest that one can come to preserving authentic prayer in the context of institutionalized religion is most probably the Quaker prayer-meeting and clearly this too does not overcome the problem completely. But even more fundamentally, the question arises whether the very structure of faith which formulates itself in the Thou-domain (and not just its manifestation of prayer *qua* address) can authentically function in an institutionalized context. All our deliberations thus far should lead us to conclude that here too the answer must be no; an institutionalized context is of necessity a context constituted in the It-domain and as such, an institutionalized context can, at best, be viewed from the perspective of the Thou-domain only as a "necessary evil." Still, we would want to suggest below that there is a way in which a structure of faith formulating itself in the Thou-domain can authentically express itself in an institutionalized context. Clearly, if our case proves tenable it will greatly help us to better understand how a structure of faith formulating itself in the Thou-domain can function in the concrete world, i.e., in the world of It.

[13]This may explain, perhaps, why in the *halachic* strand prayer does not command as prominent and central a status as one would have expected. See for example, the *halachic* ruling giving study precedence over prayer. It may also explain the marked tendency in the ethos of the strand to view prayer as an act which one is, indeed, obliged to perform but which one wants to get over with as expeditiously as possible so as to be free to attend to more important business. For clearly the prominence and centrality that one anticipates for the act of prayer is derived from the expectation that it would be the act which delineates the relating to the divine, seeing that such an act does, indeed, command the most prominent and central status in the structure of faith. But in the *halachic* strand, inasmuch as it formulates itself in the Thou-domain, the relating to the divine can be delineated only by prayer that is constituted as address. Thus, the fact that, as we have seen, the structure of prayer as address is compromised here may well explain the lessening of its status—it would certainly allow such a lessening in status.

[14]Indeed, we would suggest that the ritual legislation is encompassed within the *halacha* only because of the *halacha's* legalistic orientation. For the legalistic orientation dictates that in accepting the Pentateuchal Law in its entirety as revelatory the *halacha* is bound to encompass *all* the expressions of its legislation, and this, of course, would include its ritual legislation even though this legislation formulates itself in terms of the It-domain and is, indeed, introduced into the Pentateuchal law by the "priestly" strand. Still, it should be clear that as such the ritual legislation cannot be an essential and distinctive expression of the *halachic* strand. For the *halachic* strand formulates itself in terms of the Thou-domain and not of the It-domain and as such, indeed, is the continuation of the "prophetic" rather than of the "priestly" strand. This being the case, the essential and distinctive thrust of the *halachic* strand can find its authentic expression in the civil, political and criminal legislation but not in the ritual legislation. It would seem to us, therefore, that we are justified in seeing the *halacha* in this context as being constituted essentially by its civil, political and criminal legislation and neglecting its ritual legislation.

[15]Of course such *a priori* and universalized delineation of the manifestation and concretization of the ethical concern might well compromise its full ethical authenticity. For there is no denying that such universalization and *a priorization* of the ethical concern must

compromise the situational aspect and a case can be made that the situational aspect must be implicated for the ethical concern to be fully authentic. Still, this is not to say that in the absence of the situational aspect the ethical concern is completely undermined. No, the ethical concern can still express itself though admittedly it cannot express itself at its most authentic level. Thus, even though the *halacha* is characterized by *a priorization* and universalism, it can still express the ethical concern.

Now, this conclusion carries a further implication that is most significant. Namely, it implies that even structures of faith which formulate themselves in terms of the Thou-perspective can after all lend themselves to being institutionalized. For the *halacha* in being *a priorized*, objectified and universalized is clearly an instrument of institutionalization and this, in turn, means that any structure of faith which appropriates the *halacha* as its expression is thereby institutionalized. Thus, while it is, indeed, highly problematic, as we have seen, for structures of faith formulating themselves in the Thou-perspective (but let us note, not for structures of faith formulating themselves in the It-perspective) to lend themselves to institutionalization in terms of their direct vertical mode of relating, i.e., in terms of prayer as the mode of relating, this is not to say that these structures of faith cannot under any circumstances lend themselves to institutionalization. For, as we can see now, these structures of faith can lend themselves to institutionalization in terms of their indirect vertical mode of relating, namely, they lend themselves to institutionalization in terms of the ethical concern as the mode of relating. Seeing that religion—if it is to be an outward affair of the collectivity rather than merely an inward affair of the individual and if it is to maintain itself in the flux of history—must lend itself to institutionalization, this implication does indeed establish a most significant point with respect to structures of faith that belong to the Thou-perspective.

[16]Indeed, it is rather indicative that the Hebrew term used to signify the notion of worship is *"Avoda"* (e.g., *Avodat Elohim* or *Avodat Habore* meaning the worship of God or of the creator), a term altogether different from that which signifies prayer, i.e., the direct vertical mode of relating, that term being *"T'fila."* Namely, it is significant that the term designating the direct vertical mode of relating is not used to signify the notion of worship. This significance is further buttressed by the meaning of these terms. Thus, *T'fila* comes from a root that signifies the moving of one's lips. As such it is, indeed, an appropriate term to designate the direct vertical mode of relating, seeing that it connotes that the relating here is verbal (certainly, in terms of our analysis above, "verbal" in its first signification of being an articulation of sound but also in its second signification of being an address to a Thou). *Avoda*, on the other hand, signifies work or labor. This means, of course, that the notion of worship is designated here, in contradistinction to the designation of the notion of prayers by the signification of work or labor which, in turn, connotes that the relating is constituted here as action (certainly, in terms of its first signification according to our analysis above, i.e., in terms of its signification as bodily movement). Why is this so and how does it come about? The answer lies in the fact that the designation of the term for the category of worship originates with its reference to the category when the category was constituted by the sacrificial cult and, of course, in this context its signification of work is quite *a propos*, seeing that the sacrificial cult does indeed implicate work (indeed, the constitution of the relating here as action is not only in terms of its first signification of bodily movement but also in terms of its second signification, i.e., in terms of its signifying the manipulation or utilization of Power). The problem arises when the usage of the term is continued even though the category is no longer

constituted by the sacrificial cult, when indeed its signification would not seem to allow its being designated by a term which signifies work and which, therefore, connotes that the relating involved is constituted as action. Namely, when the category of worship is constituted by a relating that is an address (as is the case in the *halachic* strand), its designation by a term which signifies work and which connotes that the relating is constituted as action must appear questionable and contradictory. For how can the notions of work and action properly designate and describe a relating that is an address? Is it not a fact that a relating that is address implicates intention and not work and that it constitutes itself as verbal and not as action? Thus, it would appear that in using the term *Avoda* to designate the category of worship the strand is guilty of mismatching the term with the phenomenon it is supposed to designate. Of course, one can account for this by the operation of inertia. Namely, once the term has been applied (and originally when applied to the sacrificial cult the application has been quite valid) its usage will tend to continue by the force of inertia even though the nature of the activity it designates has changed. Still, such a mismatched designation cannot be sustained by the force of inertia forever—sooner or later it must lapse. If the designation holds indefinitely, as is the case in the *halachic* strand, it indicates that it must have some validity after all. Indeed, if we examine the matter more closely this will prove to be the case. Namely, upon closer examination it should be clear that the problems with the designation pointed to above really arise when the category of worship (which is, as we have seen, constituted here as a relating that is an address) expresses itself in the direct vertical mode. When the category expresses itself, however, in the indirect vertical mode, i.e., when the relating is refracted through the horizontal dimension and expresses itself as ethical action, the problem is greatly mitigated. For refraction through the horizontal dimension, specifically, ethical action, clearly implicates the notion of work and the connotation of action in its first signification, i.e., action in the sense of bodily movement. The only aspect that remains problematic is the connotation of action in its second signification, i.e., action in the sense of utilizing or manipulating Power—this clearly cannot apply here. But the term *Avoda* while necessarily having to implicate the notion of work and the connotation of action in its first signification (i.e., bodily movement) does not necessarily have to implicate the connotation of action in its second signification (i.e., action as the utilization or manipulation of Power). It is quite feasible, therefore, for the term *Avoda* to designate ethical action. Thus, we would suggest that the continued designation within the *halachic* strand of the category of worship by the term *Avoda* is due not only to the force of inertia but to the fact that in this strand the burden of expression of the category of worship lies in the indirect vertical mode, i.e., in ethical action as concretized in the *halacha*, and not in the direct vertical mode, i.e., in prayer as address. Only as such could one account for the fact that the *halachic* strand not only continued this designation but that it actually was quite comfortable with its adoption.

[17]Of course, since prayer signifies an address to the divine, it is very desirable that the act should also constitute an authentic address. Thus, indeed, the full delineation of the act of prayer in the rabbis' view implicates not only *keva'* (i.e., consistency or, in other words, the execution of the act precisely in accordance with its prescription) but also *kavanah* (i.e., intention). But as we have seen, this is a delineation of the *ideal* situation. Ideally, both criteria should characterize the act of prayer. Still, even though *kavanah* may be lacking *keva'* is nonetheless incumbent. In the last analysis, it is *keva'* which counts.

[18]The subject which prays in each one of the prayers is without exception the "we." The individual prays here only by virtue of being a member of the community, only through the "we" of the community. It is the community, i.e., the collectivity, which constitutes here, therefore, the primary category, the individual constituting merely a derived, secondary category.

[19]The fact that prayer is grounded in the divine will, i.e., in revelation, should allow us now, by the way, to understand why, as observed above, study and knowledge are invested with such great importance (indeed, taking precedence over prayer) in the *halachic* strand. For clearly, in order to be able to execute the precepts in conformity with the divine will one must first know as precisely and as fully as possible what the divine will is and this, in turn, means that one must first study and know the sources in which the communication of the divine will to man has been incorporated. It is important to note, however, that this precedence and importance accorded to the pursuit of study and knowledge is accorded specifically and exclusively to the pursuit of study and knowledge of that which incorporates the divine revelation, and for the *halachic* strand this means the study and knowledge of scriptures as interpreted and understood by the Talmud and the subsequent rabbinic commentaries. It is not accorded to the pursuit of study and knowledge in general, i.e., to the study and knowledge of secular disciplines such as the natural or social sciences.

But what is even more significant, it is important to note that this pursuit of the study and knowledge of scriptures, the Talmud and the rabbinic commentaries is not done for its own sake. It is not an end-in-itself but only a means. Namely, the act of study, the possession of knowledge, does not constitute the religious act *per se*. What constitutes the religious act *per se* is the *execution* of the deed. The religious significance and validity of the pursuit of study and knowledge are thus not inherent in the act itself but are derived. They are derived from the fact that they constitute the necessary means for the fulfillment of the religious act. As such, even though the pursuit of study and knowledge is clearly invested with essential value and significance, indeed, with logical and temporal precedence over the concrete execution of the deed, its value and significance are derived and secondary. Thus, for all the prominence and precedence accorded here to the pursuit of study and knowledge, the *halachic* strand does not constitute itself in gnosis.